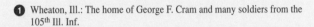

George F. Cram's Civil War Journey

1. Wheaton, Ill.: The home of George F. Cram and many soldiers from the 105th Ill. Inf.

2. Shelbyville, Ky.: Corporal Cram recuperates from fever, October 9, 1862.

3. Scottsville, Ky.: Sightings of Confederate General John Hunt Morgan's guerrilla raiders, November 12, 1862.

4. Gallatin, Tenn.: Union Fort Thomas from which companies of 105th Ill. Inf. were detailed to guard the L&N Railroad, 6 miles north at South Tunnel during the winter of 1862–63.

5. Nashville, Tenn.: Extended garrison duty at Fort Negley prevented the 105th Ill. Inf. from campaigning for several months, August 27, 1863–February 24, 1864.

6. Resaca, Ga.: Site of battle, May 15, 1864.

7. Peach Tree Creek: Site of battle, July 20–22, 1864, in which Sergeant Cram and Lieutenant Smith captured the enemy's colors.

8. Milledgeville, Ga.: On November 22, 1864, the 105th Ill. Inf. "stopped there one day and made most terrible havoc among the citizens." Expecting a conflict, Sergeant Cram's diary noted instead, "It is quite a fine place but the inhabitants look rather sour. It seemed as if we certainly would fight tonight, but we built huge fires and sat like so many toads around them."

9. Savannah, Ga.: The 105th Ill. Inf. entered Savannah on December 21, 1864. Sergeant Cram explored the city December 23–24 and noted in his diary, "It has a curious, ancient sort of appearance. The citizens seem reconciled to Federal rule."

10. Columbia, S.C.: Sergeants Cram and Wheeler and Corporal Congleton reported in varying manners that Columbia was "burned to ashes, that rebellious nest," as the Union Forces moved from Savannah towards Goldsboro, N.C.

11. Averasboro, N.C.: Site of battle, March 16, 1865.

12. Bentonville, N.C.: Site of battle, March 19, 1865.

13. Washington, D.C.: Celebratory Army parades through the streets, May 25–27, 1865, before mustering out.

14. Chicago, Ill.: Homecoming, June 11, 1865.

Soldiering with Sherman

Soldiering with Sherman

Civil War Letters of George F. Cram

Edited by Jennifer Cain Bohrnstedt

Introduction by Orville Vernon Burton

NORTHERN ILLINOIS

UNIVERSITY

PRESS

© 2000 by Northern Illinois University Press

Published by the Northern Illinois University Press, DeKalb, Illinois 60115

Manufactured in the United States using acid-free paper

All Rights Reserved

Design by Julia Fauci

Library of Congress Cataloging-in-Publication Data

Soldiering with Sherman : Civil War letters of George F. Cram / edited by

Jennifer Cain Bohrnstedt ; introduction by Orville Vernon Burton.

p. cm.

Includes bibliographical references (p.) and index.

ISBN 0-87580-261-3 (alk. paper)

✓ 1. Cram, George Franklin, 1841–1928—Correspondence. 2. United States.

Army. Illinois Infantry Regiment, 105th (1862–1865) 3. United States—His-

tory—Civil War, 1861–1865—Personal narratives. 4. Illinois—History—Civil

War, 1861–1865—Personal narratives. 5. United States—History—Civil War,

1861–1865—Regimental histories. 6. Illinois—History—Civil War,

1861–1865—Regimental Histories. 7. United States—History—Civil War,

1861–1865—Campaigns. 8. Soldiers—Illinois—Correspondence. I. Bohrnstedt,

Jennifer Cain. II. Title.

E505.5 105th .C73 2000

973.7'73'092—dc21   99-089803

Frontispiece courtesy of Deborah Hoskins Edwards and John Hoskins

Endsheet map produced by Vaupel Graphics, Genoa, Illinois.

For

A. J. Cain and Juanita Willis Cain

"That history has taken the first place in literature, is due to the exhaustless character of its subjects, among which may be found truths which foreshadow the future from the past, and leave a more abiding impression than the teachings of fiction."

—Rufus Blanchard, 1879

Contents

Editor's Note   ix

Acknowledgments   xi

Introduction   Orville Vernon Burton   xiii

1 / "Citizens No Longer"
Wyanet, July 9–Frankfort, October 20, 1862   3

2 / "If You Examine the Map"
Bowling Green, November 7–Scottsville, November 23, 1862   12

3 / "The Gentlemen's Tent"
Gallatin, November 30–South Tunnel, Dcember 25, 1862   19

4 / "Asleep in Jesus"
South Tunnel, January 1–Gallatin, February 15, 1863   32

5 / "I Would Prefer a Copy of Shakespeare"
Gallatin, April 4–Nashville, October 10, 1863   43

6 / "What Can't Be Cured Must Be Endured"
Nashville, October 28, 1863–February 7, 1864   57

7 / "The Big Brigade"
Shelbyville, February 14–Lookout Valley, April 29, 1864   75

8 / "It Was Every Man for Himself"
Gordons Mills, May 3–Battlefield, June 19, 1864   93

9 / "Perfect Terror"
Marietta, June 25–near Atlanta, July 31, 1864   111

10 / **"The Very Air Seems Full of Death and Destruction"**
Near Atlanta, August 4–Atlanta, October 23, 1864   130

11 / **"Terrible Havoc Among the Citizens"**
Near Atlanta, October 30, 1864–Raleigh, April 19, 1865   145

12 / **"Extremely Well Paid for the Trip"**
Raleigh, April 28–Washington, D.C., June 1, 1865   164

Afterword   171

Appendix: "Reminiscences: The Battle of Resaca"   175

Notes   181

Bibliography   195

Index   203

Editor's Note

Soldiering with Sherman: The Civil War Letters of George F. Cram
provides an Illinois soldier's view of the western campaigns of the
war from 1862–65. Cram was a twenty-one-year-old Wheaton College student when he enlisted in Company F of the 105th Illinois Infantry in the summer of 1862. Over the next three years he fought
his way across the breadth of the Confederacy from Kentucky to Atlanta and from Savannah to Richmond. His letters provide his keen
observations of the Battles of Resaca, Kennesaw Mountain, Peach
Tree Creek, Atlanta, Averysboro, and Bentonville. Cram also offers
his view of key figures in this era of American history, including
Generals Thomas, Hooker, Rosecrans, Howard, and Sherman. Cram
also tells the reader a profoundly different view of John Wilkes
Booth a year before the infamous night at Ford's Theater.

Cram came to Illinois in the 1850s from Lowell, Massachusetts,
with his mother, Anna Blanchard Cram, and his older sister, Juliette, in order to be near Anna's brother, Rufus Blanchard, an historian and Chicago map publisher. Cram's father, Joseph, had left the
family years before for the lure of California gold and had never returned. The depth of feeling between mother and son revealed in the
letters is all more understandable in this light; Cram not only wrote
as a faithful son but as a long-distance overseer of the family and
the family's millinery and farming businesses.

With droll humor and piercing objectivity the letters collected
here introduce us to men whose high purpose in saving the Union
also inspired them to create an honor code forbidding drinking,
swearing, and smoking. Many of George F. Cram's comrades did not
survive the war, but their road to victory was marked by more than
blood. Theirs was a community of men at war, the men of the self-
styled "gentlemen's tent" as they called their quarters.

The eighty letters printed here passed through four generations to
one of Cram's great-granddaughters, Deborah Hoskins Edwards. Two
of Cram's diaries, shared by great-grandson John Hoskins were frequently used in clarifying the context of the letters or in gauging a
closer estimate of his sentiment about particular events. The letters

required little editorial work save for the addition of punctuation and paragraphing. Omitted words and spelling errors occur only a few times and are unchanged for publication.

Several years of research have uncovered additional information useful in understanding the importance of Cram's remarks during the war and their application for the years that followed. To be certain, *Soldiering with Sherman* is indeed a book about the Civil War. But, the universal themes by which Cram's life is guided (e.g., "No one ever yet succeeded in plans of life laid by others") appeal to our sensibilities beyond that of narrowly understanding the Civil War. Understanding humanity, the value of relationships and all the ingredients by which they are bound together—truth, trust, determination and honor—is also what Cram shared. The lives of Cram and those friends, family, and comrades closest to him were examined extensively in order to understand the magnitude of impact on the many lives of one Illinois community resulting from the unforgotten days of *Soldiering with Sherman.*

Acknowledgments

In bringing the Civil War story of George F. Cram to publication, I have many friends, family, and associates to thank who have helped in this endeavor. Above all, this book could not have been undertaken without the shared vision and support of George W. Bohrnstedt.

Heartfelt appreciation and thanks additionally to: Deborah Hoskins Edwards, John Hoskins, Kassandra Chaney, Wilmer Cabezas, José Bohrnstedt, Brian Bohrnstedt, Alan Nolan, Janet Nicely, Murray Hudson, Polly Swift and Allen Grimshaw, Larry Malley, Ted Peacock, Denise Harper and Byron Wilson, Wesley Cron, Patricia McCarthy, Mary Ann Gorski, Roxann Stephens, Josh Mann, Patricia Collins, James Peñalacia, Rich Vaupel, Jack Leathers, Michael Maddux Kimball, Roger Jellinek, and Mrs. Gladys June Slater.

The breadth of research and inquiry would not have been possible without the fine assistance of the following individuals and organizations: The Special Collections and Reference Library of the U.S. Army Military History Institute, Carlisle, Pennsylvania; The Library of Congress, Washington, D.C.; Todd Butler, The National Archives, Washington, D.C.; The National Archives Midwest Region, Evanston, Illinois; The Chicago Historical Society; The Chicago Public Library Special Collections & Preservation Division; Cora Harper, The Sumner County, Tennessee Archives, Gallatin, Tennessee; Fred Prouty, The Tennessee State War Commission, Nashville, Tennessee; Terresa Sammartino, National Cemetery System, Department of Veteran Affairs, Washington, D.C.; Bettye Glover, The Highland Rim Historical Society, Portland, Tennessee; the Cumberland Valley Civil War Heritage Association; Rosemary Harper, The Allen County Kentucky Historical Society, Scottsville, Kentucky; Kentucky Library, Western Kentucky University, Bowling Green, Kentucky; Stanford University Green Library, Stanford, California; Skyline Community College, San Bruno, California; The Sutro Library of the California State Library, San Francisco; The Center for Lowell History, Lowell, Massachusetts; The DuPage County, Illinois Historical Museum; The Wheaton College Archives at Buswell Memorial Library, Wheaton,

Illinois; The Matson Public Library, Princeton, Illinois; The Wilmette, Illinois Public Library; University of Washington Archives, Seattle, Washington; Illinois State Library, Springfield, Illinois; Illinois State Historical Agency, Springfield, Illinois; and Kathleen Manning, Prints Old & Rare, Pacifica, California.

Special thanks to William L. Douthit and John S. Douthit, owners of The George F. Cram Company, Indianapolis, Indiana, for providing access to the original letters that now reside in their archives.

Introduction

Orville Vernon Burton

George F. Cram's letters document his three-year trek as a member of the 105th Illinois from Illinois through Kentucky, Tennessee, Alabama, Georgia, South Carolina, and into the final battles of the Civil War in North Carolina, culminating with a grand victory march in Washington, D.C. Cram was a twenty-one year old Wheaton College student when he joined the 105th Illinois, formed after the first year of the Civil War. As an enlisted man with a superb education, his letters offer insight from a special perspective, different from that of officers trying to justify their actions and make a place for themselves in history. *Soldiering with Sherman* is a young Union soldier's account of war that is shrewdly rendered through letters written home to his mother.

Cram's letters begin in the summer of 1862. The first year of the terrible four-year conflict between North and South had not intruded much into the young collegian's life. Yet the nation soon learned that this was not to be a short war quickly resolved. The Civil War became a life and death struggle not just for the Union, but also for the very meaning of the American experience. George Cram lived through and recorded this great national conflict after the first year.

On April 15, 1861, one day after the surrender of Fort Sumter to Confederate troops, President Abraham Lincoln began his ninety-day call for 75,000 Union volunteers to end the South's insurrection. The initial outburst of enthusiasm for enlistment was overwhelming, and the United States War Department received more volunteers than it knew how to use. In April 1862, one year later, the Union and Illinois General Ulysses S. Grant won the Battle of Shiloh (at Pittsburg Landing in Tennessee) at a price. About twenty thousand died in that bloody battle; casualties, nearly evenly distributed between North and South, were almost twice the combined casualties of the other major engagements of the war thus far. And Shiloh was a harbinger of the massive destruction and death to come. Shiloh also meant that, despite Grant's victories, the North was not going to take the West easily from the Confederates, a hope bred after the fall of Fort Henry and Fort Donaldson. The war in the West was no game, and even the victories, like Shiloh, would be ferocious and costly in manpower.

On April 16, 1862, the Confederacy enacted the first conscription law in American history, drafting men for three years' service. In that same month, Union victory looked so likely that President Lincoln ceased recruiting. In early May also it appeared only a matter of time before the Union would prevail. That very May, with his Valley Campaign in the East, Stonewall Jackson drove his Confederate Brigade into military fame and gave new optimism to the South. Then on May 31, Confederate commander of the Army of Northern Virginia, Joe Johnston, was wounded at the Battle of Seven Pines (known as Fair Oaks by the Union), and Jefferson Davis appointed Robert E. Lee as his replacement. When Lee sent cavalry Commander J.E.B. Stuart on a scouting mission, Stuart rode clear around Union Commander General George McClellan's forces in the celebrated "Stuart's Ride." Lee, Jackson, and Stuart gained an incredible psychological advantage over the Union troops. They became almost mystical, undefeatable Southern heroes as Union forces retreated under their assaults on the eastern front, especially in the Peninsular Campaign. The thirty thousand killed and wounded in the Seven Days Battles as part of the Peninsular campaign in Virginia between June 6 and July 2, 1862, dwarfed even the twenty thousand casualties at Shiloh. McClellan impudently wired President Lincoln, "If you do not know now, the game is lost. If I can save this army, I tell you I owe no thanks to you or any persons in Washington. You have done your best to sacrifice this army."[1] Following the disastrous Peninsular Campaign (where in fact the victorious Lee's smaller force lost 20,000 men to McClellan's 16,000), McClellan withdrew from the Peninsula to the upper James River. Now it was obvious to all that the Civil War would not be limited, but total war. In July of 1862, no one could predict the outcome.

Following Seven Pines and the Peninsular Campaign, the Union needed new leadership and more soldiers. For leadership Lincoln replaced McClellan with General Henry Wagner Halleck, who had been Grant's commander in the West when the Union took Forts Donaldson and Henry. Getting more soldiers on the battlefield required some finesse, as Lincoln determined that he could not appear desperate in the wake of battle losses. He refused to increase Northern disillusionment over McClellan's retreat and the seeming invincibility of Lee, Jackson, and Stuart. Secretary of State William Seward found a way to meet this political challenge. Seward convened Northern governors at a meeting in New York City and apprised them of the seriousness of the situation. Attempting to put a positive spin on the Confederate successes in the East, Seward convinced the governors to ask Lincoln to call for more troops to hasten the end of the war by following up on Union "successes." Seward actually wrote the public announcement for the Northern governors and dated the address earlier so that it would not appear to have been motivated by the Union defeat at the Seven Days Battles. Thus, using the governors' plea as an excuse, on July 2, 1862, the president asked for 300,000 more Union men to volunteer for three years' service to put a quick end to the war. The War Department assigned each state a portion of the 300,000 volunteers according to the state's population.

Recruitment was intense. The Quaker abolitionist James S. Gibbons penned the popular poem, "We are Coming, Father Abraham, Three Hundred Thousand More." The popular poem was quickly set to music by Stephen Foster.[2] Even with recruiting committees, parades, and patriotic fervor, states had problems meeting their quotas. Northerners now knew that this brutal war was no romantic fling. The U.S. government and individual state governments added incentives for enlistment. Volunteers received an immediate 25 dollars of the 100 dollar bounty they would be due after their honorable discharge. Furthermore, some states, counties, and cities offered additional bounties to volunteers. In order to encourage volunteers, the federal government on July 17, 1862, passed a militia law that allowed the president to call a state militia into service for nine months. The militia was to be composed of all fit men from eighteen to forty-five years of age.[3] Only one month after the call for the 300,000 three-year volunteers from the states, on August 4, the U.S. government used the militia act to call for an additional 300,000 militia from the states for nine months' service. If a state did not meet its three-year volunteer quota, it would be required to make up the difference in the nine-month militia call that was essentially a draft. In a blatant appropriation of state sovereignty, the U.S. government would step in and handle enforcement for a state that failed to meet its quota. However, if a state exceeded the quota of three-year volunteers, every soldier over the quota counted for four men in the militia draft. Resistance ensued in certain areas and was particularly violent in southern Indiana. Ohio, Wisconsin, and Pennsylvania also generated violent opposition, especially from the Irish and German elements. In spite of resistance, and although deadlines were extended, by 1863 the Union had 421,000 new three-year volunteers and 88,000 nine-month militiamen.[4] For many, it became a matter of local and state pride to fulfill the quota; this was especially true for Illinois, the home of Lincoln.

Why would so many men be willing to die for this war of Father Abraham's? At stake during the Civil War was the very existence of the United States. The most bloody war in our history, the Civil War also posed in a crucial way what clearly became persistent themes in American history: the character of the nation and the fate of African-Americans. Consequently, scholars have been vitally interested in the Civil War, searching out clues therein for the identity of America. From the letters of George F. Cram, we get hints of what the war meant to Midwestern soldiers fighting for the Union.

As Illinois proudly met its quota, George F. Cram was a new three-year volunteer. Cram's eighty-seven letters, all but one to his mother, provide a bird's-eye view of the Illinois 105th Regiment, and through that regiment, a window into the western theatre. Like most volunteers, Cram was recruited into a new regiment organized with commissioned officers, often whose commissions were political. Cram joined Company F, commanded by Captain Seth Daniels, the Justice of the Peace in Cram's hometown of Wheaton, Illinois. As an enlisted man, Cram offered his assessment of his officers. He noted on January 19, 1863, that "Captain Daniels is not liked here neither by his company nor by other officers." Six companies from DeKalb County and four from DuPage County comprised Colonel Daniel Dustin's 105th Illinois Infantry. Cram was one of the ninety-three volunteers of Company F, called the Bryan Blues because attorney Thomas Barbour Bryan of DuPage County helped raise and outfit the company. More than half of the company was composed of farmers, but sixteen of the soldiers in Company F were Cram's college classmates at Wheaton College. Because so many of his comrades-in-arms were his college classmates and from his hometown, these letters are also about the extended community of Wheaton, Illinois. After a soldier had returned from Wheaton back to camp, Cram wrote on April 23, 1864, "It is always a great privilege to see anyone just from our home and feel that a few hours previously, they conversed with our friends." Not only do we learn about the war and the Illinois 105th from these letters, but through them we get hints of the home front. His relatives sent him several newspapers, and his letters home often commented from a soldier's perspective on the national news of the day.

The Civil War was seen by both Northerners and Southerners as a test of manhood. And these letters tell the story of the coming of age of a sensitive, intelligent, and philosophical young man. Through his set of intimate letters to his mother, one gets a sense of what manhood meant to this Yankee transplanted to the Midwest. Cram clearly felt that manhood required bravery and willingness to undergo hardship. From the field on January 18, 1864, he explained, "Should I live to return, I shall look back with great pride upon my soldier's life. And I frequently say to myself now, 'It is good for us to be here.' We are learning much that could not be learned elsewhere." For George Cram, Wheaton College student, manhood meant Christian values of morality: no swearing, associating with camp followers, smoking, or drinking. On November 30, 1862, he bragged to his mother, "I wish you could just step into our tent and see how easy and comfortable we have things fixed. I call it the gentlemen's tent. There are four of us just like brothers who neither smoke, chew, swear nor drink. A great many of the boys are not what they were at home." Cram believed that the civilized Christian man should hold to a high standard of conduct. Civil War historian James McPherson has described midwestern soldiers as "profane,"[5] and Cram concurs with this assessment. He wrote from Murfreesboro, Tennessee, on July 25, 1863, "I do not wonder at so many young men being ruined by the army, none but minds entirely above camp vices can stand the current." All in all, however, he concluded, "Considering the morality of most of the army I am really proud to belong to Company F/105th Ill. And so long as I live I do not think I will ever regret being a soldier."

Once, when commanding four men on picket duty, Cram recited Shakespeare's *The Two Gentlemen of Verona*. Maybe this was his attempt to inspire moral rectitude because "it had an excellent effect." Cram noticed, "There was much less swearing for a long time afterward" (December 5, 1862). While in Nashville, Commissary Sergeant George Cram produced theatre, recitations, and readings for his company.

Manhood involved a sense of duty. Cram tells us what the United States meant to him and about his responsibility as a patriotic citizen willing to fight this war. On February 15, 1863, he explained, "For my own part I wish every copperhead rascal was hung and before one inch of Ill. soil shall be added to the Confederacy, I will willingly stay my 3 years and then enlist another term." And later from Nashville, Tennessee on February 7, 1864, he explained, "We who have suffered in the field have no feeling with those who play when the hour for work has come: How they can endure themselves I know not, for before I enlisted I could not look an honest patriot in the face."

Cram's letters and the annotations give the perspective of a college-educated enlisted man and spotlight the service of the Illinois 105th. There is no regimental history of these Illinoisans, a group important to Union victory. Military buffs will relish the letters on Sherman's campaign to take Atlanta, his march to the sea, his trek through South Carolina, and his fighting in the end of the war in North Carolina. Cram gives a soldier's view of the fighting of the Illinois 105th. His letters support the new interpretation of historical demographer Daniel Scott Smith. Smith (whose preliminary estimates show that a higher proportion of midwesterners served than men from other regions) found that midwesterners died at a higher rate than young men from other sections. One of the differences was disease.[6] Many midwestern farm boys, somewhat isolated, had not been exposed to contagious diseases before being thrown together in the army. These boys fell victim to childhood diseases like measles and mumps. Hygiene was also a problem. Cram wrote on December 18, 1862, "Soldiers seldom wash more than their noses and fingernails. I certainly believe that one half of the deaths in the army are caused by filth." In 1863 Cram documented a raging typhoid fever epidemic. Not inured to suffering and dying, he wrote how he had "set for hours and shuddered at the awful groans and shrieks of the sick and dying, all mingled in confusion" (January 19, 1863). At the conclusion of the war, 460 returned home, less than half of the 105th Illinois who marched away to win the war for the Union in 1862. The 105th Illinois suffered 494 casualties, either killed or disabled.

Cram also provides his perceptions into American race relations and the views of soldiers on race. George F. Cram's Wheaton College was presided over by Jonathan Blanchard, a Christian abolitionist. Wheaton's president held strong views on abolitionism and emancipation, views which stirred many of the Wheaton students. Between 1861 and 1863, sixty-six Wheaton students besides Cram joined the Union army, and many professed their president's abolitionist sentiments.[7] Less than a month after Abraham Lincoln announced the

Emancipation Proclamation,[8] George F. Cram recorded in his diary sentiments that would have warmed Wheaton President Blanchard's heart. With only a few months as a soldier in basic training, Cram wrote, "Let America set this example before the world and the time will soon come when freedom to all men of every race and color shall be universal, the long oppressed will find rest to their weary souls, wars will be few throughout the land, progress will not be impeded by the clashing of arms and a more perfect state of happiness will settle over all" (October 19, 1862). Cram's letters to his mother never reflect the abolitionist sentiment expressed in his diary. His letters from the army echo the views on race held by most white Americans at that time. In this year of the Emancipation Proclamation, the state of Illinois, home of Lincoln, Grant, and Blanchard, hearkened back to the state's antebellum efforts to keep African-Americans out of Illinois. In 1862, about two-fifths of Republican voters combined with Democrats to renew Illinois's Exclusion Law.[9]

Although Cram was opposed to slavery, from Frankfort, Kentucky, he wrote, "There are plenty of slaves and they all appear to look well and seem happy. They are as a general thing nearly as intelligent as their masters" (October 15, 1862). On February 15, 1863, just a month after the Emancipation Proclamation was to have gone into effect, Cram wrote to his mother, "I would be perfectly willing to withdraw the proclamation if the rebels would lay down their arms and come back to the Union as it was. Slavery would soon die anyhow and peace again be restored." On April 4, 1863, from Tennessee he explained, "It is Union I enlisted to fight for and not 'irrepressible Negroe.'"

Only once, when crossing into South Carolina and discovering slaves on the low-country rice plantations, did Cram describe slavery as harsh. Even here, he pointed out the harshness of slavery in South Carolina to contrast it with what he believed to be the norm. On January 16, 1865, he wrote, "The Negroes are inhumanely treated, being fed on rice and a little corn, having no meat, save on Christmas and each male and female alike whipped to a certain amount of work each day. This is the only place I have ever seen slaves really abused, except so far as it is an abuse to make them slaves and I think many novelists . . . have drawn largely on their own lively imagination for many of the horrors of slavery."

During the Battle of Atlanta, Cram expressed some of his feelings about abolitionists, less ambivalent than his feelings about abolition itself. On August 20, 1864, he criticized an abolitionist back home who wanted to avoid the draft: "Those who continually tell how they want to fight to the bitter end, etc. are always taken suddenly very ill just before a battle and find some reason for being obliged to stay in the rear, very much of course against their will. For my own part I am disgusted with Negroes although I think slavery is wrong and hope, as I believe, that the war will end it on this continent or at least in this government." Several times Cram was offered a commission to lead African-American soldiers, but he always declined. Cram blamed black troops for the loss at Petersburg although, according to McPherson, the "black troops who tested here their first combat . . . performed well."[10] Nevertheless, Cram wrote home, "Mother, the abolitionists may talk as they please, but I tell you that colored troops cannot be depended on and that evidently caused this great defeat" (August 9, 1864). Cram saw himself in the mainstream, as a moderate. He explained on April 4, 1863, "I believe there are two extremes in the North, both of which are dangerous and need watching. One, the Copperhead democrat and the other the radical abolitionist."

Such views on abolitionists in these contemplative letters of a student from an abolitionist Christian school illustrate the dilemma President Abraham Lincoln faced with these issues. Ever the master politician, who especially felt the political pulse in Illinois, Lincoln understood and shared some of these ambiguous sentiments. Such contradictory feelings help explain Lincoln's actions toward slavery, emancipation, and arming slaves and how these actions changed over the course of the war.

In contrast to Lincoln, Cram's views appear to become less sympathetic to abolitionists and African-Americans as the war progressed. The farther he marched from Wheaton, Illinois, the more sympathetic he became with poor white Southerners. Like Abraham Lincoln, George F. Cram believed that secession was the work of an oligarchy of white planters who had deluded most Southern whites into leaving the Union and fighting for the Confederacy. On January 1, 1863, from Tennessee he told his mother about soldiers' leveling a Rebel captain's "splendid mansion" with a cannon. "I wish all rebel officers were served thus. . . . The common soldiers of the south have no longer any heart in the matter, all who are taken by our men say. . . . They would gladly have the old union restored and live again in the enjoyment of peace." Cram talked to a veteran of the War of 1812 who explained that the Southern elite told the Southern people that "Lincoln's robbers" were coming south to free African-Americans, "incite insurrections, and pillage the country. Is it a wonder that the poor ignorant commoners deluded into this belief should rise and fight even without clothes, for the defense as they thought of their liberty, poor ignorant wretches! How much have the rebel chiefs to account for!" Even as late as January 1, 1865, he believed an escaped slave who said, "The private soldiers all want to come back into the Union and stop the war but the Generals won't hear a word of it."

George F. Cram often contrasted the "civilized" North with the "uncivilized" South in his letters. His early letters are the most critical of the South. It is not clear whether this is because his travels through Kentucky and Tennessee showed him Appalachia and poorer regions of the South or because his views changed as he became acquainted with white Southerners over the course of his three years of service. On November 20, 1862, he contrasted Wheaton, Illinois, and Scottsville, Kentucky. "Could you be suddenly transported from Wheaton to Scottsville it would be like an electric shock so vast is the difference." While in Nashville, he visited a family that had moved there from Wheaton; he wrote on October 10, 1863, "But like all the people of the South they worship slavery at heart and hate the North though it once was their home."

On December 5, 1862, Cram described Southerners as "a poor contemptible people and we should have whipped them long ago if we had not traitors for generals. The idea that they will fight till they are exterminated is the most absurd nonsense. They are a complete pack of cowards and were it not for a few of their leaders they would have given up long ago." A certain grudging respect for Confederate leadership, almost a mystique, permeated some of Cram's letters, even early ones like that of February 15, 1863, wherein he spoke of the "redoubtable Morgan." John Hunt Morgan, successful scout for the Confederates, nicknamed "Morgan the Raider," was already something of a legend among his enemies.

In women Cram preferred intelligence, which he found more likely in the North. He thought that in the South "the women have an ignorant careless expression." "Some of them are very beautiful but lack that look of intelligence that so characterizes our northern girls." Later he discovered at least one Southern woman to admire. In March 1864 when a friend accidentally delivered some of Cram's belongings to his mother and she found a picture of a Southern woman among Cram's possessions, we learn that he had changed at least some of his views when he affectionately described her as a "very fine young girl and had one brother die in the rebel army. Her mother also recently died, leaving herself and older sister alone with an aged father, who was at one time wealthy and in good circumstance." On May 16, 1864, he writes about Southern women's hospitality: "The inhabitants of Georgia are much more hospitable and intelligent than those of Tenn. & KY though they acknowledge themselves our enemy. The women are kind and brought many nice eatables to our wounded at Resaca."

On June 15, 1864, Cram defended Southern soldiers accused in the *New York Tribune* of scalping Union dead at the Battle of Resaca, even though the 105th had seen no barbarity inflicted upon their dead and wounded. Cram wrote, "I know the rebels are savage enough," but he resented the newspaper report and the motives behind it. He went on to explain that "Very frequently the rebel skirmishers and ours meet each other half way and spend an hour talking quite amicable, when not ordered to fire our boys sometimes trade coffee to them for tobacco." In the same letter he told about three Rebels who followed a "yankee pig" into camp. They "had enough of fighting against the old flag." That flag, Old Glory, had been loved in the South prior to the war, whereas the Confederate flag was a new symbol. In North Carolina on March 12, 1865, he wrote that the "best possible feeling seems to exist between the citizens and our army. The houses were not plundered and a guard was sent to each." By May 1900 when he published his "Reminiscences: The Battle of Resaca" in *Cram's Magazine: A Monthly Journal of History, Geography and Topics of the Day,* he referred to his former enemies with respect: "Americans are opposed to Americans, and both sides with natural pride and courage are determined to snatch victory from defeat."

Cram's letters describing the battles at Atlanta are one of the best accounts we have from the Union side. One historian has declared that the Battle of Atlanta, from May 3 to September 2, 1864, is "one of the hardest battles of the war to define."[11] Cram helps define that battle, as he explains in vivid detail why it was the "Battle 'for' Atlanta" rather than the "Battle 'of' Atlanta." On May 16, 1864, he optimistically wrote, "I am in the very best of spirits and feel it is the greatest honor to have a hand in this great campaign, which I trust will be the last of the war." It was at Goldsboro that the 105th Illinois joined up with Sherman.

After Chattanooga Sherman's army fought against Confederate troops commanded by General Joseph E. Johnston as it progressed toward Atlanta. Then the aggressive John Bell Hood replaced Johnston in Atlanta. The Confederates always knew that Atlanta, at their backs, had to be defended, and Sherman certainly understood Atlanta's importance. The significance of the taking of Atlanta cannot be overstated. According to McPherson, the Confederacy put so much effort into defending Atlanta that the city "became a symbol of resistance and nationality second only to Richmond."[12] Cram reported on June 17, 1864, that two captured Rebels explained that if the Union took Richmond and Atlanta "and re-elected 'Abe,' their only hope was gone." Historians agree that the fall of Atlanta foreclosed the possibility of political victory by the Democratic Party and ensured the reelection of Lincoln as President. Electoral victory for the Democrats would have meant the end of the war and acceptance of Southern secession.

Cram's account goes into the nitty-gritty of battling for Atlanta. On May 27, 1864, Cram described charging Confederate breastworks: "The scene was grand and awful beyond description; a terrible sheet of lead bridged the air above us and leaden hail flew threw our ranks. Man after man went down, but no fear entered the hearts of the others." He felt that "The many escapes, the many acts of bravery I saw, and the thousand little things . . . might afford conversation a lifetime." On June 7, 1864, he recounted, "The loss of our brigade during the month of May was 99 killed and 385 wounded, making an aggregate of 484 most of who received their wounds in that charge." His mother was worried about the constant artillery bombardments, but Cram comforted her by writing that it was not the artillery but "little leaden messengers sped from rebel muskets that decimate our ranks and find so many southern graves for our boys" (June 17, 1864). After the 105th left Lookout Mountain for the Battle of Atlanta, Cram noted that he had passed "Sixty long weary days, everyone of which has been in itself a lifetime. During that time our regiment has lost in killed and wounded about one hundred and twenty-five men" (July 1, 1864). On July 4, 1864, he described what it was like in the midst of a battle: "Now a poor boy has his leg shot away, another has his face blown off by a shell, and one by one they fall." Over the guns' roar the soldiers could hear the captain's commands "in a loud clear voice, and the men obeyed them as if they were unconscious that the next moment might be their last on earth. Noble fellow! Everyone a hero." On August 9, 1864, he wrote, "Bullets are continually whistling and monster shells flying form line to line. . . . The very air seems full of death and destruction."

Cram documents a string of Confederate desertions and captured Rebel soldiers, conversations with them, and observations about them. On Independence Day, 1864, he noted "a continual string of prisoners, coming in most of them giving themselves up, declaring that they would follow the running army no farther." He answered inquiries of his mother and erroneous newspaper reports on July 31, 1864, when he argued that the deserters "are not foreigners but mostly Georgians and are as intelligent as any. The foreigners we captured are the most rabid, particularly Irishmen . . . most of the deserters and prisoners are only anxious for peace on any terms." One wounded Confederate "said if we could only kill their generals, that they made them fight against their will, etc." It does not occur to young Cram that these captured soldiers were spouting what they thought the Union soldiers wanted to hear.

Soldiers both North and South saw firsthand the devastation of war. On January 24, 1864, Cram wrote, "You cannot realize the terrible destruction which attends those countries where active war exists, but I have seen it. All traffic ceases except a little in the largest towns. The work of a lifetime is destroyed in a few minutes, fences are burned down; education ceases; whole towns are in ruins and in others beautiful buildings, once used for thriving business, are now filled with dirty soldiers for a large percent of soldiers will be dirty— but were I to undertake to tell of one half the awful ruin and devaluation exhibited even in Tenn. I should want four such sheets of paper as this." When the 105th Illinois entered South Carolina, where they laid the blame for the war, they took their vengeance. "As soon as we stacked arms, the whole brigade rushed hell upon these houses and in half an hour not a vestige of them remained save the chimneys and one house for headquarters. They made us excellent fires and warmed us thoroughly. Such was our entrance in the state" (January 5, 1865). On March 12, 1865, he worried that "in South Carolina we ruined the principle railroads and I am sorry to say, destroyed a great percent of dwelling houses; this kind of campaigning is just as vicious to our army in its discipline as it is to the enemy."

As an enlisted soldier, George F. Cram exercised that inalienable right of troops to complain about their officers. On October 20, 1862, he wrote, "We are now soldiers, citizens no longer, and are subject to the orders of superiors. . . . Strange that officers are not selected from men of real merit and moral character." On December 5, 1862, he noted that officers "sit in their nice warm tents, faring like kings, and caring no more for us than though we were so many dogs." Five days later he wrote, "Our soldiers are fast losing confidence in their leaders." On April 23, 1864, he criticized officers and surgeons who "ride by in perfect indifference" to exhausted soldiers who had marched until they "lay groaning by the side of the road."

For some of the officers, Cram expressed admiration. He described fellow Illinoisan General Ulysses S. Grant, whom he saw in Nashville, as a "plain man, and deals in a plain way, especially with rebels" (January 1, 1864). And a month later he exclaimed, "We have full confidence in Grant" (February 14, 1864). Cram was pleased to fight under corps commander General Joseph (Fighting Joe) Hooker: "Everybody loves him and to see him as he rides along our lines is only to like him more each time." When Sherman bypassed him for promotion, and Hooker resigned, Cram assessed that "the soldiers, who fight battles will always love him" (July 31, 1864). Cram was especially fond of General William Starke Rosecrans. When Rosecrans replaced General Don Carlos Buell, Cram noted excitedly, "The soldiers all think everything of him and are much elated that Buell is superseded" (November 7, 1862). And when, after Chicamauga, General George Thomas replaced Rosecrans, Cram despaired that "one of the best, if not the very best military commanders" was removed (September 1, 1863).

Cram was never fond of his Brigade commander General Ward. On October 20, 1862, he reported "Our brigadier general is seldom or never seen sober after ten o'clock in the morning." When the 105th Illinois was reorganized as 1st Brigade, 3rd Division, 20th army corps, Cram commented, "The brigade is commanded by Brig. Genl. Ward, a regular old Falstaff whose sheer delight is to swill whisky, etc. No one respects him." On March 6, 1864, he wrote that "Our Brigade Com is Col. Harrison, who is a most able man and well liked by us all, but our division Genl. is a regular sot." Yet, years later, when he published his memoir of the Battle of Resaca, he generously described his commander: "For here is brave old General Ward waving his sword and shouting words of encouragement. He is holding up one arm, for a bullet has passed through it, and the grand old man is more proud of that wound than is the mother of her first born."

Cram's views of Sherman evolved over the course of his service under him. He commented on July 31, 1864, that "I have little faith in Sherman's ability, but a wooden General ought to succeed here against an army one half our strength commanded by a rash man." A few months later he explained, "I cannot say that I like Sherman much or all his actions but he is our Genl., and we have to submit" (September 9, 1864). After Sherman had mess with the 105th Illinois, Cram reported, "He is a very nervous man and can't keep still a moment. . . . I begin to think much more of his generalship than I ever have before" (October 18, 1864). By the end of the war, Cram was devoted to Sherman and awed with respect for "Uncle Billy" (May 26, 1865).

Among the political leaders Cram discussed was John Charles Frémont, of whom the soldiers had long been his "strongest supporters." This good opinion changed when Frémont declared his candidacy as a Radical Republican to run against Lincoln for President. Although Frémont withdrew when it became obvious that he had very little support from other Republicans or from the general population, his willingness to go against Lincoln harmed him in public opinion. "The news of Abe's renomination was received with intense joy by the army, but the addition of Frémont blasts him forever in the eyes of the soldiers" (June 15, 1864). Soldiers now ranked Frémont "with the enemies of the country and the special enemy of the soldier." The soldiers supported Lincoln, even with some misgivings. Cram wrote of politics, "I am almost disgusted Mother with politics, there is so much rottenness in it. I want Lincoln to be reelected for the benefit of the country, because I think it would be a benefit to the country at the *present time,* but I am far from being satisfied with him or his administration" (August 30, 1864). He reported in September that the army held "a few McClellan men. Alas, copperheads in our regiment, but they are weak-kneed cowards who want him elected merely to stop the fighting so they may not have to endanger their worthless necks anymore." He reported that in his company, "all are loved for Lincoln and the Union." He mentioned his hometown soldiers: "Wheaton boys generally are well, hopeful and earnest for Lincoln."

In his letter dated April 19, 1865, Cram told of the grief over Lincoln's death. "Yesterday our camps were filled with intense sorrow over the death of Mr. Lincoln. . . . The feeling in the entire army is deep mourning." In his writing about the assassination of Lincoln,

Cram appears even sympathetic to the North Carolina secessionists whom he had despised at the time of his enlistment. "The citizens of this place held a meeting yesterday and made some resolutions expressing their sorrow at the occurrence and even the old rebels seem to feel a kind of horror at such a dastardly deed."

Covering such life-and-death issues, this volume of letters by George F. Cram also provides details of the everyday life of a soldier. Answering his mother's wish "to know how I managed to spend my time," he carefully logged the soldier's life (November 23, 1862). Cram's record, made over the course of his service of three years, enlarges our understanding of the Illinois 105th and of the history of the Civil War. From these intimate letters we learn an Illinois soldier's perspective on events of national importance and about those insignificant moments that made up most of a soldier's life during the Civil War. In a letter to his uncle early in his journey, he referred to struggling across the Kentucky mountains with a heavy knapsack as "the hardest work I ever did" (November 7, 1862). But as George F. Cram's letters vividly illuminate, that was just the beginning of what hardship would mean.

NOTES

ACKNOWLEDGMENTS: Portions of this introduction are much indebted to material supplied by Jennifer Cain Bohrnstedt.

1. *War of the Rebellion . . . Official Records of the Union and Confederate Armies,* Set 1, Vol. 11, pt. 1, p. 61. An officer deleted these harsh words before sending the telegram.

2. James M. McPherson, *Battle Cry of Freedom: The Civil War Era* (New York: Oxford University Press, 1988), p. 491. Luther O. Emerson and others as well wrote music for the poem.

3. *U.S. Statutes at Large,* 12, p. 597.

4. McPherson, *Battle Cry of Freedom,* pp. 492–93.

5. McPherson, *Battle Cry of Freedom,* p. 754.

6. Daniel Scott Smith, "Military Participation in Union Forces during the Civil War: A Comprehensive Demographic Portrait and Analysis," unpublished paper to be presented at the American Historical Association Annual Meeting, Chicago, IL, January 2000.

7. Richard S. Taylor, "Beyond Immediate Emancipation: Jonathan Blanchard, Abolitionism, and the Emergence of American Fundamentalism," *Civil*

War History 27 (September 1981); Paul M. Bechtel, *Wheaton College: A Heritage Remembered, 1860–1984* (Wheaton, 1984); Clyde S. Kilby, *Minority of One: The Biography of Jonathan Blanchard* (Grand Rapids, 1959); Warren Wyeth Willard, *Fire on the Prairie: The Story of Wheaton College* (Van Kampen Press, 1950).

8. The classic account is John Hope Franklin, *The Emancipation Proclamation* (Garden City, N.Y.: Doubleday, 1963).

9. V. Jacque Voegeli, *Free But Not Equal: The Midwest and the Negro during the Civil War* (Chicago: University of Chicago Press, 1967).

10. McPherson, *Battle Cry of Freedom,* p. 740.

11. Henry E. Simmons, comp., *A Concise Encyclopedia of the Civil War* (New York: A.S. Barnes and Company, 1965), p. 25.

12. McPherson, *Battle Cry of Freedom,* p. 751.

Soldiering with Sherman

Anna Damon Blanchard Cram (Mrs. Cram)

(Courtesy of John Hoskins)

CHAPTER 1

"Citizens No Longer"

Wyanet, July 9–Frankfort, October 20, 1862

Corporal George F. Cram began his correspondence with friends and family back in Wheaton from Camp Dixon in northwestern Illinois, one of the nine camps in the state for training new Union soldiers. Photographs of camp life would have shown enthusiasm and camaraderie among recruits like George F. Cram in newly forming regiments like the 105th Illinois Infantry. If it had not been July 1862, the image of that excitement could have been confused with a revivalist's camp meeting.

George became feverishly ill before leaving Illinois and the 105th Illinois Infantry's march to Kentucky only exacerbated his misery. The regimental surgeon, Doctor Potter, who had treated George before in civilian life, left him at a private home in Shelbyville, Kentucky to recover while the regiment continued to Frankfort.

While recuperating in Shelbyville, George saw hundreds of Union soldiers who had become separated from their regiments. The errant soldiers seemed to feel at home there—a town that George suspected was full of Southern secessionist sympathizers. According to his diary (October 7, 1862), the wild scenes of drinking, carousing, and the playing of "Dixie," the Confederate anthem, made George uncomfortable. Furthermore, he was lonesome for his comrades. Upon learning that several soldiers who had also convalesced in Shelbyville were planning to march to Frankfort to join their regiments, George mustered his strength and accompanied them.

The 105th Illinois Infantry was only in Frankfort, Kentucky for seventeen days, but during that time Colonel Dustin drilled them rigorously. Drilling was about all they could do because, like in nearly every other new Union regiment at the time, the 105th had been issued shoddy firearms which were either unsafe or inoperable. As a newspaper editor back home, Colonel Dustin was familiar with the power of the press and took his complaint about the firearms to the *Chicago Tribune* (October 28, 1862): "Never was there a more intelligent, active and energetic regiment sent into the fields than the

105th, but the officers and men have been extremely mortified and chagrined at the miserable apology for arms turned out to them from the Springfield armory. We had the most positive assurances that Enfield rifles should be ours, but instead we have Austrian rifled muskets of the most bungling and defective character."

Perhaps inspired by President Lincoln's Emancipation Proclamation the month before, George wrote eloquently in his diary on October 19, 1862, "Let America set this example before the world and the time will soon come when freedom to all men of every race and color shall be universal, the long oppressed will find rest to their weary souls, wars will be few throughout the land, progress will not be impeded by the clashing of arms and a more perfect state of happiness will settle over all." George's description of the war as a crusade to end slavery was unique in his writings during the early months in the army. The further south he marched, the stronger he articulated his desire for restoring the Union.

After leaving Frankfort he noted in his diary (October 31, 1862) that "the poetry of war has now worn off and we have come to the prose part." His accounts to his mother began to withhold some of the more unpleasant observations of a soldier's life. While his letter mentioned that the men were hobbling on sore feet, his diary (October 28, 1862) was more direct: "Many of the boys are nearly used up, their feet are sore and their backs are most broke carrying those heavy knapsacks. I have seen them walking along encumbered by nearly 60 lb. weight, the tears rolling down their cheeks from fellows I know . . . there is no one here to care for them, all is selfishness here, everyone for himself." By the time the 105th Illinois Infantry arrived in Kentucky, George and his comrades had left poetic illusions of soldiering far behind.

Wyanet, Ill.
July 9, 1862

Dear Mother,

I have just arrived at Wyanet[1] and hasten to give you the particulars so far. Monday I met Ellis, Blake and another student (Bean) and I got off the train and went home with them to Ellis's.[2] I passed the day yesterday there and came over here today.

Everything is in as good condition as could be expected; 20 acres of the best land are in wheat; the rest in corn. The wheat looks as well as any around here (but, all wheat is light this season owing to the bad weather) the corn is very weedy but there is no corn in this country what is so. I think it will be an average crop all around. Harvest will not commence before 2 weeks.[3]

I am at Mrs. Basses, she is married to a Mr. Shurtleffe, a fine looking man. She thinks of coming to Wheaton with me when I go back to look around and if she likes the place she wants to buy property there and go there to live. She was very much pleased to see me.

The people here all thought I was dead. They had heard I was killed in the army but I have assured them that I am yet alive and expect to be for some time to come.[4]

I do not think I am going to be able to work much. The sun hurts my head. I have had a very severe headache all day and my ear is worse than it was. I think the doctor will have to send me something stronger for it. He spoke of using the acetate of copperas,[5] I think, if this did not cure it. When you go to Chicago you can tell him what I say.

Wyanet has two temperance societies established now and has got rid of all the lager beer saloons but one, which I think is doing pretty well, for so drunken a place as this was.

I have not seen many of the people yet but expect to tonight when I go to take this to the P.O. Old Mr. Giles and Annie tend the office together now. She has not been to Chicago since last summer. Henry Giles is in the army selling confectionary. Miss Parker is still in the old stand and Mrs. Stubb has a shop also, so the town is well supplied with ribbons.

Well I believe I have written you all the news I have at present so I will write you what I learn hereafter the next time.

Mrs. Bass (Shurtleffe now) sends her very best respects to you.

From your affectionate son George

Dixon [Ill.]
Aug. 31, 1862

Dear Mother,

I have but just now got time to write since we arrived here and I have now but a very few minutes to write. After a ride of about three hours we arrived here last Friday, nothing unusual occurring on the road with the exception of one or two men getting slightly drunk. We found no place had been prepared for us and have taken up our quarters at the passenger freight house, eating at the former and sleeping at the latter.

Immediately upon our arrival, myself, Kingsley, Leonard Dewolf, and three others were detailed for special duty and were handed over to the Commandant for directions.[6] We are the cooks for two companies. We get extra pay and extra fare having the very best the house affords while the rest can get nothing but bread, butter, meat, potatoes and coffee. We have a good bed also and are not obliged to sleep on the floor, but tomorrow ends our special duty as we are going into barracks.

The camp here contains about two thousand men and present a very fine appearance. We went down last night to the river and passed right by the camp, which, all lighted up looked beautifully.

Today a few of us went there and heard their chaplain preach. He is rather a dry preacher and we were poorly paid for the walk. I have in my mess eleven, all good fellows among whom are Dewolf, Kingsley, Griswold and Whitlock. Most of them are church members and we shall have evening worship. We commenced it last night.

I expect I shall be able to get a furlough and if I do I shall probably be home next Sunday, which will without doubt be the last Sunday I shall spend in Wheaton till after the war.

We have not received our bounty yet but expect it daily.[7]

Today we are going to have a regular old fashioned dinner of pork and beans. Our landlord is a very fine man. He told us to eat anything we could find about the house and we contrived to do so. Our boys are a very quiet sort and make no disturbance. They are all well and in the best of spirits, we cannot tell as yet anything about the length of time we shall stay here, but I think it will be three or four weeks.

You can have no idea of the amount we eat up here, whole stacks of bread and meat at about the rate of one ox per day with other provisions in proportion. There are woods full of plums, grapes, and wild cherries about half a mile from here, and after we get once settled we shall live well, but I must close as it is now time to get dinner.

Give my respect to all the friends.
Your affectionate son George.
Direct to Dixon, Ill. 105th Regiment, Ill. Volunteers

Camp Childs[8]
Sept. 25th, 1862

Dear Mother,

I have rec'd several letters from you since I came from Wheaton and also a night cap and jar of pickles. I should have written yesterday but I thought from what you wrote in your last letter that you would be here.

Frank Ellis has enlisted. I saw him a day or two since in Camp Douglas.[9] He enlisted with a company from Princeton.[10] We do not know when we shall leave here but all of us are anxious to go. Our guns have come but are not yet distributed.

Last Monday we had a good post review; 9 regiments were drawn up in line of battle and inspected by the commandant of the post (Col. Tucker). It was a beautiful sight.

Our officers are very strict now. Capt. Daniels is still in Wheaton, nobody regrets it.[11] The men, many of them, openly express their disapprobation of his treatment of them. He has done nothing at all for the company.

Last Saturday after he was gone the sentinels allowed about twenty-five of the men to go home and spend the Sabbath, but since that time the Col. has issued orders that none of them shall go home without a furlough signed by him. So it is very difficult now to get off.

We are at present very comfortably situated. Our tents are warm and shed the rain well. We are supplied with sufficient bedding and more clothing than we can use so you need not be at all anxious for our physical welfare.

The boys in our company are all doing well. Dewolf is a nurse in the hospital. Tirtlot and Kingsley are both well and we are all seemingly in the best of spirits.

A few days ago there was a man in the company next to us [who] had his arm shot off by carelessly leaning upon his gun while on guard. He was not expected to live, but I believe he is better and possibly may recover.

Mr. Blanchard was here and staid all night with us night before last.[12] He looks as natural as ever.

When you come in I wish you would bring my pants (those which I wore at Dixon). They will be very serviceable to me. You might patch up the knees a trifle and they will last longer.

Uncle Sam and Alice came here last night. He slept in our tent and seems to like it pretty well. I shall send this letter out by her.

By your last letter you seem to have heard some very singular report the purpose of which you did not write. I have not deserted nor do I expect to and I am not aware of having done anything to have displeased you or anyone so your "horrible rumors" are simply the result of some very lively imagination. I have nothing more to add at present and must close for drill.

Your affectionate son George.

Shelbyville [Ky.]
Oct. 9th, 1862

Dear Mother,

I am very much better than when I last sent word to you. Dr. Potter had myself and another sick man removed to this place. He thought it was better than to remain at camp. I am at a private house here and the landlady is very kind to me. She says she is a sister of Mr. Powell's wife (the jeweler in Wheaton).

Our regiment has gone on to Frankfort and I expect to follow them in a few days. The boys have been very kind while I have been sick and I feel very lonesome here without them.

We have had a great many little incidents on the road but I do not feel able to write more now. Give my love to Ettie. Tell Mrs. Gary we were ordered off so soon I could not see her son but I sent her letter to him.[13]

Love to Uncle Rufus and all the friends,
Your affectionate son George
SEND ME SOME STAMPS.

Camp at Frankfort [Ky.]
Oct. 15th, 1862

Dear Mother,

I rec'd two letters from you today the first I have had since I left Chicago. I left Shelbyville last Sat., and arrived here Sunday night. I did not expect to come so soon, but I got so very lonesome there with none of my friends around me that I concluded I must try and make the journey. I came through with fifty other men just out of the hospital there.

We came slow (only ten miles a day). Sat. night we stopped halfway between here and S——. We had only 15 guns and were much afraid of being captured by the rebels as there had already been nearly 1000 men taken by them on the road. We made a soup for our supper and then made up our beds as best we could. I spread my blankets on a side hill with the rest and laid down. The night was dark as pitch. I kept slipping down the hill all night and woke up every half hour. About two o'clock a lot of cattle came rushing down the hill on the opposite side and we all thought it was rebel cavalry but it proved nothing more than a good scare.

The next morning (Sunday) we started on buying our provisions on the road. They charged us terrible prices and I was more than once tempted to refuse to pay them anything (about half the inhabitants are secesh[14]) but I got into camp that night about five o'clock very tired and sore. The boys were all much pleased to see me again, many of them had thought I would never be able to rejoin them. I am much better and shall soon be able to do duty again.

Today I visited the country. There is a beautiful monument erected to the brave sons of Kentucky. Also I saw the monument of the celebrated Daniel Boone. I send you with this letter a piece of wood which I cut from the stump of one of the first trees that he felled in this state. It is a great curiosity. Also I send a leaf which I picked up in front of the monument where ly his remains. I saw the coffin which enclosed him and also the one which lies his wife. His monument is erected on the very spot where he built his first house. It must have been a very wild spot.

Frankfort (the capital of the state) is a very miserable little town surrounded by the most rugged hills I ever saw—so steep they can hardly be climbed. In the valley runs the Kentucky River, a very insignificant little stream. The State House is a very old and shabby looking building. The State prison has fairly gone to rack and ruin (a portion of it took fire and burned down this evening).

The entire state, at least that part through which we have passed, presents a scene of desolation, nearly half the houses are unoccupied, large and beautiful looking orchards, entirely stripped of fruit (scarcely an apple can be bought here at all), corn fields have been ravaged by the hordes of soldiers that have passed through, the country is generally rough and presents little appearance of agriculture.

There are plenty of slaves and they all appear to look well and seem happy. They are as a general thing nearly as intelligent as their masters.

We have it pretty hard for now but hope for the best. Dr. Potter sends respects. Goodbye, love to Uncle Rufus. I will write to him as soon as I get a little further.

Your affectionate son George

Camp at Frankfort [Ky.]
Oct. 20th, 1862

Dear Mother,

It is now Monday evening. I am sitting on my blankets up to a long box which we use for eating on and doing all our writing. For a light I have a candle fastened down by means of dropping some of the tallow on the box and setting the other end of the candle in it—it hardens and holds the light firmly. On my left in the corner is a smaller box in which we place our dishes and eatables, what we have for our tent is very small, calculated to contain four, although five are crowded into them all now. I will now endeavor to describe our manner of living as nearly as possible.

At four o'clock in the morning, the regiment is called out and with their knapsacks strapped upon their backs, their guns in their hands, they are obliged to stand until six o'clock, then they are called to breakfast. Each man at once takes his cup, fills it with coffee, breaks up a hard cracker into it, takes a piece of pork and that is the sum total of the soldier's breakfast. Then the guards are detailed and those who have nothing to do go to their tents to write to their friends, talk among themselves about the probabilities of the war's soon ending and in various other ways pass away the time till noon.

Our dinner programme is the same as breakfast with the exception of beans once in about a week. In the afternoon we have a battalion drill which is simply a drill of the whole reg't conducted by the Colonel. Our supper is a repetition of breakfast and dinner and consequently needs no description.

Early in the evening those who have no guard duty to perform retire to their tents, spread their blankets and while some sink at once into the arms of Morpheus, others write to their friends in the far off, and fully appreciated land of the North.

Yesterday our regiment was called out and marched from camp at one o'clock in the morning, I was not well enough to march and staid behind with about one hundred others. Our boys were marched fifteen miles to a town in which a lot of guerrillas were encamped. They arrived their about nine o'clock just in time to find that the birds had flown, covered with dust from head to foot, tired and half starved they reached camp about dark, having marched thirty miles with nothing to eat and without accomplishing anything at all. Poor fellows, how I pitied them. There is a rumor tonight that those same rebels are all captured.

My health is improving, but I do not yet perform any duty and have not since we left Chicago. We do not know how long we shall stop here in camp.

We are now soldiers, citizens no longer, and are subject to the orders of superiors. Our brigadier general[15] is seldom or never seen sober after ten o'clock in the morning. Strange that our officers are not selected from men of real merit and moral character.

This afternoon a shooting affray took place in the camp next to us. Two men shot at each other with revolvers, some ten or twelve shots were fired, resulting in one of them being wounded in the hand and a horse standing by being killed.

But I must close my letter. Good night,
Your affectionate son George.

CHAPTER 2

"If You Examine the Map"

On October 30, 1862, General William S. Rosecrans assumed command of the Army of the Cumberland. Under his command, the 105th Illinois was part of Ward's Brigade under Brigadier General Paine at the post of Gallatin, Tennessee. Rosecrans's task was to continue moving south and defeat Confederate General Bragg. The troops were kept busy and none were busier than the musicians who played the death march as typhoid fever spread quickly at Bowling Green and Scottsville, Kentucky. The Army of the Cumberland's migration into Secesh territory added rebel guerrillas to their growing list of dangers. Confederate General John Hunt Morgan was supported by many Confederates who came from nearby Sumner County, Tennessee. A *New York Times* correspondent reported while at Gallatin, the county seat of Sumner County (November 24, 1862), that "The citizens of this section regard Morgan as some ubiquitous demi-god, possessing all the qualities of manliness and chivalry, as well as a charmed life against the steel and bullets of the Union forces."

Union cavalry captured some of Morgan's men between Scottsville and Gallatin during the winter of 1862–63, adding validity to the rumors of Morgan's proximity. Colonel Basil Duke who served under General Morgan said that in times of danger, Morgan seemed possessed of a coolness and "a quality even higher than courage. . . . It was almost mesmeric." Morgan's list of attacks and escapades grew and in August 1862, his destruction of the strategically important tunnel of the Louisville & Nashville Railroad nearby underscored the vulnerability of Union troops at the hands of Morgan and his men near Scottsville.

By the late Fall, the list of Union deserters was growing rapidly, and more than a dozen men of the 105th Illinois Infantry had deserted. By December 1862 the count of desertions among the Union Army's enlisted men and officers was well into the thousands. The *New York Times* (December 15, 1862) chided the War Department for tolerating this growing problem: "General

Halleck has announced, either twelve or fourteen times, that desertion from the Union Army is not permissible. If he continues to reiterate this statement long enough, there is hardly a doubt, that some of the twenty thousand men and officers who are now said to be absent without leave, will finally get indoctrinated with the notion that quitting the army without the knowledge of their superiors is an objectionable practice."

Although keeping desertions a secret was impossible, George did not use names when he wrote about deserters. Private Robert Hale Strong, Company B, 105th Illinois Infantry, deserted twice during the first year and fled to Canada, probably to escape the bounty hunters who would take him back to face court-martial and punishment. Another soldier, Private Nelson Samples, originally a member of Company K, was not as lucky as Private Strong. Private Samples deserted from the 105th, then enlisted in an Illinois cavalry unit. When he deserted from the cavalry, he was apprehended and executed without the benefit of a court-martial.

With an early winter nipping at their heels and supplies running low, George's letters to his Mother remained buoyant, yet his diary (November 2, 1862) was more candid, "I have got so I can drink out of mud puddles and eat raw pork. Dear me, what are we coming to?"

Camp near Bowling Green [Ky.]
Nov. 7, 1862

Dear Uncle,[1]

Today is the first opportunity I have had of writing for the last two weeks. We have just passed through a ten-day march from Frankfort to this place, a distance of 150 miles. Although we traveled slowly, still the march was a severe one, and a large number of our troops fell out on the way and were left behind. We were encumbered with heavy knapsacks, blankets, overcoats, cartridge boxes filled, guns, canteens and haversacks making in all a weight of about 60 lb.[2] Carrying this over a mountainous country, you may well imagine was no easy task. It was the hardest work I ever did.

We passed over some grand and beautiful places, and it put me in mind of the time when I used to visit Grandfather's and ride up that long hill near East Wilton.[3] We met with no incidents of any consequence on the march and are now encamped on a large plain surrounded by woods, upon the top of a mountain, about three miles from the town.

Bowling Green is a place of, I should judge, about five thousand inhabitants. It is a poor looking place, like all the Kentucky towns, the houses are old, poorly built and seem just ready to fall to pieces though there are a few very handsome buildings in it.

Yesterday afternoon our division was reviewed by Gen. Rosecrans. It presented a most beautiful appearance. The infantry were all drawn up in line of battle and formed a line as far as the eye could reach, their bayonets all glistening in the departing sunlight. It was really grand. Our reg't has the post of honor, on the right flank and our company is second on the right wing of the reg't so you see we have the most important position. The Genl. stopped in front of us and made us the following speech, "Soldiers, fire deliberately, aim well and shoot to kill."

The soldiers all think everything of him and are much elated that Buell is superseded.[4] The troops here are in good spirits and though marching is the hardest part of a soldier's life, they all wish to press forward and close the war. The rebel troops have all left or are leaving Kentucky but a few guerrillas under Morgan. And we expect every day to march for Nashville.

The health of the reg't is excellent, considering the hardships we have endured, but few have died; only one in our company. My own health is now good, though I have been quite sick with bilious fever.[5]

The greatest trouble I have is not knowing what is being done and how the war is going on. We do not get papers until they are so old. We are not yet supplied with good guns and tents, both important articles. Those we have are of an inferior quality.

I am in need of nothing at present and am as comfortable as a soldier can expect.

Love to all,
Your affectionate nephew George.

Camp near Bowling Green [Ky.]
Nov. 9th, 1862

Dear Mother,

Well we have at last arrived at this famous place after ten mortal days marching over space of some 150 miles. We got here yesterday and have now got our tents up. The march was indeed the hardest thing I ever went through. Many of our men fell out on the road and hundreds of others hobbled along on very sore feet.[6]

We started Sunday morning the 27th Oct., marching that day through the snow which was about three inches deep encamping that night about 18 miles from Frankfort. We slept on the damp ground with no covering but our blankets. The ground froze that night two inches. The country through which we have passed is mountainous and we saw but very little farming land.

I cannot imagine how the people here continue to live. I saw many most beautiful places. We marched for miles over high mountains, great huge rocks jutting out over our heads and in some spots trees were growing out as it were from the rocks on the side of the hills. I cannot possibly describe it in a letter and will not try.

The country bears the marks of devastation, houses all along the road are deserted and those which are inhabited are mostly filled with secesh, they beat all for ignorance. We scarcely saw a school house on the road. There is no enterprise nor ambition whatever here. The Negroes as a general thing know about as much as their masters.

Bowling Green, instead of being the beautiful place I had supposed, is a shabby built town of about five thousand inhabitants. The houses are mostly very old looking and poorly built.

We are now camped in a good place and are comfortable. There is a large cave where we get water.[7] I explored it yesterday about a quarter of a mile it is a beautiful place entering into the side of a mountain and the huge rocks arching out above all form a picturesque and grand appearance. We do not know how long we shall remain here but expect soon to be on our way to Nashville.

I am well as ever. My feet are not at all sore and the only discomfort I feel from the long march is in being very tired.

I rec'd a letter from you the day before we started by Capt. Daniels, and had rec'd three others before. I'm glad [for] the things you sent me in Chicago two lemons and a large piece of beef. I wish you would send me some gloves by Lieut. Adams when he comes if you can.[8] You need not send stockings. I have plenty for this winter. Do not send anything that will burden me to carry.

I am keeping a diary and shall send it home when I have an opportunity. Tell Mrs. Grant that David and Orris are well.[9] Isaac [Grant] was sick at Frankfort but I hear he has recovered. The boys generally are in good health, but many are very homesick.

Send what papers you can, some of them will come through and with the principle war news, we know but very little what is going on here and when we get papers they are old ones.

Griswold, Kingsley, Whitlock and I tent together.[10] Dewolf is detailed as cook to the quarters.

Muster any nice little thing you can send by Lieut. Adams; will be acceptable and be sure and eat a Thanksgiving dinner for me.

From your affectionate son George

Camp at Scottsville [Ky.]
Nov. 20th, 1862

Dear Mother,

It is a dull rainy morning and we are allowed a little time to ourselves which I will improve by writing. You will see by the heading of this letter that we have again marched, we arrived here one week ago and have been kept in perpetual motion drilling and performing other camp duties all the time. Scottsville is a little old town of very few inhabitants. Most of the homes are deserted. It is the county seat of this Co. and the courthouse looks very much like a water tank on one of our Northern railroads.[11]

If you examine the map you will see that we are now near the border of the state, but a few miles from the Tennessee line, and are forming a line of defense from Cumberland Gap to the Mississippi having driven the rebels out of the state. The country where we now are encamped is almost wholly Secesh though they are all Union Men just at present. There is also an unfortunate number of young widows with enormous families.

The ignorance of the people is really amusing. An apparently intelligent woman yesterday was trying to sell us some pies. One of our boys asked her if she would take postage stamps for them. "Postage stamps!" said she, "what's them, them are little things what you puts on letters." Such little incidents occur every day.[12] Could you be suddenly transported from Wheaton to Scottsville it would be like an electric shock so vast is the difference. The men are all slim, small and of a pale, sickly color, generally having long black hair and the women have an ignorant careless expression. The men all dress in their "Butternut" coat, vest, and pants and we see them sitting around on fences standing with their mouths wide open, their hands in their pockets listening to our musicians. The country for miles around is one vast forest.

Our reg't has the post of honor in the brigade, being on the right flank. We are the best drilled reg't in the division and have the credit of it. I wish you could see us sometime as we go out on drill.

The health of the boys is generally good, but two deaths have occurred in our company and we report the fewest sick of any company in the reg't. My own health is most excellent. I am fatter than I ever was in my life and I hardly think you would know me now.

Our Col. was presented with a beautiful sword day before yesterday. He made a few appropriate remarks on the occasion. We were in a hollow square and after he had concluded his remarks, one of our Lieut's gave us a song.[13] Gen. Ward made us a small speech which gained him the respect of the whole reg't. He was followed by others and after another song we went back to camp in the best of spirits. The boys are looking forward eagerly to the speedy ending of the war, but I think they are rather fast with their anticipation.

We are almost wholly destitute of war news. I wish when you write you would mention the general summary of news. Tirtlot, Griswold, Kingsley, Batchelder and all the Wheaton boys, I believe, are in good health.[14] Martin Griswold and I chum together and continue to make ourselves quite comfortable. I rec'd several letters from you while at Bowling Green but none since.

Lieut. Adams has not yet arrived, though I hear he is at Bowling Green.

Your affectionate son George

Camp at Scottsville [Ky.]
Nov. 23, 1862

Dear Mother,

I rec'd the things which you sent by Lieut. Adams—butter, strawberries, apples, socks, gloves, pickles, water filter, etc. together with several letters and papers for all of which I am of course very thankful. The butter and fruit will chase down many a hard cracker. I wrote to you a few days since but write again now to acknowledge the receipt of the things.

Affairs here are going on very well. You wished to know how I managed to spend my time. I will tell you. At five o'clock we get up to roll call then go to bed until daylight. At half past seven we eat breakfast then we have two hours for cleaning guns, folding blankets and various other like duties. At ten we go out to company drill which lasts till twelve, then we take our dinner and have a little rest. At half past one we have battalion drill and that lasts till four. At half past four we have roll call and dress parade which lasts till about quarter past five. Then we eat our suppers and retire to our tents, sometimes we have candles to write by and sometimes we do not. At night we have another roll call and then go to bed. Sat. afternoon is allowed us for washing purposes, but Sundays we have general inspection and sometimes drill. You will see at once that we have but few idle moments.

You wrote that some one had written home that Gen. Ward had caused a soldier here to be gagged and to lay on his back three days. The statement was wholly false, no such thing occurred. You must not believe but two thirds of the rumors you hear. They are as thick here as flies in the summer.

I am not at all desponding, but believe I shall be home safe and before long. It is true that I have passed through many hardships but I expected that before I enlisted. I know what it is to make a dinner of hard crackers and raw pork, to drink out of a mudhole and sleep without tent when the ground froze hard, but I keep constantly thinking that all these things will only make me enjoy life the more when I again get into the civilized world.

We are now quite comfortably situated. Martin Griswold got a lot of butter and we have enough to last our tent nearly a month. Nicholas Kenyon is well;[15] I see him occasionally. Dewolf is at Bowling Green. John Batchelder is promoted to a corporal.

The young men you mentioned who were paroled are here held in almost as great dishonor as if they had deserted. It is evident they wished to be taken prisoners and lagged behind for that purpose. But I must close,

Your affectionate son George

CHAPTER 3

"The Gentlemen's Tent"

Gallatin, November 30–South Tunnel, December 25, 1862

The men of the 105th Illinois Infantry had come a long way during their three months away from home. By December they were making winter camp in Sumner County in northern Tennessee, secesh home soil. The Union Army camp was located two miles south of Gallatin on the Cumberland River. In Gallatin the soldiers first encountered former slaves, freedmen. Many of the freedmen clung to the Union Army for sustenance and protection, but the army could hardly provide for itself. However, the troops built a primitive camp for them in the town, inhabited mostly by women and children, and posted guards around the perimeter.

The bleakness of Gallatin at the time was described by a *New York Times* reporter (November 24, 1862): "The whole country about this place is a picture of desolation; but few dwelling houses are to be seen, and they appear denuded of everything which makes life comfortable. No stacks of hay or corn are visible in the fields, scarcely a fence within the limit of vision is discernable." By December 26, with blockades preventing shipments of goods to the South, a *New York Times* correspondent claimed that this region was in a state of famine.

Some seven miles north of the fort at Gallatin, hundreds of Union soldiers guarded the strategic South Tunnel where the Louisville & Nashville Railroad burrowed through the Highland Rim. The L&N was literally the Union Army's lifeline to rations, supplies, and munitions as General Rosecrans's army dug further into the hostile South. Remote, wooded, and with high ridges, the terrain was physically challenging for soldiers on picket. And the rugged landscape offered hiding places for Confederate sharp-shooters.

South Tunnel consisted of two tunnels: the north tunnel was 930 feet long and the south tunnel was 650 feet long. Union troops established small fortifications on both sides of the tunnels' entrances to prevent further sabotage of the line. Guards kept large fires at night and posted themselves no further than fifty yards away. Just weeks before the 105th Illinois Infantry arrived, General Morgan's men had captured Union guards stationed at South Tunnel and caused severe damage by sending blazing freight cars deep inside the tunnel, burning supporting timbers and causing tons of earthen debris to cover the track.

Nervousness at South Tunnel was well placed. In the early morning hours of Sunday, December 7, 1862, General Morgan's men crossed the icy Cumberland River and after a short but deadly battle overtook the sleeping camp of the Union's 39th Brigade near Hartsville, Tennessee, less than fifteen miles away from the camp of the 105th. The 39th Brigade, under the command of Colonel Absalom Moore (104th Illinois Infantry), lost 135 men; more than 1,800 were taken prisoners.

The battle at Hartsville shocked Union leaders. Late on December 7, General Rosecrans telegraphed General George H. Thomas who was based nearby at Gallatin: "Do I understand that they have captured an entire brigade of our troops without our knowing it, or a good fight? It seems to me impossible that the entire brigade could have surrendered. Are there none left?" Reporters dispatched many reports about the Union's humiliation at Hartsville, such as the column in the *New York Times* (December 9, 1862): "We trust that Gen. Halleck or President Lincoln will at once find means of putting each of them [isolated brigades and regiments] on their guard, else Morgan will soon half extinguish our armies in the Southwest." Adding insult to injury, five days later the newspapers featured Morgan parading the captured prisoners of the 39th Brigade past the home of his Murfreesboro, Tennessee fiancée, Mattie Ready. General Bragg likely regretted that the Hartsville raid was not targeted more productively at the destruction of the tunnels once again—an act that would have stopped the Union Army's supplies from getting through to Nashville.[1]

The 105th's winter of 1862–63 at South Tunnel was a turning point in the men's lives. The tunnels seemed to winnow the weak from the strong as large numbers of soldiers began to die. And it was there that George and the other soldiers began to challenge the politics of war and to question the capabilities and integrity of their leaders. In spite of the abnormal circumstances of his winter at South Tunnel, George maintained some normalcy. True to his character, he organized Shakespearian readings among the men and collected botanical specimens to send home. He also stayed abreast of the news once again thanks to the diligence of his mother and his uncles. Newspapers were received more frequently, making his quarters a primary place for others to learn of foreign and domestic affairs. And by staying connected with the business affairs of the nation, George, through his letters and diary, began to develop a stronger voice as he speculated about life after the war.

George's letters were calming in tone and had a positive attitude regarding the regiment's preparedness and his own unwavering devotion to high moral conduct and principled behavior. As assuring as this report must have been to his mother, the war extracted a heavy price from many, including some of the men who shared "the gentlemen's tent."

———

Camp at Gallatin [Tenn.]
Nov. 30, 1862

Dear Mother,

I rec'd since I have been here several papers, two *Independents and three Tribunes* but no letters yet, though I am expecting some every day.[2]

I am glad you continue to send papers. A great many of them come through especially when we are on the railroad and they are a source of a great deal of comfort to a soldier. In the last two papers you sent I see there are some very excellent news and hope they will keep on getting better till we at last conquer the rebel states.

We started from Scottsville last Tuesday morning at about nine o'clock and marched twenty miles that day arriving at this place Wednesday evening. We succeeded in getting a large quantity of straw for our tents and I slept better that night than I had before any night since being in camp. We are indeed very comfortably off being now entirely in an enemy's country we occasionally have a piece of fresh meat for dinner.

Yesterday our regt. was detailed to work on fortifications here, we left our arms in camp and shouldered spades and picks and Irishman fashion pitched into the dirt. I think we shall not be obliged to work any more however as they have sent some men from Nashville for that purpose.

I wish you could just step into our tent and see how easy and comfortable we have things fixed. I call it the gentlemen's tent.

There are four of us just like brothers who neither smoke, chew, swear nor drink. A great many of the boys are not what they were at home.

One of our Wheaton boys, Marshall Meacham, died at Scottsville the night before we left.[3] We did not have time to attend his funeral but had to leave behind some of our number to bury him. He was sick but a few days and gave way to despondency.

Four of our boys have now died and more are yet very feeble. My health continues good and I feel confident of again returning home. We cannot of course tell how long we shall stay here but it will not probably be long.

I wish you would try and send in your next letter one half an ounce of cayenne pepper and ground ginger in equal proportions as I am now in some need of it.

I saw Mrs. Kenyon's son today, he is in good health and in fine spirits. Leonard Dewolf is still at Bowling Green and I do not hear from him at all. I have received all the good things which you sent by Lieut. Adams and they come very opportune.

We are to have preaching tonight and I will now close to hear it.

Your affectionate son George

Camp at Gallatin [Tenn.]
Dec. 5th, 1862

Dear Mother,

I am sitting in our little tent with my feet covered up in blankets and trying to write on my knapsack. Outside the snow is falling very fast and the air is cold and damp. Griswold is sitting beside me writing home also.

I rec'd yesterday an *Illinoian* and today an *Independent* from you. In the *Illinoian* I noticed a piece from Lieut. Col. Vallette written principally against those boys who were paroled, which was not strictly true.[4] He stated that there were no armed rebels in the vicinity. There were over 1,000 Morgan's men all around us. He said that the sick were all allowed to fall back and ride in the ambulances. You will at once see how false this statement was for we have only two ambulances, each containing but two men and there were a hundred at least sick on the march, many of whom were left behind. I have seen on that march men who at home were strong and hearty, actually drop to the ground, perfectly exhausted. I have seen them lay groaning by the side of the road while our officers and too often our surgeons ride by in perfect indifference. I do not of course excuse those boys. There is no doubt but what they wished to be paroled, but I do think such a tirade of abuse against erring boys was entirely uncalled for by a Lieut. Col.

I do not exactly agree with you in believing this war is to hold out very long. The *Illinoian* speaks of them wearing such poor uniforms as a mark of their determination. You should see the clothes they wear at home and then you would think they would be glad to wear anything. They are a poor contemptible people and we should have whipped them long ago if we had not traitors for generals. The idea that they will fight till they are exterminated is the most absurd nonsense. They are a complete pack of cowards and were it not for a few of their leaders they would have given up long ago. I have some faith in Burnside and believe he is not afraid to risk a battle.[5]

I rec'd a long letter from you day before yesterday. You wished me to write a description of my life since leaving Chicago. I have not sufficient paper nor time to do so but I keep a diary which you will sometime see. You also asked quite a number of questions which I will answer here.

I get a large proportion of the papers you send. As a general thing we have had pleasant weather. I have had no difficulty yet in keeping my feet dry. We do not eat at a dining table anymore but take it in our hands and eat it in our tents sitting on the ground. I do not know the number of papers I have read, but think about twenty. Our work is not so hard as steady. We have no literary debates.

I do not get homesick, though when the war is closed none will be more glad to get home than myself. We have not been paid off yet and do not know when we shall be. I know no more how long we shall stay here than you do. Our movements depend upon those of other forces.

Our hospital here is in a very bad state. They are getting out of medicine. I have had a bad diarrhea for a week past and I went there day before yesterday to get some cayenne pepper for it. They have nothing for it but some turpentine and opium mixed. Of course, I wouldn't take that and I came back and starved it out.

We are on short allowance now of everything but crackers. We have drawn no soft bread since leaving Chicago. If an officer cared one jot for the comfort of the men we might have good bread. A bake oven could be built in a few hours and flour plenty could be brought on the railroad, but they sit in their nice warm tents, faring like kings, and caring no more for us than as though we were so many dogs. But I reason thus, the greater our deprivations are here, much more will be our ability to enjoy life hereafter.

After I close I will tell you one pleasant little incident which occurred a few nights since. Our company were all placed on picket duty. I was in command of a post, having four men in the evening I related to them one of Shakespeare's plays *(The Two Gentlemen of Verona)*. It had an excellent effect—they listened attentively and I noticed there was much less swearing for a long time afterward.

From your affectionate son George

Gallatin [Tenn.]
December 10th, 1862

Dear Mother,

You have doubtless heard long before this letter reaches you of the surprise and capture of a federal brigade stationed a short distance from this place last Sunday morning.[6] It was a most disgraceful affair to our army.

Two Ohio regt's stacked arms and fled without firing a gun. Well the affair put our officers all in a great flutter. Sunday evening news first came into camp and we were at once ordered out. After ascertaining our fighting number they ordered us to hold ourselves in readiness to fight or march at a moment's warning. That night (Sunday) we were ordered up at three and ordered to take three days rations and be ready to march any moment. The teams also were harnessed up. Well we got our three days rations, went back to bed and lay in anxious suspense till morning. The sun rose bright and clear and seemed to disperse some of the fears of our officers for no order for march was given. The day passed away quickly but yesterday a report was brought into camp that 2,000 rebels under Morgan were advancing to attack us. Our Col. examined our guns and we were obliged to wash them all out. In the afternoon we drilled to make ourselves more efficient and finally night came but brought no enemy.

I spent the event in writing to Ellis and at the usual hour we retired for the night.[7] About one o'clock woke up and the 102nd regt. (adjoining ours) was sounding the long roll (the battle call). A minute more and our drums rolled out the alarm upon the still midnight air. In an instant all was noise and bustle in camp. Our coats were hastily donned and cartridge boxes and bayonets were quickly put on. I had just buckled on all the accouterments of war, picked up my gun and stepped out of the tent when the alarm was found to be false. It originated by a regt. of men sounding the call for their men to get up to work on the fortifications. The call was mistaken by the 102nd Ill, for the long roll and thus it was taken up by one regt. after another till the camp was fully aroused. Well we threw off our warlike apparel and went back to bed again like sensible men. I cannot speak for the other companies in our regiment but our company promptly responded to the call, turning out to a man. The boys were cool and self-possessed although none knew what scenes of bloodshed the next hour would bring forth. We are getting used, as much as can be, to this wild roving kind of a life and nothing at all surprises or startles us now.

Our cavalry are still scouring the country by day and the fortifications are being rapidly completed. It is evident that our General does not intend being caught asleep.

There is a great spirit of peace prevailing in the army. The closing of the war and getting home again with their friends are the constant topics of conversation. They are all heartily sick of the war and many are looking to Congress to settle it. I had a letter yesterday from Ellis. He writes from Holly Springs,[8] speaks of his journey there and of the hardships he has endured since leaving Chicago. He has more yet to see and I am afraid he cannot endure them.

Our soldiers are fast losing confidence in their leaders. They have been fooled so many times that they no longer have faith in them and unless our government puts down the rebellion this winter, my own opinion is that it never can do it, the army will lose all its energy and vigor and our movements after that time will be attended with defeat. The soldiers are now being used far more roughly than ever before during the war and very many are giving way under it.

I still continue however to be hopeful and always look on the brightest side. I live now wholly for the future for there is certainly no enjoyment in a soldier's life. I do not however expect to resume my studies again should I live to come out of this struggle.[9] My health will not permit of it. I shall endeavor to get into some business in which I can raise myself up.

I wish you would have that thirty-five dollar order of mine collected as soon as possible so that it may draw interest. If you wish to use it, do so, I do not want you to be straitened for means neither shall you be so long as I have any. I hope we shall be paid again by the first of Jan. and then I will try to send home some, I have been without a cent for last six weeks, but good by,

Your affectionate son George
I rec'd two papers from you today.

Camp of the 105th [South Tunnel, Tenn.]
December 18th, 1862

Dear Mother,

Well, we have again moved. We started one week ago today from Gallatin for this place and arrived here a distance of seven miles in the evening of the same day.

We are now, they tell us, guarding the tunnel which the rebels partly demolished in their last raid into Kentucky, but it seems to me we are guarding the entire country around here. Five companies of our regt are out at one time. We have to go three miles to guard a bridge in one direction and four miles in another besides the picket which are extended from a mile to a mile and a half beyond our regular camp. Before they sent us here they had two regts and a battery to defend the place but they have been withdrawn and the 105th is alone and we never have in camp more than two hundred fighting men the rest being scattered over the country doing the guard duty.

Morgan is now said to be advancing to attack the railroad somewhere and as this is a very important point. I should not be at all surprised when he finds out our limited numbers if he paid us a visit. This is the soil over which all of Rosecrans' army supplies go and at this point it could be so seriously damaged by blowing up the tunnel that it would take months to repair it. Meanwhile Rosecrans' army might either starve or retreat. Of course our generals know best but I think the place is not half defended, for if Morgan could capture an entire brigade at Hartsville (which he did do) certainly he could easily defeat the two hundred men who are here in camp.

Yesterday we received news through the Nashville papers of Burnside's repulse at Fredericksburg. It greatly depressed the spirits of the soldiers generally but we all hope for the best and as the darkest hour is just before the dawn, it may be that some of the numerous expeditions underfoot will finally accomplish something.

While we are here we occasionally hear the news first from the front and could buy a newspaper daily were it not for the poverty which Uncle Sam compels us to endure. Yesterday we were coming in from picket and as we passed the mail train they threw us out a couple of papers, which although they contained bad news were nevertheless a rare treat.

We were sent out day before yesterday to guard a bridge three miles from here. It was one which Morgan had burned and had been reconstructed. I was up four hours in the night. We built up large fires on each side of the bridge at night and established our head-quarters off to the left about forty rods, posting the guards some ten rods from the fire in the forest so they could see every movement around the bridge.

It was the corporal's business to post the guard, keep up the fires and visit each one of the guards in succession to see that all was right with them. We had also a reserve of some twelve men at headquarters in case of an attack. I was up from eight till ten and from four till six. Nothing occurred during the night of any movement but in the morning our second lieutenant shot himself in the foot while getting over a fence.[10] The wound disables him for a time but is not serious.

Last Friday I was out also on picket and I had a glorious bath in a little brook nearby and my companion (Whitlock[11]) and myself succeeded by example and persuasion in getting all but one of the other guards to wash themselves from head to foot. This is a historical fact and might almost be put on record for soldiers seldom wash more than their noses and fingernails. I certainly believe that one half of the deaths in the army are caused by filth. We have some even in our own company who only wash their faces about once in a week and who *never* wash their bodies at the same time. They just pour down the grease and coffee cooked in iron kettles which spoils it. I have stopped drinking coffee except when on picket and then we are allowed to draw it and cook it in our tin cup. I eat no more pork also than I can favorably help. But to do wholly without is impossible as we have nothing else most of the time but crackers.

You wrote in your last letter of sending some more things if you had a chance. If you should send anything send with it some writing paper (I have only three sheets left) and a little tea. I have received the pepper and ginger you sent and also have got several papers lately, an *Independent* in which was Beecher's Thanksgiving sermon, which I think was the best thing I ever read.

You need not be anyway alarmed about me. I think I am as well able to stand it as any of the soldiers. My health still continues good. Mrs. Vallette is now here visiting the camp. I do not know when she returns home.

I recd a letter from Ettie yesterday, shall answer it this afternoon. Goodby,

Your affectionate son George
Give to Ettie

Camp of the 105th, South Tunnel [Tenn.]
Dec. 25th, 1862

Dear Mother,

Merry Christmas, Merry Christmas. This is our first Christmas in the army and supposing perhaps you might like to know the manner of our spending it I concluded to write you a Christmas letter beginning with that happy exclamation which I fancy has in this made jubilant the homes of the North and the far off lands to which the thoughts of the "soldier boys" are directed by day, and their dreams by night.

Well, this morning, our quartermaster having sent a barrel of flour, our orderly sergeant, Tirtlot, issued to us one quart each and the first thing our mess did was to mix a batter and cook some griddle cakes for breakfast and although they were not exactly such cakes as I told the boys "My Mother" used to make at home, still they were to us, without butter, an excellent Christmas meal.

After we had eaten our Adjutant came to the company and informed us that we were detailed to work on some fortifications which we are making; as we do not know what moment Morgan may attack us, it was necessary that work should go on today. So the company turned out and spent the forenoon in the use of the spade and shovel. I did not work as I have done an over amount of picket duty lately and the officers cannot make me on account of my office, but I went down to the tunnel and had a glorious good bath, put on a nice clean shirt and pair of socks and thus prepared to pass the day in as gentlemanly manner as possible. Then I went back to the tent and taking out my "work box" I sewed on a button with a needle full of thread which you threaded and put in my pocket-book before I left home. I also did all the repairing to my clothes which was necessary and then read awhile in one of the papers which you sent me. Then I set myself to work to get dinner for the boys, they being at work.

I made another lot of pancakes and these with our rations of boiled beans made us a Christmas dinner. This will without doubt seem to you to have been a very meager dinner, for this celebrated day as compared with the roast turkey, nice potatoes and accompanying sauces together with the fine cakes and never to be forgotten plum pudding, which usually overload our tables at home. But I assure you to us this simple repast was a rare treat after living for months upon those antiquated hard crackers which infest our armies.

After dinner I took a little walk around the camp grounds and in a short time the mail came in and with it two papers for me. The *Chicago Tribune* and the *Illinoian*. At three o'clock the Col. insisted upon our usual drill, but I came to the conclusion that I would put off all world cares and army drills and as I have always been prompt to attend to duty, the officers allow me to do pretty much as I please. So I resolved to sit down and write a Christmas letter home, a resolution which I am now putting into effect.

The *Illinoian* which I received today had much in it to remind me of home and the festivities of the holidays. I hope you will enjoy them both in the usual manner. Certainly the thoughts of absent ones should not deter the friends at home from any enjoyment and although we cannot be with you in person, still our thoughts are there and certainly it is a great pleasure to us to know that at home the same happy scenes are transpiring in which we were want to engage, and in which we hope and indeed expect to participate when another year shall have rolled around. Do not omit anything, but keep up the old customs in remembrances of the past and in anticipation of the future.

The weather here today is almost like summer, so warm and pleasant, but still I do not enjoy it as I should a regular Christmas day in the North and as I sit here writing with the tent door thrown wide open, I have to let my mind run back to the cheerful fire within and the snow and howling wind without; I much prefer the cold blasts of the Northern winter than the insipid seasons in the South.

Yesterday morning I came in from picket after a night of considerable excitement and little sleep. It was my turn to keep watch from eight to ten and had to stand about ten rods from our reserve on the railroad, the reserve being posted on the main road. The main object was to guard the road against an attack and skirmish sufficiently long to give the regiment time to get in line but it would be easy for spies and bushwhackers to creep along the railroad and hence the necessity of guarding that also. Well after watching my two hours out and seeing nothing worse than myself, as our laughable Irishman says, I had called the relief and ascended the hill to the reserve where we slept while not on duty. After warming my feet from the few coals which were left, I wrapped my blankets around and settled down for a good nap when suddenly the report of a gun quickly followed by two others broke the stillness of the night. I instantly jumped to my feet but not quicker than our sergeant who threw his blankets right and left in his haste to get up and seizing our guns we proceeded first to rouse up the rest of the boys (there were ten of us) and then to make a short reconnaissance. One of the boys had seen a light off in the bushes and another had heard a noise off over a hill, so after reconnoitering the ground and finding nothing we went back and held a council of war which came to the following conclusion. That in as much as the firing was in the direction of camp and that only three guns were fired, and that the long roll had not been sounded, a general engagement was not imminent and the firing must have been done by some frightened sentinels, so we again lay down with our guns besides us.

I got occasional snatches of sleep till four o'clock and as that is the time Morgan generally makes his attacks, we all got up and kept vigilant watch till morning. The fact is we don't intend that the 105th regiment is going to be taken asleep. The next morning when we got into camp we found that some of them had shot at what they said was a bear whether it was or not I cannot say, but there are numerous black dogs around here and I surmise it was one of them, but I must leave off now to get supper.

Well we have partaken of our evening repast consisting of another lot of pancakes and have lighted up our little tent preparatory to a very literary evening. There are three of us writing home on a little cracker box with a couple of boards over the top.

The boys keep coming to our tent to hear the news and borrow papers. I am about the only one in the company that gets papers regularly. I believe I receive the most of the papers you have sent and all the letters and the papers in them. I did not think it necessary to mention the receipt of them all for if I had not received them I should have said so. I rec'd one from you yesterday and one day before.

Tomorrow we go again on picket and as the weather is now so warm, it will be about as pleasant there as to remain in camp with the exception of being up at night. I sent you last Sunday by Capt. Jones a letter containing some very rare mementos of my sojourn in the army.[12] I hope they will interest you, certainly it will be a pleasure for me to see them when I return. I am collecting all the specimens I find and shall send them along as I get a chance.

The Wheaton boys are all well. Griswold is now cooking for the captain. He has not been well lately and it is a good place for him relieving him from all other duty. John Bachelder is well. I have not seen Nick Kenyon for a few days but I believe he is well and in good spirits. Dewolf is at Bowling Green. Tirtlot is always well and is generally liked.

But I see my space is getting limited so as I commenced by wishing you a "Merry Christmas" and as this letter will probably reach you in about a week, I will end by wishing you and Ettie a very Happy New Year.

Your affectionate son George

CHAPTER 4

"Asleep in Jesus"

South Tunnel, January 1–Gallatin, February 15, 1863

The new year opened explosively just sixty miles south at Murfreesboro, Tennessee. General Rosecrans's Army of the Cumberland met Confederate General Bragg's Army of Tennessee on the banks of Stone's River where both lost nearly one-third of their troops. The news of the battle was embellished by the time it reached the 105th Illinois Infantry at South Tunnel. George's diary (January 5, 1863) grossly overstated the outcome when he wrote, "We heard news that Rosecrans had completely whipped the rebels."

While a soldier's life at South Tunnel was not filled with Stone's River's gory scenes of carnage, it was not without its own horror. George's writing during the first weeks of 1863 reflected the harsh times, documenting the deaths of his close friends to the sweeping typhoid fever epidemic. Seventeen men of the 105th Illinois Infantry Regiment and untold numbers of soldiers from other regiments "fell asleep in Jesus" during their detail at South Tunnel and at Buck Lodge, a nearby camp.

George's diary (January 9, 1863) showed a paternal concern for his tentmate, Henry Kingsley: "I think he exercises too little." Within the next two days, though, Henry had unmistakable symptoms of typhoid fever. With the approval of Captain Daniels and Doctor Potter, George was assigned oversight of Henry and the rest of the sick soldiers in their makeshift hospital. Soon, however, even the practitioners became patients; Doctor Potter developed typhus symptoms.

George was not alone in forlornly watching the South Tunnel hills become a graveyard for Union soldiers. Comrade James Congleton also wrote, "Day after day and even some days two of our dear boys would be carried back of our camp on a hill which we used for a burying place."[1] It was not surprising that a regimental bugler filed a pension claim in the years ahead, claiming that his lungs had no chance for rest here due to continuous playing of the death march.[2]

The rank-and-file soldier of the Grand Army was not alone with his troubles. General Rosecrans felt that ensuring the certainty of provisions for his troops, now more than 200 miles from their base of supplies, was a critical factor for the army's success. While General Rosecrans contended in dispatches to General Halleck that controlling river transportation was as important as the railroads, the control of gunboats on the Cumberland and Tennessee Rivers had been transferred to Admiral Porter and the Navy Department. Despite Rosecrans's appeal, President Lincoln chose to stay clear of the growing contentiousness among his generals, chiding Rosecrans in a telegram (January 29, 1863), "Your dispatch about 'river patrolling' received. I have called the Secretary of Navy, Secretary of War, and General-in-Chief together and submitted it to them, who promise to do their very best in the case. I cannot take it into my own hands without producing inextricable confusion."[3]

George began to reveal signs of the stress he was enduring in a manner that would appear again in his writing—through the use of somewhat nonplused and incongruous remarks. While waiting for his turn at war as he mourned the death of friends dying around him, George wrote to his Mother about his biscuit-making skills confirming a singular fact: soft bread was savior.

Camp of the 105th, South Tunnel, Tenn.
January 1st, 1863

Dear Mother,

"Happy New Year." The day that ushers in the new year has at last come, and as I wrote you a Christmas letter I concluded to make you a New Year's present, alas, the best that I can give in the army. You have without doubt heard of the late Morgan raid into Kentucky tearing up seventeen miles of our railroad and stopping the mail, thereby getting not the most enviable wishes of our soldiers. And you have not yet received my last letter, which I very much wished you should get today. Well in war we have to take things as they come, at least such is my experience, and I have had some little chance of finding out war's realities as well as its poetry.

It has been one week today since I have heard a word from home. No mail having found its way here since Christmas, and it is yet uncertain when it will again go through, but I mean to keep writing and if you don't get my letters now, you will sometime.

The past week has been one of little interest and has dragged wearily away. The boys have daily watched the coming of the regimental post master, but alas, only to turn away disappointed at sight of his empty mail bag. Occasionally during the week we have had exciting rumors of an expected attack here, and a few nights since our Col. received a dispatch from Gallatin, that Breckinridge with a large army was trying to cross the Cumberland a few miles below Gallatin and that we might expect an attack any moment.[4] We had orders that night to have our guns in the best condition and where we could put our hands on them at a moment's notice. But the night passed away and morning brought a dispatch that the rumor was false. A few little incidents of this nature have served to keep us alive as it were.

They have had, however, quite exciting times at Gallatin, having been drawn up in line of battle nearly every day in expectation of an immediate attack and being started out of their sleep by the long roll in the still hour of night, only to find that the alarm was false. Last Monday part of a rebel company fired up the pickets there, the captain of the rebels had a splendid mansion about three miles out from the town, and our enraged soldiers, wheeled out a cannon and leveled it with the ground. I wish all rebel officers were served thus; that the war, already prolonged too much by the imbecility of our administration and the cowardice of our officers, might end. The common soldiers of the south have no longer any heart in the matter, as all who are taken by our men say. I have myself talked with several of them and they say, to a man, that they would gladly have the old union restored and live again in the enjoyment of peace.

Yesterday I was talking with a very aged man who was a soldier in 1812. He said that when the excitement first broke out about this war the "big men" went around the country telling the people that Lincoln's robbers were coming down here for no other purpose than to set the Negroes free, incite insurrections, and pillage the country. Is it a wonder that the poor ignorant commoners deluded into this belief should rise and fight even without clothes, for the defense as they thought of their liberty, poor ignorant wretches! How much have the rebel chiefs to account for!

You cannot have the remotest idea of the sufferings of this part of rebeldom. I never did when at home and never should had I not actually seen it. If the war lasts a year longer, many of the inhabitants must actually starve and go entirely naked. The government you are aware allows no trade with the land beyond Nashville; no supplies from the southern sources can reach here. The young men are mostly off to the war, and I have seen many an old couple just tottering on the verge of the grave with a son in either army and no possible means of support the coming year. Their clothes already covered with patches, no others to buy and *no money to buy them.* (One old man told me he had not seen ten dollars since the war broke out.) Living in little log houses, the only thing they can have plenty of is wood and that the country abounds in.

The health of the regiment is not so good as it has been. Four have died already this week, one a day. The disease is principally diarrhea, which has so far almost wholly baffled the surgeons skill, owing to the villainous food they give us. The hard crackers, when eaten dry, swell up in the stomach and when soaked previous to eating are heavy as lead entirely indigestible. Last week our quarter master got us a lot of bacon that was so *rotten* you could smell it all over the camp. If we could only get salt beef, a great many of the boys now sick would be well. Another man has just died, while I was writing the above. He had been sick for some time and suddenly dropped dead. My health continues pretty good for I take care of myself and keep as far from the Dr. as possible.

Last night I was out doing picket duty. It was very cold and as it was New Years Eve, I could not be blamed for thinking of home and contrasting my present position with that I had occupied a year ago. I paced the wood in that lonely old forest. I thought of the cheerful fires and the happy faces at home, but I have one consolation, and that is, the more hardships I undergo here and the more dangers I encounter, so much the more shall I at some future day enjoy the comforts and pleasures of a home. I slept last night on some corn stalks and you may well imagine they were not so soft as feathers, but still they kept us off the cold damp ground.

This morning we received news of a federal success at Murfreesboro. It gives the camp a cheerful aspect to hear good news, but still we are now expecting a summer campaign, as there are little signs of any more forward movement in the East. The enemy must be crushed at its front before the war will end and the army before Richmond must be shattered before anything very great will happen. Nevertheless I do not feel at all despondent and intend while I stay in the army and have my life to be contented and live with the expectation of sometime returning home. I believe we should today have one half the men with us, who are now dead, had they not given way to homesickness.

In one of your letters you said you did not think I could get that thirty-five dollars which my order calls for at present on account of a new law that volunteers should not receive the one hundred dollars bounty, when discharged before two years service, unless the war closed previous to that time. That law was a late act, I believe of Congress, and relates only to the *government bounty*. That thirty-five dollar order is *County bounty* and can be collected whenever the county taxes are paid, and I believe it is now time for payment.

When you collect it you can use it if you wish, if not, let Uncle Rufus have it and take his note at whatever interest he can afford to pay. We have not been paid anything yet since we left Chicago and I do not think there are any prospects of our being paid at present, but I must close.

Give my love to Ettie and all the friends.
From your affectionate son George

Camp of the 105th, South Tunnel [Tenn.]
Jan. 19th, 1863

Dear Mother,

Since writing my last letter, which I sent you by Mr. Brennan,[5] our company has been again diminished by two deaths and my own tent made desolate by the loss of Henry Kingsley. He was taken sick one week ago yesterday with typhus fever in its most malignant form. I myself went to the hospital with him and to care of him till he died. Four long weary days the fever raged within him. The fifth day it was broken, but his system was too weak to rally; at ten minutes before six in the morning of the seventh day he went peacefully to sleep, "asleep in Jesus." He died so easily that we could scarcely tell when he drew the last breath. I closed his eyes and we laid him out in his soldiers clothes and buried him in a soldier's grave, one more added to the fearful list recorded against the leaders of this awful rebellion.

I secured the services of a sergeant in another company who had been a minister at home to perform the funeral ceremony and marched in company to his grave. Sadly we laid him there and firing three volleys over his grave we went back with subdued spirits to our quarters.

The other one who died was a private by the name of Geer, from Winfield.[6] He cursed and swore to the very hour of his death and died in the most fearful agony tearing himself and screaming, "I'm burning up. I'm burning up."

Henry was out of his mind during his sickness and it was difficult to tell whether he became rational or not before death. He called for his Mother several times the evening before he died and the last thing we heard him say was, "You pray, I can't."

Oh, it was terrible that week among the sick, and I tremble when I feel how little the soldiers sufferings are realized in the North, they *cannot* be realized unless actually seen and felt. I have sat for hours and shuddered at the awful groans and shrieks of the sick and dying, all mingled in confusion, and I have *stood* for hours at Henry's couch to keep him from leaping out. I was left alone with them all once and one of them, the moment my back was turned, jumped out on the floor. His weight was about 170 lbs. and he struggled with the strength of a maniac, but in the excitement of the moment I lifted him by main strength, up to his bed, almost on a level with my head.

I was obliged to be there constantly, as Henry would be quiet with no one else. I got only four hours sleep at night and had also all of the orderly's writing to do as he is off to a private house sick and there is no one else in the company who can do it. So you will see I have had a week of work, but my health still is excellent for which I am truly thankful.

After having been a week exposed to every kind of disease, experience has taught me what perhaps I should have learned at home, to be careful of myself. I am very particular in regard to diet, and eat as little as I can get along with. Disease is thinning our ranks fearfully; two were buried day before yesterday and two more will probably be today. Doctor Potter is himself sick and we have now but one surgeon to attend to the regiment.[7] Discharged soldiers are going home every week, and what the end of the 105th will be is difficult to see.

My tent was left, by the death of Kingsley with no occupant but myself. Griswold is cooking for the Captain and Whitlock is appointed regimental postmaster. I could not live alone in a place rendered so lonesome by death and the sergeants have invited me to tent with them, at which place I am now stopping. It is a much more comfortable place.

The boys are as a general thing terribly homesick and talk of nothing but home, home. Many of them lay in their tents and brood over it, thus inviting disease. They are applying for discharges by dozens and half the regiment would be glad to end the war upon *almost any terms of compromise*. I never for a moment allow myself to think of being homesick and keep constantly busy about something, which I find the best preventative for it. I have attended diligently to duty and am always prompt which has secured the compliments of all my officers and of the officers of other companies also, but that is perhaps writing egotistically, though you know I would say so to none but you.

Captain Daniels is not liked here neither by his company nor by other officers and it is doubtful if he stays with us over six months longer. Our first lieutenant is a good man, but far from being a military man.[8] He is old and feeble and cannot stay with us long. Such are the changes of war and should the war last, the company will have an entire new set of officers in one year.

But to write of another subject, we have drawn some flour and perhaps shall draw some more and I want a little instruction about cooking. I have made pretty fair pancakes by mixing with water, a little salt and vinegar and letting the batter stand over night then putting in a little saleratus,[9] but saleratus is hard to get here and costs 50 cents per pound. While we are out of cash and if you can send me any or some yeast if you ever have a chance and also directions for using, it will perhaps add to my health. I have baked biscuits by mixing with salt, water, a little grease and saleratus when I had it and when I did not I mixed them without. They would hardly be considered eatable at home but we make them disappear very readily here.

I am still in good spirits and however hard the fare or severe the duty I never allow myself to complain but have ever found that it is better to laugh than cry.

But I must close, with much love,
I am your affectionate son George.

[p.s.] I rec'd ten newspapers from you a few days since.

The ground is covered with four or five inches of snow and it is quite cold but it will probably soon be off. The mail has been stopped a few days again owing to some tracks being washed away below Gallatin. Fourteen discharged men are waiting to go home. We have had no news lately. Give my love to Ettie and best respects Prof. Beardsley and all the friends.

We had an election for Chaplain last night as ours has left us and the Rev. Mr. Chapman of Bloomingdale was elected. You will of course remember him. He is a good man and preaches practical sermons. We have been without one for a long time and a great deal of immorality has cursed the regiment. I am now going out on picket. Goodby.

Gallatin [Tenn.]
Feb. 15th, 1863

Dear Mother,

Yesterday I received a nice lot of things from you by Dr. Waterman among which was a pair of boots. They came very acceptable and fitted well. I have this morning greased them well and put them on. The other things were so numerous that I almost thought of starting a grocery store. The nice yellow butter above all was such a luxury and looked so much like home. In short I am very thankful for all and fully appreciate your kindness. I made yesterday some cream of tarter biscuits which were so light and nice and the butter was so sweet on them, it almost made me homesick.

Well we have got comfortably situated here and notwithstanding the mud are making ourselves quite contented. We occasionally have a little romance intermingled with daily routine by way of frequent expectations of the redoubtable Morgan. Now he is reported off South a few miles, and now he is coming from the North or West with a tremendous force to overwhelm us. Almost every other night the streets are barricaded and we await his coming but, alas, he never comes. Now there is daily expected a battle at Tullahoma, but it may be delayed a long time. Our business here is simply to hold the place and we have again commenced drilling daily and have the regular inspections and reviews. Today although Sunday, we are to pass in a review.

We have not been paid yet, but are told that we soon will be, whether or not soon means a few days or few weeks or a few months, I can't say, for we have been expecting our money so long that our faith is getting very weak. In fact the base idea of our being paid off is ridiculed by the boys but still we may soon get a portion of what is due us, though I very much doubt the financial ability of government to pay us the full amount.

You spoke in your last letter of two men who went out after provisions and were never afterwards heard of. The fact of the case was they didn't want to be heard of very soon by us, for they deserted as did also a number of others and went over to some guerillas to get paroled. We sent a large cavalry force after but they had gained the protection of the rebels and had been hurried away where our force dared not follow. They will probably soon be North seeking the protection of their natural friends, the Copperheads.[10] There is a great deal said here about those copperheads and as a general thing, at least among the more intelligent class of soldiers, they are now being denounced, but still there is a majority who secretly hope they will conclude a peace with the rebels at almost any price.

For my own part I wish every copperhead rascal was hung and before one inch of Ill. soil shall be added to the confederacy, I will willingly stay my 3 years and then enlist another term. I would like to have the 105th Regt set to work among the Northern villains awhile and perhaps we might straighten out their disordered brains a little. I believe they are at work in our armies and have no doubt that after the soldiers are paid off, there will be a multitude of desertions as a large portion of our army is composed of unprincipled and ignorant men. I almost blush to say it, but such is the melancholy fact. However, I still have a little faith in the administration, although I think they have shown themselves totally unfit for the position.

I received a letter from Aunt Annie a day or two since and shall answer it today.[11] She speaks very hopefully of the speedy close of the war and thought it was at its crisis. I hope so, but I have no clear idea on the subject though. The increasing maze of difficulties have made up my mind not to worry on the subject whatever turn it may take. I believe I am about as cheerful and contented as any soldier I have ever seen and I certainly know I have enjoyed better health for it.

And speaking of health you remember I mentioned in my last letter one of my tent mates who was suddenly taken down with fever. Dr. Potter gave him five powders containing quinine and calomel. He did not like to take them and I advised him not to, so they went hissing and spitting forth venom into the fire. I gave him an injection often enough to keep his bowels loose and the next day he was better. Potter again left him another lot of calomel which shared the fate of its predecessors and in two days time he was walking around. Accidentally he came across Potter who seemed to think that his medicine had worked such wonderful effect and actually said that he did not expect to see him up for a long time to come.

Potter is not liked here as he was in Chicago and he rarely cures anyone taken with any very *dangerous* fever. His first medicine, calomel and second quinine, which generally saves his nurses the trouble of long watches, for the patient soon dies. There is now in our tent a man slowly dying with the consumption but Potter refuses to discharge him. I was hospital steward about three weeks and had to go through the hospital with the Dr. and write off the prescriptions as he gave them so I had a good chance to know his method of treatment and the different medicines used for different diseases. I think of studying for a physician when I get home for I believe a mount of good can be done by those who understand the business.[12]

I received a letter yesterday from Henry Kingsley's sister. She wrote a very feeling letter and wished to know all the particulars of his death. I answered it last night, giving her as minute a detail as to the commencement of his illness to his death, as possible. She appeared to be perfectly broken hearted, and the whole family seemed so bound up in him, too much so I think. Mr. Kingsley is quite a fine old gentleman and seemed to be very intelligent.[13]

The weather is very stormy yet and it rains a great deal, still we have had some days during the last week which were pleasant and seemed more like June weather than February. Nick Kenyon is expecting to go home very soon and I shall see if I can send my diary[14] and if we get paid I shall send all I can spare which will be the most of what I get, for I find I have little use for money here. There is no fruit or anything of that nature we can get without paying three or four prices for it and I do not believe in wasting so hard earned money.

Tirtlot was never taken prisoner and I can't see how such foolish reports find their way home. He has been very sick but is now almost well and is at a private house where he is as well cared for as is possible to be in a slave state. We expect him into camp in about a week or ten days.

I am now acting commissary sergeant, but cannot have the position permanent unless our sick sergeant is discharged. Capt. D. is thought but very little of either by his brother officers or his company. He is continually quarreling with his lieutenants and our commissioned officers are more like cats and dogs than respectable officers. They all hate each other and all seek every occasion to slander the other.

My health is most surprisingly good and I continually complain of being very well. I always make up my mind to be well at any rate and as a natural consequence am so. I have received two letters from you the last week with the good things you sent and also have got an *Independent* and weekly *Chicago Tribune*. I think the *Tribune* is a little too radical and goes to extremes too much for my part. I would be perfectly willing to withdraw the proclamation if the rebels would lay down their arms and come back to the Union as it was. Slavery would soon die anyhow and peace again be restored. I think always the middle course should be pursued in preference to either extreme.

If you get a chance to send anything more, you may send me two blue shirts for summer. They will be much more comfortable than these flannels.

Give my love to Ettie.
Your affectionate son George

CHAPTER 5

"I Would Prefer a Copy of Shakespeare"

Gallatin, April 4–Nashville, October 10, 1863

By mid-1863, army courts and hospitals began to fill with cases of desertion, rape, plunder, and murder. To help alleviate some of the problems that resulted from having thousands of armed men in an occupied city without an immediate battle to fight, the U.S. Christian Commission implemented loan libraries throughout many army installations. The chaplains in charge of these libraries claimed many benefits including reduced boisterous and rude conduct and improved correspondence between camps and the home front. When Chaplain Daniel Chapman joined the 105th Illinois Infantry, hope was restored once again for improving upon the morale and moral conduct of the men.

Unlike the months at the tunnels, the 105th Illinois Infantry's time in Nashville provided the men an opportunity for some socializing. Sergeant Cram had the opportunity to reestablish old friendships and to make new acquaintances. He may have been more motivated for establishing new relationships; during his first year away from home, Sergeant Cram and his girlfriend, Mattie Hiatt, broke off their engagement. While he did not write about having a broken heart, perhaps sharing this news with his mother was unnecessary. According to letters of Mattie's brother, Luther of Company F, Mrs. Cram was to blame for coming between the two sweethearts.[1]

But, Mrs. Cram wasn't so influential with her son on all fronts. After more than a year since George had seen his mother, his voice spoke with more authority. However, he kept one promise to his mother; he refused opportunities for commission as an officer. This did not prevent him, though, from having to act in an officer's capacity, but without the pay or benefits.

Sergeant Cram was troubled by his comrades' conduct. His letters indicated that he suspected that some soldiers' gunshot wounds were not accidental as alleged. He was especially bothered by the behavior of one friend, Lieutenant William Tirtlot, who was meddling in camp politics. Worse, he thought that Tirtlot may have overstayed his sick leave in a private home while claiming that he was too ill for duty. Arrangements in those "private houses" distant from camp were described by another Illinois soldier in a letter to his wife: "Nothing but shoulder straps & uniforms of blue coats and brass buttons are to be seen anywhere except of course in the boarding houses where the officers play cards & drink whiskey with their friends male & female."[2]

As the summer of 1863 approached the fall, General Rosecrans continued to build up a tremendous army of men and supplies near Chattanooga. Fort Negley in Nashville, the headquarters for the Union Army's communications and supply links, needed continuous garrison duty. The 105th would stay at Nashville for the time, in the 2nd Brigade, 3rd Division of the Reserve Corps of the Department of the Cumberland under Major General Gordon Granger. It was not their time at the front yet.

With little evidence of military action on the horizon, General Halleck complained to General Rosecrans that he wasn't following orders. Distracting as this message must have been in the face of up-coming battles, General Rosecrans may have overplayed his hand with a prophetic reply (August 1, 1863): "I say to you frankly that whenever the government can replace me by a commander in whom they have more confidence, they ought to do so, and take the responsibility of the result."[3] And so they did.

———————————

Gallatin, Tennessee
April 4th, 1863

Dear Mother,

I rec'd yours of Mar. 2 this morning containing one also from Rufus. In my last letter I mentioned the things I most needed, I forgot to tell you to send my hat. I left one almost new and as we are all going to wear hats this summer, I would much prefer that to the poor ones which we shall draw.

I have been thinking the last few days of the most suitable book or the one that would be the greatest relief to lonesome hours, and I think of several that I would like but as I cannot be burdened with many, I would prefer a copy of Shakespeare. Cover it well with strong muslin and send at the first opportunity. My facilities for taking care of a book are now much better than they have been. I do not think of anything else now that I want more than what I have told you if you received my last letter. Anything you may happen to find in the way of light literature, that would be interesting but not worth preserving, send it and we will try and make it useful here.

I am very glad your health is enabling you to go out more and I known by experience it is not good to be penned up too much. I am not a member of the Union League;[4] were I there I should think it the least to do to become a member, but soldiers who are openly working for the cause are doing I think enough and really I don't see as they could do much good were they all to become members. Inasmuch as the League is, as I understand, more for work in the popular sentiment and political arena North than in the field. I rejoice however to hear of their success and great increase, which I read of in almost every paper. I see that the people are getting worked up to a sense of the necessity of concentrating their energies on the war.

I believe there are two extremes in the North, both of which are dangerous and need watching. One, the Copperhead democrat and the other the radical abolitionists. The loyal democrats, republicans and reasonable abolitionists are the ones who will save the Union. I have just been reading a letter from Judge Patton of Ill. (an old time democrat) to Gov. Seymour, his sentiments must be endorsed by every lover of the country. He says "victories must be won before they (the south) listen to reason from any party and accept reunion on any terms. Were the democrats in power today, they must win victories before they could save the Union." He does not seem to recognize the copperheads as belonging to his party for he says again, "To excite a reasonable hope that the South will return to the Union on the old basis, it is indispensable that they should be disabused of the opinion that the democratic party is a fierce party on the basis of separation." These are my sentiments exactly although I don't claim to be a democrat, but I am with every democrat heart and soul, who rejects peace on the basis of separation but seeks adjustment and reunion, for it is Union I enlisted to fight for and not "irrepressible Negroe" but I am getting too long for a simple letter and will change the subject.

A few days since our little city was visited by a fire which broke out in a house some to the rear of our building. The first idea was that the fire was a ruse to cover an attack by the rebels. Part of the 70th Ind. Regt was sitting down and stacked arms in front of the burning building. Our company was then marched down and ordered to clear the ground of some eight hundred or more persons who had congregated there, which we set about so vigorously that in minutes not a soul was to be seen except guards who patrolled the grounds. The building burned to the ground but we succeeded in stopping the fire from spreading, though the day was windy. Two men were seriously injured by timbers but are doing well now.

We are guarding Gallatin with great vigilance and our earthworks are being strengthened by the timbers to protect our cannon and for the protection of those who support the battery. I do not believe any amount of well drilled troops would take the town but should have few fears for the result unless we are attacked by fifteen thousand.

I have a great contempt for the fighting qualities of lank lean southerners and attribute their defect in so many engagements to the severity of their generals. Napoleon in his Italian campaign with 40,000 men whipped three of the largest armies that all the wealth and resources of Austria could bring against him, each one of which was double his own numerical strength, but he was a military general while too many of our big guns have been political favorites.

We are to be paid day after tomorrow up to the first of March and I shall send it all home with the exception of a few dollars. I shall not be able to comply with my promise in my last letter, of sending you my photographs, for I have since learned that I cannot get any taken here.

I had a letter from Ettie last night, she wrote in good spirits.

Tirtlot is very much better and will soon I think be able for duty. I continue to get the NY dailies from Uncle Calvin and shall always feel most grateful for them. My health remains good. Give my love to Uncle Rufus. I shall answer his kind letter in a few days.

Your affectionate son George

[p.s.] Don't forget to send me Shakespeare.

LaVergne, Tenn.
June 4th, 1863

Dear Mother,

You will see by the superscription that we have again moved. The opening days of summer have been momentous ones to us. Last Monday afternoon at three o'clock our brigade marched to the depot and were filed into freight cars. After about an hours delay we started en route for this place (if we may call it a place), we reached Nashville just before dark, and were there marched off upon the Murfreesboro road, the iron horse again started and about nine o'clock found us at our journeys end, we immediately debarked and gazed upon our new home, but had not long to look for soon the old Col's voice rang out, "Form battalion, On center dress. Guides post by company, right wheel. Stack arms. Rest." The last command we obeyed by spreading our blankets and stretching our tired bodies inside of them.

Early in the morning we arose and after performing our ablutions at a neighboring spring, took a view of the scenery. First, we are 15 miles in the rear of the grand army, just half way from Nashville to Murfreesboro. The town of LaVergne has suffered the extreme rigors of war. It is burned to the ground, but three houses remain which are used as hospitals. It was there that the great battle of Stone River began.[5] All around us lay the remnants of wagon trains which the rebels burned and the decayed remains of mules and horses, while little piles of bricks and crumbled masonry are significant of the terrible fate and swift destruction that overtook a rebellious city. It's a terrible sight to contemplate and though it was a just retribution, I cannot help feeling sad at the fate of the misled inhabitants, once as happy and joyous as those of our Northern villages, now exiles, with no home on earth.

Tuesday afternoon we were ordered out on picket and shouldering our guns were soon again on duty. At night we fixed a sort of shelter with our rubber blankets and about midnight were aroused by a drenching rain, but did not get very wet and the coming morn put a more lively aspect upon our affairs, we were relieved at nine o'clock Wednesday morning and went to our new camp. The boys at once commenced the work of building log huts and the sound of the axe is heard in every direction as I write. Our house is about half-completed and we are now at a stand for the want of an axe, a want which we hope soon to supply so when I next write I should be able to give you a description of our soldier built house.

We have been short of rations for a few days as our supplies have not come up. All I have had to eat for five days was a loaf and a half of bakers bread but we are all cheerful and the work goes merrily on. Our camp is situated in a very hilly place, just in the skirts of the timber and after we get it cleared up I have no doubt we shall like it very well and we may stop here sometime as our General has obtained command of the post.

Yesterday I received a copy of the *Illinoian* and of the *Independent* but have had no letter from you for some time. I had one from Frank Ellis just before we left Gallatin. He was in General Grant's army at Big Black River when he wrote and I suppose he is in the army before Vicksburg.

My health is now good though I was quite unwell a few days before leaving Gallatin. I have great reason to be thankful for my health ever since I have been in the army.

You must excuse my using a pencil as I am sitting out in the woods and have no place yet where I can write from. Give my love to Uncle Rufus. I have not heard from him for some time.

Your affectionate son George.

> Murfreesboro [Tenn.]
> July 25, 1863

Dear Mother,

I received a letter from you a few days since in which you wished to know how our army subsisted. We live as we always have on army rations sent from the North consisting of bread, sometimes soft and sometimes hard, pork, coffee, dried peas, sugar, rice and once in a while a little beef. Just now we are regaling on blackberries which abound here. The woods are full of them. I went out yesterday and picked twelve quarts in about two hours. They are an excellent preventative of scurvy and I indulge large in them. I eat no meat at all except when we get beef and I have never seen the time since being in the army that my health has been so good as now, while twenty-five percent of our company are constantly sick.

I go in the river every day and have a good wash. The Drs. say it is bad and so a great many of the boys go weeks and some months without washing their bodies. Some already have the scurvy and very many the symptoms.

I had quite a time gathering berries yesterday. I had charge of twenty-five men, all armed, we went out about four miles, picked our dishes full of the nice large berries and returned to camp via several Secesh orchards without having the satisfaction of seeing a rebel. Fruit trees hang full of apples, pears and peaches but they are not yet ripe.

Mr. Chapman is very much liked here, but like all chaplains in an active campaign, he is of very little benefit. We never get a chance to hear preaching on an average of more than once a month and then for only a few minutes and as for prayer meetings, they are indistinctly remembered as long ago occurrences. It's bad I know and I do not wonder at so many young men being ruined by the army. None but minds entirely above camp vices can stand the current.

Today there is a rumor in camp that we are to move back to LaVergne next week. I am inclined to think it is true and we are only waiting to be paid off again, to start where we shall go next nobody knows. But certainly we shall go no nearer the enemy till we get another General. I think I shall date my next letter at LaVergne. I sent home by Tirtlot $30 and shall send more if we are paid off as we now expect at the earliest opportunity.

We all feel very cheerful and happy here at the brilliant success that have lately carried our arms. I think now that six months more will see us again, of course, if we have no further drawback. But though history of the past teaches us not to be too sanguine. I received a letter from Annie and Edwin containing one of Uncle's photographs.[6] Our weekly papers are most all rec'd though when we change positions as we have recently done, many are lost. I wrote to Aunt Sofia some time again and am now expecting an answer.

The weather here is intensely hot and very rainy. I should think this climate must be very unhealthy and do not wonder at the slim, sickly looking wretches that inhabit it.

Your affectionate son George.

LaVergne [Tenn.]
Aug. 17th, 1863

Dear Mother,

I received your last letter day before yesterday in which you expressed much anxiety for my situation. You need not be at all concerned. My health is as good as any one could expect and I am never troubled with summer complaint, nor do I think any one need be if a few degrees of common sense and a little care were used for we can now buy plenty of good vegetables at moderate prices and an abundance of fruit for almost nothing,[7] but there are a great many soldiers who never think and these are the ones who are always sick. Some keep themselves swimming in grease. Some never wash themselves and others make a regular swill barrel of their stomachs. Of course, such imprudence must be paid for in some way or other.

You wished to know our business here. It is simply to guard the communications of the Grand Army. Extending from Louisville to Nashville is a regular line of guards always increasing in force as they near the army. Were it not for such forces as ours, guerillas would cut the railroad and speedily cause a retreat of the whole army for want of subsistence.

Our duty is principally picketing, which is done in a very soldier like manner. Pickets keep their coats on all day and also their accouterments[8] with their gun in reach. I went out a short time since acting as 1st. Lieut.—in command of a company owing to our scarcity of com. officers. I am now acting orderly sergeant during the sickness of our present orderly.[9] I have pretty much control over the entire company owing to the imbecility of superior officers. My rank is now 2nd sergt. or what is sometimes called commissary sergt. I have the rations to draw and issue to the men and all the provisions accts. to keep. There is but one non commissioned officer in the company higher, and that is the orderly.

Our daily routine is as follows. At five in the morning, drill. At half-past six, breakfast. At nine, non com. officers school. At 12, dinner. At half-past five, supper. At six, dress parade and battalion drill which lasts till dark. Once there occasionally we frequently form in a hollow square and pass the twilight hours with speeches and songs.

There is considerable romance about this kind of a life and many soldiers who now long for home will be just as eager for the army again even when the war is over.

I think in your earnestness for me to become a follower of the law, "volens, volens" you quite mistake the natural turn of affairs. At the expiration of the war, I cannot see that thousands of broken down soldiers stand ready to step into every branch of business and fill up every opening. The army is not made up of clerks and the worlds favorites; it is composed of the lower classes. Not that I wish to speak disparagingly of our soldiers, but two thirds of the rank and file are men totally incapable of anything but the most ordinary pursuits of life. Enclosed with this you will find Henry Clay's ideas of business men. I do not at all see the necessity of business men becoming mere machines or counter jumpers, on the contrary, they are the ones who form our society and who are really the practical men. In viewing any subject, we should not be led astray by our preconceived ideas but give both sides a careful consideration, always remembering that no one ever yet succeeded in plans of life laid by others, but prosperity attends those who enter with determination upon that path which their own impulses lead them.

Our country has not yet done with military affairs and I do not think it at all certain that we are not to have a war with the European powers, and it is already reported that Cassius M. Clay has promised our assistance to Russia.[10] The mind of the people is warlike and they are ready with the close of our present war to wipe out the insults put upon us by England and France.

I expect almost every day those things will come which were sent last Spring. Dr. Potter has sent for them to be shipped here at once. Tell Ettie I have not forgotten her, and she must be a good girl and always mind her Mother. You need not send any more ginger at present; I have a large quantity on hand.

Your affectionate son George.

Nashville [Tenn.]
August 27th, 1863

Dear Mother,

I wrote you a short letter Sunday evening and promised another in a few days since then. I have returned from a trip south which I will describe.

We started (thirty in all) at one o'clock Monday morning in fine spirits and arrived at Murfreesboro just at sunrise. Here our dutiful haversacks were called into service to answer the prompting of the inner man. Starting from M—— we passed through a fine level country well stocked with provisions and fruit, at intervals of two and three miles we passed little old villages that looked more like a lot of old dry goods boxes filled up promiscuously than anything else I can imagine, occasionally seeing where Bragg's soldiers had been encamped.

About nine o'clock we came in sight of Tullahoma. Here we prepared ourselves to witness some great things in the shape of rebel fortifications. Here was the famous retreat of a great rebel army, but astonishing enough, they had no works whatever except one small line of rifle pits around the limits of their camp and two very small earth works while Murfreesboro the headquarters of our fine army under Rosecrans at that time, was a complete fortress with a splendid line of earth works around it and numberless forts so contrived that any point of ground within firing distance could be brought under a concentrated fire.

Well, the great Tullahoma of which we have heard so much of the last six months consists of one hotel, a few small stores and some shops and perhaps a dozen or fifteen of the oldest, dirtiest, roughest looking houses I ever saw. The country around it is very level and was last Fall covered with a heavy growth of timber which has now been felled to prevent the approach in regular order of our army.

We stopped here long enough to take on wood and water, and were seen bounding on through woods and openings far down into the enemy's country. At noon we came in sight of the Cumberland mountains stretching their blue tops up to the region of clouds and after running to the foot of it, we stopped and another engine fastened itself to our rear. On we again went, both engines huffing clouds of smoke and shooting us forward at a higher rate of speed till suddenly we commenced ascending the mountains. It seemed as though we were just going right up to the very top when suddenly we came to a deep cut—and in another moment we were capitulated into a tunnel darker than Egyptian darkness; went [we] went through all right and at the other side our extra engine left us and we began descending one of the steepest grades I ever saw. All around us were high hills, mountain gorges, deep valleys and in short—a scenery, romantic enough for the most lively imagination.

On we went—now around a curve, now through a tremendous cut where huge rocks from above seemed just ready to drop down upon us, now and then passing car wrecks till finally our steed gave a prolonged whistle and we soon came to a stop at our destination, Stevenson, Alabama, the present headquarters of Gen. Rosecrans. It consists of a depot and a few little poor-looking houses on the side of the mountain. Some two or three railroads connect here with different points both North and South. We arrived there at four o'clock and after looking around what we wished, spread our blankets in an empty car and were soon in the arms of Morpheus.[11]

At midnight we started home and arrived here next day at noon, well satisfied with our trip. If we stay here we shall go down as guards about once a week. I like it much better than army duty for although it is hard, still it is more like civilized business and for a time almost, makes us forget that we are soldiers.

Our camp is situated here on the hill where stands Fort Negley. Four companies of our regt. are stationed inside the fort and remaining six outside. They drew lots to decide who should go in and we were fortunate enough to remain out. Fort Negley is a beautiful fort and of immense strength properly manned it would be next to an impossibility to take it.

Nashville is one of the finest cities of the South and has all the advantages that an advantageous position, a river navigation and three railroads can give it. The state house here is well worthy of a whole letter, it is really the finest specimen of modern architecture I ever saw and is of itself a strong fort. The hill on which it stands is strongly fortified and several guns of large calabre stand frowning down upon the city. Steamboats run now from here to Cairo and a great amount of supplies for the army are brought around that way. But I must now close as we are to be inspected in a few minutes.

Your affectionate son, George

Nashville [Tenn.]
Sept. 1st, 1863

Dear Mother,

Yesterday I received a letter from you and Ettie which I hasten to answer. I wrote to Ettie day before yesterday.

Since I last wrote we have met with no change and are still encamped at Fort Negley, one mile from town. Yesterday afternoon we had a grand review conducted by Gen. Granger. There were seven regiments and a battery of us. We formed on a large parade ground a mile from here and extended a line over a mile in length. It would have been a very beautiful sight for you to have seen us as we stood with bayonets glistening in the sun and indeed half the city was out to see us, but it was more fun for them than for us who had to stand like posts holding up about seventy-five pounds. After standing about an hour, we marched in review and were allowed to retire. Reviews are splendid affairs but are much dreaded by soldiers.

Last night I visited a family in Nashville that were formerly from Wheaton by the name of Westerville. He is a doctor and one of very little repute too, I guess, but it seemed like old times to see them. They were acquainted with President Blanchard and almost all the families at Wheaton but like all the people of the South they worship slavery at heart and hate the North though it was once their home. They have lived here but three years and have in that time acquired all the southern style. The ladies here all take pride in looking like marble statues and I have yet to see the first one who had the least particle of color in her face unless it was one of the lower classes or poor whites as they are here called.

Some of them are very beautiful but lack that look of intelligence that so characterizes our northern girls and all of them have in a greater or less degree the Negroe dialect in their speech. They have a very fashionable habit of dipping which means ramming snuff into their mouths and chewing it like tobacco. This is indulged in by all classes. Nice lady-like practice, ain't it?

Sunday night—I went to church here and heard a very sleepy sermon preached to a sleepy congregation. The war was not mentioned at all in it.

We have about as curious a trio of officers as ever was together in our company. The captain is simply a nobody but is ugly as sin when he gets prejudiced against anyone, and when he punishes any of the boys our first Lieut. Adams runs right to him (the boy) and makes him believe he [presumably Capt. Daniels] is the most absurd person in the world thus keeping the company in a continual fervent. The two hate each other intensely, but neither will resign on account of pay.

Tirtlot stands on the fence ready to join on the strongest side. He is very deceitful and owes his present position to his hypocrisy. Last winter he tried to get me to write a petition and circulate it to get D—— out (not daring to himself). Had I done so I should have subjected myself to trial by court martial. In various little things he has shown himself a friend only so far as his own interest is concerned, but I never pretend to notice it and treat him as friendly as ever. Well I must close as I have much to do today.

Your affectionate son George

Nashville [Tenn.]
Oct. 10th, 1863

Dear Mother,

I received a letter from you a few days since dated Sept. 21st. It had been delayed on the road. I shall answer Aunt Sophia's letter just as soon as I possibly can, but you have no idea how busy they keep us now. Wheeler's Cavalry are scattered all around the country and one of our regiments is taken away to watch them so it makes the duty come so much heavier.[12] We are on picket every other day besides our train guards.

Today I had the pleasure of seeing one of my old school mates at Wheaton, named McLellan. He is now a Lieutenant, we had quite a fine little chat about old times. It is really refreshing to see one friend once in awhile whom the war has not spoiled.

Yesterday I went down to the city and engaged some photography. I will send you one when they are finished which will be next week sometime.

We are having now very exciting times looking out for the rebels. Every morning we get up at four o'clock and stand at arms till seven that being the usual time of cavalry attacks. Last week we expected an attack and ten days rations and water were drawn into the fort but the rebels haven't come yet.

Yesterday we took in a tremendous siege-gun which you would be astonished to see. It took six pairs of mules to draw it up to the fort and carries a forty-two pound solid shot—so you may imagine what kind of a breakfast we would give the rascals if they venture to come upon us.

We have not been to the front as guards for some little time as the road has been taken up for troops, reinforcements to Rosecrans. Hookers Corps. passed through last week.[13] And I have myself seen at least thirty five thousand men go through here en route for

Chattanooga, some from the Potomac and some from Vicksburg. Rosecrans must now have nearly one hundred and fifty thousand men and all who come from there represent them in good spirits and eager to again meet the rebels. I have not the least doubt of the issue of the next battle there, when I believe Rosecrans will give them a terrible thrashing.

We are all pretty comfortably situated now here, have drawn our winter clothing and I have bought some, in addition, which I could not draw.

Quite a number of the officers' wives are here on a visit, but it is terrible expensive for them as they have to pay at the rate of $16 each per week for gentlemen & lady.

I wrote a letter to Hamrick about two weeks ago telling them to sell the wheat and send the money to Rufus. I have not yet rec'd a reply from him.

I will write again the first of the week and send you a picture.

Your affectionate son George.

CHAPTER 6

"What Can't Be Cured Must Be Endured"

Nashville, October 28, 1863–February 7, 1864

The 105th, part of Ward's Brigade, was under the control of Brigadier General R. S. Granger and the Post of Nashville. Sergeant Cram's duties took him to Stevenson, Alabama by train. His letters from there were in sharp contrast to those written weeks earlier during enjoyable treks to Rosecrans's headquarters. With the battle of Chickamauga over, Sergeant Cram wrote grimly of the effects of the battle's devastation that claimed one-third of the Union soldiers. By late October 1863, General Rosecrans was removed from the command of the Army of the Cumberland and was replaced by General George Thomas.

While Cram was sad about this military and political decision, he had reason to be sad on a personal level as well. With the change in leadership, General Thomas canceled all leaves that were previously approved by General Rosecrans. Sergeant Cram could not go home on furlough after all. But his sorrows were trivial compared to those of his comrade, Private Lewis Stover, who became a double amputee in the blink of an eye while guarding the train between Nashville and Stevenson.

With the war lingering during the winter of 1863–1864, his disenchantment with military affairs increased. His writing assumed a more strident tone, challenging the wisdom of political and military figures, and captured the conflicts among generals, especially between Ward and Rousseau. His notice of General Ulysses S. Grant in Nashville preceded the general's historic appointment. In just days President Lincoln and his cabinet would promote him to the rank of Lieutenant General of the entire United States armies. And although the 105th had not suffered losses in battle yet, death still worked among the troops of occupied Nashville from the start of the new year. Detailed to tend those sick with smallpox, Sergeant Cram wrote with frustration of the lax medical protocol.

Sergeant Cram and his comrades were relatively comfortable in Nashville and spared the assaults of war for awhile, but the signs of the upcoming spring campaign were impossible to ignore. While a veteran regiment, the 105th still had not experienced the rites of passage of war firsthand. By late February 1864, the regiment was brigaded under Colonel Benjamin Harrison, under the 1st Division (Brigadier General William T. Ward), of the 11th Army Corps of the Department of the Cumberland, under Major General Carl Schurz's command at the time.

Sergeant Cram's letters from Nashville, rich in philosophy, as much as in tactical observation, represented his halcyon days in the army. His diary noted the first occasions of potential romantic interest—perhaps casual courtship—of one or two of the "beautiful girls of Nashville." As there was time to fill in spite of his duties as commissary sergeant, George enjoyed Nashville's theater—"Willow Copse," "Gilbert Judd," and "Richard III" played that season. Perhaps influenced by the performances they saw, Sergeant Cram and his comrades hosted their own renditions of Shakespearean plays. But then, how could he not have been inspired to host theatrical performances after multiple visits to see the "fine actor" he wrote about in his diary (February 1, 1864) who played the lead in "Richard III," John Wilkes Booth?

Nashville [Tenn.]
Oct. 28th, 1863

Dear Mother,

Your two last letters have been received and would have been answered sooner had I not expected to answer them in person. Our calculations are like chaff here, blown away by every new wind. I had my papers all made out for a furlough, all that was lacking was one man's name, the Adjutant Genl. of the Department, but I was two days too late, for immediately upon Gen. Rosecrans' removal, Genl. Thomas issued orders to allow no more furloughs. So, having received my papers back, very respectfully disapproved, I proceed to make my visit home in the shape of a letter.

I had heard of your accident and loss by fire before you wrote concerning it, but am very glad to know it was no worse. It seems a wonder to one that the house and everything in it was not burned down. If your business continues good, probably you will be able to make it good this Fall. I feel better satisfied also that you have heard from Hamrick, though his years labor don't seem to promise anything very remunerative.

You write in your last letter, which I rec'd today that Aunt Sophia has come back. Has she got my letter? I am so glad she is there, it will be so much company for you during the winter.

I am still staffing at the hospital but expect to be relieved in a few days as my patient is nearly recovered.[1] Are there any enlistments going on up there under the late call for 300,000 volunteers? Or has the spirit of war all died out? If it was not for the effect it would have on our government, I should almost wish our army would get driven clear back to the Ohio River. Perhaps then someone would be scared into it.

I feel perfectly disgruntled with the way this war is carried on. The fact that someone or some party has succeeded in depriving one of the best, if not the very best military commanders of his command is enough to disgrunt anybody. Fairly idolized by his army, he [Rosecrans] was becoming too popular to escape the malice of political schemers, but it can't be helped and what "can't be cured must be endured."[2]

I have nothing new this time to write. My experience at the hospital is pretty much the same from day to day. I have now one more to see to. A young man from our company who had both legs taken off by falling between the car of a freight train while it was in motion.[3] He bears it like a mystic, poor fellow, five cars ran over him, as he lay with his legs on the rails and his body between them. It is enough to bring tears from a stone to see him lay there so terribly mangled. The company will present him a pair of cork legs as soon as he can wear them.

Before I write again I shall have returned to regular duty and hope to have something more interesting to say. Good night.

Love to Aunt Sophia and Ettie.
Your affectionate son George

Nashville [Tenn.]
Nov. 3rd, 1863

Dear Mother,

I have just finished a letter to Ettie and have a short time to my-self before the bugle call for inspection in which to write to you.

Since I last wrote, I have returned from the hospital and am at the present moment sitting at a small stand in our little tent. The sick boy whom I nursed has nearly recovered and I have little doubt but what I saved his life.

Two of our sergeants—Wheeler and Boutwell—have got commis-sions in Negroe regiments and gone to their commands. I could have held one also just as well as not, but to please you, I did not go be-fore the examining board.

I received a commencement of a letter from you, a few days ago which was finished by Ettie. I am glad to hear you are so drove in business and that your loss in goods by fire was so small. Business seems to be good everywhere now and merchants are just counting money here. I think it will be a great help to you also in the way of company to have Aunt Sophia with you. She is always so full of life. But I shall be obliged to postpone my letter till evening for they are calling us.

Sat. Nov. 7th—Before I could finish my letter I was called away to the front, we made the trip in two days meeting with no trouble ex-cept a few trifling accidents. I was much struck during the journey with the changed appearance of things since I was last down. All along the road lay the wrecks of cars and engines while at the differ-ent stations buildings had been burned down by the guerrillas. The country also looked more barren and desolate. The leaves were falling from the trees and the mountains looked like great dreary piles of ruck.

Arrived at Stevenson, I hardly knew the place. There were broken wagons scattered all over the place, dead and dying mules and horses were congregated together, the soldiers there looked ragged and horribly filthy, and I saw crowds of them standing to catch water in drops as it came from the spring. Everything was covered with mud, but things will probably be better now, then will be more provi-sion for them and forage will not have to be drawn by famished mules so far through the mountains.

Yesterday afternoon we had a brigade drill, all four regiments being present, they kept us going till sundown and tomorrow we are to have another general inspection. When the regiment is brought out for inspection they are first formed in line of battle, then in columns of companies by a wheel to the right. After that they examine each man to see if his gun is bright, whether he has the requisite amount of cartridges or not, then his knapsack is overhauled and his clothes examined to see if they are clean and whole. If any man is found with dirty clothes or a rusty gun or with less than 40 rounds of cartridges he is reprimanded publicly. All these things are necessary to make good soldiers, but they are very humiliating.

I have just this moment received a letter from you and Ettie jointly. I am very glad the babies are doing so finely and cause so little trouble. You must have a very lively time at home now with such a large family.[4]

I cannot see the policy in removing such a fighting man as Rosecrans at this time and I think his conduct since his removal shows that he is not afraid of the most rigid investigation. But as Ellis once said in a letter to me, "The ways of our rulers are more mysterious that the ways of Providence."

We are not at all discouraged and fully expect to get home in one year and ten months. True it seems a long while to look forward, but time soon passes away.

We are well clothed and have been at all times since being in the service. This winter we are to draw boots.

Day before yesterday I received a letter from Wm. Henry. He is at Corinth, Miss., and has 9 months longer to serve.

I do not think it probable that I shall yet be home this winter on a furlough, but shall do it if a chance offers.

Your affectionate son George
Love to Aunt Sophia.

Nashville [Tenn.]
Jan. 3, 1864

Dear Mother,

We are all 'froze' up here and this is the first day we could keep the ink thawed long enough to write a letter. New Year's morning found us without a stick of wood and such weather I never saw. Six soldiers were frozen to death coming up on the train from Franklin the night before. Poor fellows—they had enlisted in the Veteran Corps and were going home on furlough expecting to meet their friends and have a happy visit at home, there were about three hundred of them and a great many had to ride on top of the cars, some of them got off the train and came in on foot the next morning, others were frozen in such a manner that they will never fully get over it, while six poor boys were found *dead*.

We spent New Years day shivering over a few little fires; we managed to pick up enough wood to keep up but it was not a very pleasant New Year's day to us.

I have bought me a fine pair of boots and got out of money. The probabilities at present are that we shall not be paid again till Spring so I borrowed fifteen dollars and gave an order on you for it.

I think you did well in not going to Chicago at present. It is hard to get along in our old city especially alone. Twenty months will sometime come around and then certainly I shall be enabled to come home and assist you, I hope before, and indeed it does seem as if the war would not last much longer.

I sent Uncle Calvin one of my photographs and will try and send one to Uncle Rufus but cannot just now, this last lot I have taken were spoken for long before they were finished and about a dozen more have spoken for one. You see all the boys in the company want the sergt's pictures and I find it is rather expensive for we can't get them here as cheap as you can up North.[5]

New Year's Eve the Union men of Tennessee had a meeting in the statehouse and everybody was for "Old Abe" and Andy Johnson of Tenn. for our next Chief Magistrate. I think Tenn. will soon be returned to the Union. Old rebels are daily coming around to the right track and many are disposed to take advantage of the President's proclamation.

While I write it is snowing and the ground is covered already but to us soldiers it contains no charm for sleigh rides and snowballs are things of the past, however we hope sometime to enjoy them again.

Give my love to Uncle & Aunt, the cold weather must excuse this letter for my fingers are now aching,

Your affectionate son George

Nashville [Tenn.]
Jan. 10th, 1864

Dear Mother,

I have not received anything from you since I last wrote, but conclude you have written and the recent storms have delayed it. I think I told you in my last to send the dried beef to Tirtlot by express. You had better send as soon as you can, for goods are sometimes a long while in getting through and our staying here is very uncertain.

The weather here is cold and stormy, very unpleasant for soldiers but it will soon be over and the warm sun again shines out. We have now better arrangements for getting wood however and are comparatively comfortable. It is most severe on pickets, who have to watch a dreary walk without regard to wind or weather. The orders are to have no fires in our forts, but, of course these are disobeyed, for men would freeze without them.

The Genl. Comd. [Commander of Nashville Post] (Genl. Granger) is a contemptible scoundrel and he has no mercy for a soldier while he hits the rebel citizens. This is R. S. Granger and not Gordon Granger, who is fairly worshiped by his soldiers.

Our brigade has been reorganized and our Genl. (Ward) is placed in command of the division which puts the ranking Col. (Col. Harrison of Ind.[6]) in command of this brigade. We have now orders to go to the front as soon as needed there, but I do not think that will be until Spring. We are now in the 1st Brigade, 3rd Division, 11th Army Corps commanded by Maj. Genl. Hooker.[7] The troops at the front have all been moving forward towards Huntsville and I have not heard from Ellis since the movement began but I learn that his corps (the 15th Army Corps) is one that has moved. It is the general opinion here that they will go into winter quarters at Huntsville and be ready to take a general start in the Spring.

We are living very comfortably now, draw soft-bread, 3/5 beef and 2/5 pork, beans, rice, sugar, coffee (sometimes tea), candles, soap, vinegar and frequently molasses. Draw clothes every month, of a good quality. We cook in messes, in our mess there are four Sergts., Grant, Smith, Sergt. Mjr. Whitlock and myself. Of course we have as lively a time as soldiers could. When the paymaster comes around again we shall have some photographs of our mess taken and then I will show you how we look.

There is considerable sickness in the regiment now, the cold weather seems to be productive of disease when we are not sufficiently prepared against it. Small pox is alarmingly prevalent and scarcely any measures are taken to check or control it. Men just recovering are running at large over the whole regiment and those just taken down remain in their own tents, exposing their comrades, frequently several days before going to the sick house. I have been exposed several times but do not fear it. One boy in our company died with it a short time since and another is now sick. Other companies are worse, some having five or six sick ones.[8]

I received a very pleasant letter from Uncle Calvin last week which I shall answer today. He is still writing and I guess will always have a book going so long as he is able to write.

Mr. Pool also wrote me a very friendly letter which I answered yesterday.[9]

Last Thursday night the officers here had a grand military ball for the benefit of the sick and wounded soldiers of the Army of the Cumberland. Almost all of the officers of the regiment attended, leaving their command deserted. Capt. D—— and Lt. T—— both went and danced till morning which probably neither would have done had they been in Wheaton.[10]

Here comes the mornings mail and I stop to examine it. Nothing for me! So I continue my letter. On the night of the eighth, there was a general Union meeting, at the state house, where speeches were made by Gov. Johnson, Col. Dustin and several others. Gov. J made a strong appeal to the southern women to work as hard for the old Union as they had previously done for the rebellion. Prominent men in Tennessee are doing all they can to bring about a restoration of the old Union, which I have no doubt they will effect before many months.

Day before yesterday I attended the funeral of Dr. Potter's little girl who died of diphtheria. She was a very bright intelligent little girl and her last words were, "If I die, shall I see anybody[?]" Our good Chaplain spoke very feelingly from those words at the funeral. Col. Dustin sent an escort of 50 men who marched to the grave with arms reversed, while muffled drums were beating. She was the Dr.'s only child and it seems to almost kill him. They buried her body in a vault, preparatory to conveying it with which I suppose they will do as soon as possible.

My health is pretty fair and I consider myself fortunate in that respect above many of my comrades, I am cheerful also and confident as to the final end of this war which I think will come soon.

Give my love to uncle and aunt, I will write soon to Aunt Sophia.
Your affectionate son George

Nashville [Tenn.]
Jan. 18th, 1864

Dear Mother,

I received your letter of Jan. 6 & 7 day before yesterday, it having been delayed, probably on account of the heavy snows up North. The New Year opened very cold with us even here, and I feared at the time that much suffering and loss of life and property would ensue. Further North a great many soldiers suffered severely for lack of sufficient fuel and those standing guard were entirely exposed to the storm.

We had a good sleighing here for about a week, a most unusual occurrence, but of course it did not profit us soldiers any, only reminding us of the comforts of home. I look forward with pleasant anticipation to the coming of another New Year's anniversary, as the herald of my approaching freedom and return to citizenship.

I have very nearly come to the same conclusion with you that the war will not so end that we soldiers can return to our homes for a long period of time. Military affairs drag slowly and some already think that we shall be obliged to carry on a war of invasion till all the rebellious states are subjugated one by one. I do think however, that all the severe fighting will be over before the coming of another year. I saw that Mr. Shanks of Arkansas is doing his utmost to bring back his state. And there are many men in Tenn. who are doing likewise, but there is still a strong undercurrent here in favor of rebellion by those who have friends and relatives in the southern army.

Last week a tremendous rebel printing establishment was found here. It was left when our troops came some two years ago and never discovered until now. Everything was all in readiness for work, type set and huge stacks of paper waiting to receive the impress of rebellion and southern treason to the gaping traitors of Tennessee. It is thought to be as large as any such establishment in the south. The type and presses are very valuable to the government and will now be used for the support of our cause.

There has been great excitement throughout our regiment for the past few days with regard to enlisting as veterans, getting a furlough home and four hundred ($400.00) dollars bounty. Colonel Dustin made us the proposition that he would endeavor to re-enlist us if we so desired. The regiment voted almost unanimously to reenlist, but I do not entertain any idea that we shall be allowed to do so. I think the offer of the War Department only refers to those regiments whose terms of service expires in 1864. For my own part, I do not desire to again bind myself for another term of three years, but the prospect of a furlough makes the majority of the regiment mad. They do not stop to reason on it at all, and never once reflect that a month at home is soon passed and then a dreary three years campaign in view, during which time a great number will die, while others will be ruined in health and morals. How fickle is the common mind! "Pleased with a feather and tickled with a straw!"

Last week I was downtown and going into a barber's shop to get my hair cut. I saw one of our veterans pay three dollars to a Negroe for working over him about half an hour. He had just received about $200.00 bounty and back pay and I warrant before he reaches his home one half of it will be gone.

I received a letter from Ellis not long ago since which I answered yesterday. He has left Bridgeport and gone further south. The whole army is, I think, preparing for a grand forward movement—though it may not take place yet for a long while but when it does take place, woe be to the rebels in the Southwest.

Genl. Grant is now here at Nashville, and were one to meet him on the street, he would not have the slightest idea that it was the great Genl. Grant that he saw. He is a plain man, and deals in a plain way, especially with rebels.

I do not have to stand guard at present, my commissary duties are now such that I am exempted from other duties and probably will be until about the first of April. The men all cook by messes now and I have to issue to each mess of four, separately, which is considerable of a job.

You speak of having a chance to send to me soon. I do not know of anything I need so much as paper. I shall soon be out of that article. We can buy pretty much everything here and I would get paper but it is very dear, and not a good quality.

The weather here is terrible, considerable cold, some wind, much rain, and much in the superlative degree. We can hardly stir outside of our tents without being in danger of sticking fast in this nasty, slimy soil. The company have just come in from picket. They were out all night in a cold rain. We shall all be glad when we are released from this exposure, though we don't feel at all discouraged and shall while duty keeps us here. I often think, should I live to return, I shall look back with great pride upon my soldier's life. And I frequently say to myself now, "It is good for us to be here." We are learning much that could not be learned elsewhere.

But I must close for I am not very well today and my sheet is nearly full. Love to all.

Your affectionate son George

Nashville [Tenn.]
Jan. 24th, 1864

Dear Mother,

I received your letter of the 15th day before yesterday. The mail is very badly delayed now on account of the recent blocking up of the trains, but although our letters come slowly, they are just as gladly welcomed when they do come.

Before I go further, I must explain my using so dirty a sheet of paper; the fact is, it is all I have this morning and we have to be economical of paper here.

This morning is very lovely; seems just like Spring, the frost is all out of the ground the mud fast drying up; little birds are singing and we can almost forget that we are engaged in a bloody war while looking out on the calm, bright face of nature. It really seems to me that the weather here is more changeable than in Ill. and I do not think you would like living in a southern climate at all.

Speaking of going to Virginia to live, I cannot but think it is a wild prospect, knowing what I do about these border states.[11] Virginia has received a check from which she cannot recover in fifty years, to speak within bounds, I might safely say a hundred. Two of the largest armies have countermarched over her soil for nearly three years and none can tell how much longer they will continue it. You cannot realize the terrible destruction which attends those countries where active war exists, but I have seen it. All traffic ceases except a little in the largest towns. The work of a lifetime is destroyed in a few minutes, fences are burned down; education ceases; whole towns are in ruins and in others beautiful buildings, once used for thriving business, are now filled with dirty soldiers for a large percent of soldiers will be dirty—but were I to undertake to tell of one half the awful ruin and devaluation exhibited even in Tenn., I should want four such sheets of paper as this.

The beef you sent Tirtlot has not yet arrived, and I understand from last accounts the box had not started from Wheaton; perhaps it has before now though.

I believe I gave you in one of my last letters our bill of fare so I will now show you how we pass our time.

In the morning, I am the first up in our mess. I at once get on the coffee hot and in due course of time have the meat frying; breakfast being ready I call my comrades who by this time are busily engaged performing their usual duties and toilet, we then partake of a good cup of coffee and whatever else our table affords. Sometimes we live well and sometimes not. After breakfast, the dishes are washed and set away. The house swept and blankets spread, then we each enjoy ourselves as best we can till noon, some by writing, some reading, others playing checkers and in anyway proper by which we can pleasantly pass away the time. Our dinner is not essentially different from the morning repast, and the afternoon is spent pretty much the same as the forenoon.

In the evening we very frequently get a few of the more intelligent ones in our tent and read Shakespeare, each taking a part. The last play was *Juliet & Romeo* and our next cast is laid for *Julius Caesar*. At eight o'clock we have roll call and then almost instantly go to our beds which consists of a few blankets and a few soft boards; probably such a bed would not afford a great degree of sleep to some of our college chaps in Wheaton, but there is nothing like a good conscience and getting used to a thing. So we drop asleep as quickly and dream as swiftly as though we had beds of softest down.

I cannot but think business will be good after the war is over, for I am not able to see what causes can conspire to make it otherwise. In case the European powers become involved in war, which now is almost certain to be the case, we must certainly have a great increase of all kinds of business, besides a better currency established. Grain must be exported in enormous quantities, this gives the laboring classes, who return from our army, a bountiful source of business, besides raising the price of land, and must in connection with other results give us a great commercial and inland traffic on a specie basis.

I will write to Hamrick with regard to arranging the sale of the land,[12] but did not think it best to act hastily. Land must rise, I feel confident of this fact, and we are not now in need of money. I think the prospect ahead is brightest and believe we shall all yet see happiness, fairs, trains; such too, and such will be the result of the war. Everything speaks more hopefully and every newspaper gives us the dying groans of the slave-ocracy.

I believe the end is approaching and may it come speedily. Let us at any rate, look on the bright side, and whatever the result may be, we shall always have cheerful faces. Life is made up of bright spots for us while we but look at them.

Love to all,
Your affectionate son George

Hardeville[13]
Jan. 27, 1864

Dear Mother,

I have not written to you before since reaching this place, but sent a letter to Aunt Sophia and not long since by the first mail which went out from here. When we first came, it was not expected our stay would be more than two days but a severe rainstorm was coming on; the country all around was overflowed and it has been impossible for our trains to move. We get rations by way of the river, from which we are distant four miles. The weather has cleared up and the water is fast disappearing so a move is expected any day. There is already a rumor that we shall start tomorrow, but I think not before the first of next week.

I have within the past week received two letters from you, one of Jan. 1st and another of the 8th, the latter containing one from Uncle Edwin to you. Does it not strike you that his mind is much impaired?

I received the letter containing $2.00 from Uncle Calvin and one since that with the same. Dr. Waterman has reached us bringing many little things and letters. I was very glad you did not send my overcoat as it would have been thrown away entirely since I could not possibly have been burdened with it on the march and we have nothing now before us but campaigning.

I am so pleased that Frank Ellis got home. He is an excellent friend and it does one almost as much good to hear of his being well treated as if it was myself.

Grant and Wilcox arrived here safely without sustaining any injury from their capture by the rebels. They brought me the three dollars in stamps. Both are entering well upon their respective duties and I believe this time Isaac is going to endure camp life as well as the toughest among us.

My friend Whitlock has just entered the tent and seeing me writing said, "Give her my love." Being answered that it was to my Mother, he modified it by sending his respects. He is another of the really worthy young men.

During the last year I have kept a diary not omitting a single day and I shall send it home the first opportunity.[14] Also I have commenced one for this year.

I am glad to hear from one of your last letters that you are getting some nice clothing apparel. I do love to see a person dressed finely and especially my Mother.

I have just learned that the mail must go out immediately owing to the uncertainty of its being got off as Hdqrtrs. are expecting marching orders. I am almost disgruntled with writing any letters. I have to hurry them so and disjoint and disconnect them, but perhaps you will get a general idea of our whereabouts from them. I expect to next write from some other point in the confederacy.

Your affectionate son George

Nashville [Tenn.]
Jan. 30th, 1864

Dear Mother,

In the midst of all our hurry, I take a portion of the forenoon to write to you not knowing when I shall again have a chance to do so. We are ordered to set out tomorrow morning for Bridgeport and shall march all the way. So you may imagine what disorder and con-fusion we are in this morning getting ready.

I have packed up my overcoat, blanket, and all clothing not ab-solutely needed to wear and leave them here to be forwarded or sent to Wheaton as shall see fit hereafter. Everything we take will have to be carried on our backs. The distance is 130 miles, we are ordered to take 10 days rations, two cooked in our haversacks and eight on the wagons. We take also 100 rounds of ammunition to each man. The idea of marching is not so very disagreeable to us. Though we would rather have transportation furnished us on the cars, still we are willing to endure it if we can help to shorten the war.

The report is here now that the two armies are confronting each other at Knoxville. We are all anxious to have the fighting over and will not be backward to have a hand in if needful. We are going pre-pared for anything that may happen, and do not expect any more soldiering in the rear.

I received your letter containing also Aunt Sophia's a few days since. There is no sort of danger of our enlisting as veterans until we have been in service two years and at that time I do not think any will be so foolish as to try it, even if the war lasts which I hope will not be the case. Day before yesterday I received an order from the board of examiners to appear before them to be examined for a commission in a colored regiment but did not go, though I should have done so had it not been for you and have no doubt what I could have gotten a captaincy. However I do not regret it, for I don't think any commission would tempt me to remain in the service after the war is over.

My health is now good and I feel well able to endure the fatigues of the coming march, so do not worry about me for I shall be enabled to get safely through I know. I will write as soon as we get there and before if possible though it will not be easy to do so on the march. I feel new vigor in starting out as everything beckons activity in the coming campaign and I shall not allow myself to become despondent whatever we may have to pass through.

The weather is still warm, with some rain this morning but not enough yet to materially injure the roads. We are to take along in our train a large number of pontoons and ordnance items. The road is not at all difficult till we get to the mountains and then our jour-ney will necessarily be slow on account of the wagons. I send you in this two photographs of my companions.

Tell Aunt Sophia I will answer her letter as soon as we get a little settled again. I wrote one to her not but a few days ago. Have received several lately from Uncle Calvin and Aunt Annie.

I have just invested my last cent in postage stamps of which I have 60.[15] We shall not need money at the front for there is nothing to buy, so we all expect to get rich.

Now, do not be at all uneasy. I feel strong both in mind and body and shall march through without difficulty. I must now close as I have yet much to do to get well ready. If this letter is full of mistakes you must remember I have only had a few minutes to write it.

Love to all,
Your affectionate son George

Nashville [Tenn.]
Feb. 7th, 1864

Dear Mother,

Well "all is quiet at Nashville" and the 105th is still safely camped at the old fort. Spite of all our desperate attempts to get away to a hotter clime, we are still far in the rear, our general made several furious attempts to get us off and so far succeeded to have ordnance and supply trains all loaded and driven part way out, tents turned over to the quartermasters and ten days rations drawn for the march.

But as our good fortune would have it, just about four hours before we were ready to start, a telegraph dispatch was received from Brig. Genl. Thomas advising us not to move. Genl. Ward is in a peck of trouble to get to the front and was going to leave this place wholly unguarded. Maj. Genl. Rousseau, commanding officer of this district, told him that if he marched his troops out of town, he would put him under arrest. Rousseau telegraphed at once to Thomas and he settled the matter. Genl. Grant has since arrived here and says we cannot be spared to leave Nashville within a month so there the matter rests.

Our ordnance and supply trains are unloading today and we are eating up our ten days marching rations with as good a grace as possible. We have drawn new tents so taking it all around I think we rather gained some as is the affair has cost government about five thousand dollars and General Ward has lost the confidence and respect of both officers and men.

Capt. Daniels has been detailed as A.C.S. on the staff of the brigade commander and takes our orderly (Smith) with him as clerk. This leaves me acting orderly and as our First Lieutenant is in command, I have all the company business also to attend to and in reality am about the same as captain only I don't get the pay. Tirtlot has been detailed off on an expedition about fifteen miles up the river and will not be back for ten or fifteen days, if then. I gave him your letter which I received in one of mine last week.

We are all very cheerful and even enthusiastic over our good fortune in not marching for although a few complaints were uttered, yet all dreaded the terrible march at this time of year. I never felt really so discouraged in my life as I did at the prospect before us, although I wrote cheerfully concerning it and when we ascertained we were not to go, I tell you the shouts from brave regiments filled the air, and all seemed drunk with joy. I had my haversack all packed and blanket folded ready to start.

We are gratified also with the President's call for more men. Now I begin to see peace dawning. We want a perfect avalanche of men to pour down upon the South and end the war with one glorious sweep. Now some of the sneaks will have to come; thank Heaven for that.

I have just received a fine letter from Frank Ellis and I assure you he is down on that class of young men who stay at home, much worse than I am. We who have suffered in the field have no feeling with those who play when the hour for work has come: how they can endure themselves I know not, for before I enlisted I could not look an honest patriot in the face.

We hope much from the Spring campaign and I do think that it will so stagger the rebellion that a few months more will end it, but yet we cannot tell and must await the coming blow with anxious hearts.

There is much demoralization in the army and thousands of young men here are ruined. Still there is no excuse for it, I do not think I have depreciated in the least and it is my boast now that I can return home as much a gentleman as when I left. I have never been tempted to follow the vices of camp and cannot see how one who has any respect for himself or his friends at home can so degrade themselves as many do.

I have bought me a fine lot of paper as cheap as you could get it North so you need not send any at present. Send a few envelopes should you have an opportunity and also two summer shirts like those you sent last year. I find them much more comfortable than these army shirts especially for summer. I wore those others eight months. I need them more than anything else.

My health is excellent and indeed there is very little sickness among our soldiers. We have become acclimated and pretty well accustomed to camp life and most all the disease is confined to a few sneaks who are sometimes taken suddenly ill, when called on for duty. This class I am happy to say is small and is becoming daily beautifully less.

I will answer Uncle Rufus' and Aunt Sophia's letter soon. We are now in 1st Brig., 1st Div. 11 Army Corps commanded by Mjr. Genl. Howard.[16]

Your affectionate son George

Rufus Blanchard, George F. Cram's uncle, was a prominent historian and Chicago map publisher. As a surrogate father, Uncle Rufus had a significant influence on George's life.
(Courtesy of John Hoskins)

Sergeant Cram, like many soldiers, held the highest respect for General William Stark Rosecrans, seen here in 1864.
(Ambrotype by Mathew Brady, Carlisle Military History Institute)

Above: During March–April 1864, Cram wrote of the great care
troops gave to the construction and appearance of their pine cottages
near Wauhatchie, which were probably similar to this one.

(Library of Congress)

Left: Unidentified soldiers of the
105th Illinois Infantry pose
for a photograph on "grim"
Lookout Mountain. Sergeant Cram
also posed for a photograph
there, on April 6, 1864.

(Carlisle Military History Institute)

Above: Officers of the 105th Illinois Infantry.

Standing: Chaplain Daniel Chapman, Quartermaster Timothy Wells, Adjutant David Chandler, Assistant Surgeon George Beggs.

Left to right, seated: Major Everell F. Dutton, Assistant Surgeon Alfred Waterman, Colonel Daniel Dustin, Surgeon Horace Potter, Lieutenant Colonel Henry F. Vallette.

(Carlisle Military History Institute)

Below: The Battle of Resaca,

Georgia, May 15, 1864.

(*Cram's Magazine,* 1901)

THE BATTLE OF RESACA.

Martha "Mattie" Hiatt, of Wheaton, Illinois, became the wife of George F. Cram. Mattie's brother, Luther Hiatt was also a member of Co. F.
(Courtesy of John Hoskins)

George F. Cram after the war.
(Courtesy of Deborah Hoskins Edwards and John Hoskins)

CHAPTER 7

"The Big Brigade"

Shelbyville, February 14–Lookout Valley, April 29, 1864

For many weeks, Sergeant Cram had noted the makings of a serious campaign attentively from the relative comforts of Nashville. The 105th was part of the 1st Brigade of the 1st Division of the 11th Army Corps during their advance to "grim Lookout." By the time the regiment was comfortably quartered in their pine camp in Lookout Valley they were part of the 1st Brigade, 3rd Division of the newly formed 20th Army Corps under Major General Joseph Hooker.

Rain, mud, and reduced rations made conditions rugged as the troops began their march southward. The sight and stench of leftover carnage and destruction from the battles of Chickamauga and Chattanooga framed the backdrop of the march. But, by April 1864 the heavy rains finally ended which signaled the re-flowering of the war. As the roads dried, heavy artillery could be transported. The wheels of war were rolling towards Atlanta.

During the spring of 1864, Western troops such as the 105th Illinois Infantry were joined in Lookout Valley by veteran regiments from the eastern campaigns whose own numbers had been decimated. Some men of the 105th Illinois Infantry complained of the new styles foisted upon them by the easterners. Corporal James Congleton wrote (May 1, 1864) that there were rumors that the 79th Ohio was even wearing white collars and gloves. Sergeant Cram noted in his diary (March 31, 1864) that the men were required to salute an officer whenever they met him; "the boys are quite indignant. . . ." And when the men were subjected to the return of regular inspections Cram wrote in his diary (April 4, 1864), "It is a bad thing and gotten up by men of limited judgment." The newly arrived soldiers at Lookout Valley engaged in continuous preparation, proudly conducting make-believe, "sham" battles in front of several generals. The sights and sounds of the army's beautifully executed rehearsals were just preludes to the performances in which one out of ten of them would be counted among Sherman's aggregate losses during the next month's reports.

General Ward, however, was finally a happy man. He was in position to move his men to the front after imploring headquarters that they were ready for the test. General Ward felt it only fair that his men could show friends and foes alike how well they were prepared for battle. General Ward, the "Old Falstaff," as Sergeant Cram called him, hungered for the heat of battle, the only pathway to stand apart from a throng of lesser generals. General Ward's wishes soon came true.

Sergeant Cram wrote his mother nostalgically from their camp among the pine trees in Lookout Valley. Whether it was part of a well-considered plan, or, simply hope for a life after the war, he wrote about joining his uncle, Rufus Blanchard, in map publishing in Chicago. Perhaps he discussed this with his friend, Private Frank Ellis, when they finally reunited. After so much concern for his friend's welfare, Sergeant Cram reunited with Private Ellis for a bit of dinner, nearly two years after they parted for their separate regiments. With little more than hard tack and pork belly, this dinner was surely in contrast to the bounty of Mrs. Cram's dinner table so long ago. But the meal itself probably didn't matter to Sergeant Cram on the eve of the Atlanta Campaign; he was nourished by the company of his friend.

Nashville [Tenn.]
Feb. 14th, 1864

Dear Mother,

It is again Sunday morning, my day for writing to you, so I seat myself to begin my letter. Mr. Whitlock and I are warming some water with which we intend to enjoy a good bath. Whitlock is one of those neat and tidy young men that it does a man good to be with. Here comes the mail!

After looking it over I see there is nothing for me, so after distributing to the others I resume my letter.

Yesterday I was pleasantly surprised to see one of my old Wheaton college school mates, Lt. Rood. I do not know whether you will recollect him or not. He is a Lt. in the 104th Reg. Ill. Vol. And coming to Nashville on duty with his regiment he called up to see us Wheaton boys. I enjoyed a very pleasing conversation with him on the times and scenes that were. He has seen more of active service in the field than our regiment has, but still looks just as he did when a student, with the exception of course of the regimentals. You may readily imagine the amount of pleasure we find in seeing old acquaintances here in the army.

A few days since I received the things you sent by express. Tirtlot was on a detail about fifteen miles up the river, guarding some wood choppers and there being a probability of his remaining there some time, I sent all the beef to him. The other things came very opportune and I have saved them for future use. Seven letters also are received. If you have a good chance to send to me again you might send two summer shirts, but in case you do not I can do very well without them.

Yesterday our regiment received two months pay, which comes very timely as we were all completely out of funds. Pay day with us is a great day and jubilant faces can now be seen all over the camp. You would laugh to see the boys pocket their "green backs" as the paymaster hands them out. And it is especially amusing to see with what alacrity the boys fall in line when ordered to "Fall in for pay." We muster on that occasion a much larger company than at any other time. You see, there are no sick men then.

I am still acting orderly sergeant and have pretty much all the company business to do. Capt. Daniels is on the Genl's staff and Tirtlot off on duty so only one commissioned officer remains with the company. I get along with him finely, he is no military man at all, but is an excellent man at heart. Everything is much more harmonious in the company now that the other two are away.

It is still uncertain when we shall leave here, but we expect it will be decided in a few days and it would not surprise me at all if we were ordered to march any day and still we may stay possibly for months yet. We are all willing that the latter may be the case, but if ordered to go, will do so cheerfully. You speak of the war soon closing, we think here very much as you do that the Spring campaign must wind it up, but everything in war is so uncertain that I do not allow myself to set a time anymore for the war to close though I am full of hope.

I see by the papers that resolutions have been brought into the rebel congress to send delegates to Washington to attempt a settlement. This looks to me as if they were willing to lay down their arms, certainly they know that with our prospect, we will not consent to a division and hence we must infer that their desire to meet us with peace propositions is really for the purpose of affecting their pardon and then laying down their arms. I place more dependence, however, on our armies than in any repentance of the rebel leaders, and it does me good to see that Lincoln at last is determined to bring out the sneaks. That last call together with the continued enlistment of veteran troops is worth more than victorious battle.

There are great preparations making in this western department, though you don't know much about it up North. Genl. Grant is omnipresent. He is now here at Nashville but no one save himself knows what for or what he is doing. Long and heavily laden trains are continually rolling over the Chattanooga rail now and an immense amount of supplies must have already accumulated there. Veteran soldiers are beginning to report back and are sent right through to the front. And although we do not know anything about the programme yet, we have full confidence in Grant.

Our regimental hospital has been vacated and the sick sent to brigade hospital so our good Chaplain, ever on the lookout for a chance to do some good, has had the building (which was formerly a church) cleaned up and will preach to us there hereafter, whenever occasion offers. He is a model man and well fitted for an army chaplain, very frequently he comes into our tent and spends the evening with us, always talking hopefully of the future.

The health of the regiment is good, but very few are under medical treatment and most of these are men who became sick to avoid duty.

I wrote a letter to Uncle Rufus a few days ago and also one to Uncle Calvin. If I have a good opportunity to send some I shall send you $25 but would rather keep a little more than run the risk of sending it by mail. Give my love to all.

Your affectionate son George

In camp, five miles south of Shelbyville [Tenn.]
Sunday afternoon, four o'clock
Feb. 28th, 1864

Dear Mother,

I have just got nicely washed up and finished a cup of coffee in time to write my customary Sunday letter to you. Last Wednesday morning our brigade left Nashville under orders to report to Maj. Genl. Hooker at Lookout Valley. We commenced the journey by slow marches going only ten miles the first day; even this we found tired us much, on account of our heavy load. Arriving at Murfreesboro, we took the Shelbyville Pike because it led through the best watered country. Tomorrow, we shall reach Tullahoma, distant fifteen miles. We have marched sixteen today. I feel somewhat tired but the march is not so exhausting as the one we made eighteen months ago through Kentuck.

Today's march was especially cheering to us as we passed through the most loyal section I have seen in the South. Many of the homes we passed were decorated with Union banners and at almost every gate groups of men and women stood waving their handkerchiefs to cheer us on. I remember one little girl in particular, who came out with a beautiful flag and as she unfolded it we gave her three rousing cheers. Passing through S— it seemed as though every girl in town was waving her handkerchief to us. I shall long recollect our passage through that loyal town.

A thousand little incidents occur every day that I cannot write. The main thing however I want to let you know is that we are all in good spirits and health. Not a man from our company has fallen out or been left behind and we are confident of reaching our destination safe and sound. The worst thing we have to contend with is the dirt which envelopes us in huge clouds as we march along. Every night when we file into camp the first thing is to have a good scrub then pitch our tent, pull up some grass or weeds to lay on, make up our bed nicely and after making coffee, go to writing or whatever else we may wish to do. And right here I want to call your attention to the value of coffee, it is to us soldiers absolutely indispensable, as all who have ever marched will testify.

The country we passed through today is flat and low, good for farming. Many loads of cotton passed by us on their way by Nashville. The rebel fortifications here at Shelbyville amounted to simply a few rifle pits. We have passed by many soldiers' graves in the last two days. It seems almost as though this whole country was covered with the graves of our brave boys. I can never pass lightly by one of them, but always think that there is some Mother mourning a dead soldier boy.

We left all our sick in Nashville. They will probably come through on the cars. I received the shirts; and some other things you sent by

Parker[1] just two days before we started. Also some letters in which you spoke of selling out; I think perhaps you cannot do better than to take the price you set upon your goods and let him have them.

I left all my things with a friend in Nashville who will bring them through on the car except my overcoat which I shall send home or rather, he will send it from Nashville. Tirtlot and I sleep together and are fully well off for clothing.

Your affectionate son George

[p.s.] I have written a disconnected letter but I had a bad place to write and but little time. Don't be anxious, George

Camp of the 105th, Two miles north of Stevenson [Ala.]
March 6th, 1864

Dear Mother,

Well you see we have not yet arrived at our journey's end. Since I last wrote you from Shelbyville we have seen camp life in all its different forms but are still all well and cheerful. Not a man has had to be left yet from our company and all look forward to active service with eagerness.

Last Monday we started for Tullahoma in the midst of a driving rain which did not cease for forty hours. We reached T—— at dusk, built up large fires and pitched our tents but twas no use to try to sleep for the waters ran under us and soaked us through. By keeping close to the fires however, we managed to keep from freezing and at noon next day it ceased and we were enabled to dry our clothes and blankets. I tell you if ever I was thankful to see the blessed sunlight it was then. It would [have] amused you to see us reading the letters which we got that morning, while the cold rain was pouring down on us.

Last Friday we began ascending the mountains and after traveling about five miles our drunken old Genl. found he was on the wrong road, so after retreating about a mile we left the path and struck right across the unbroken mountains. We traveled this way about an hour over huge rocks, down steep hills, across ravines, amid all sorts of laughable casualties. When we came to the right road and began to file into it, the companies and even regiment were so mixed up that we could scarcely find our places. Here I was much amused at one fellow who after looking in vain for his company, stepped up to a soldier just ahead of me and said he, "Soldier, can you tell me what my name is?" Such little incidents occur often and tend much to break the monotony of the march.

We have got along very well so far over the mountains. The first day troubled us the most. The roads were then awful and although we camped at night, seven miles from our camp in the morning, yet the teams did not all get in till two o'clock the next day and three wagons were broken to pieces and abandoned. We did not start in consequence yesterday till along in the afternoon and only went four miles. Today the roads were pretty good and we have marched fifteen miles.

We have not had any mail since leaving Tullahoma but are expecting to get it tonight or in the morning. I am writing now, on a box which Tirtlot and I brought into our tent for that purpose. He sits on the ground at one side and I at the other.

We shall continue our march tomorrow and may halt a few days at Bridgeport but expect to soon be camped on Lookout Valley. There has been some talk of our being transferred to Genl. Sherman's Second Division but I don't know how it will end. We are at present in the 1st Brigade, 1st Division, 11th Army Corps. Our Brigade Com. is Col. Harrison, who is a most able man and well liked by us all, but our division Genl. (Ward) is a regular sot.

I shall write again as soon as we get fairly settled, that is if we ever do settle down again. Now don't be anxious. I never was more healthy and contented and no money would tempt me to change positions with some of those young men at home.

Your affectionate son George

Lookout Valley [Tenn.]
March 12, 1864

Dear Mother,

We have at last got to our present destination, and are more busily engaged getting our camp fixed up conveniently and making it as comfortable as we can while we stay here. The name of the station here is Wauhautchie. We are located about one mile from it. Our camp is in the valley right at the base of Lookout Mountain whose grim and rocky sides stretch out so far above us that they almost seem to reach the sky. Here the extreme right of our army under Hooker drove the rebels like sheep from the mountains. Lookout itself is a high mountainous ridge extending for many miles in a southwesterly direction and completely commanding the river and railroad running from Bridgeport. The main part of the fighting however was done on the Northern extremity situated about two miles from here.

Lookout Valley is a marginal tract of land extending for some miles in length and reaching in width from the base of Lookout to the high ridge of hills on the northern side. On the south side of Lookout is Mission Ridge where Sherman's army engaged the rebel posts. Here Ellis was engaged and it is especially interesting to me to look over the fields where those so well known fought and suffered. I never in my whole life saw country so rocky and mountainous and can now more correctly judge the brilliancy of Rosecrans' campaign for the possession of Chattanooga.

The last two days of our march were the most difficult of all. Leaving Bridgeport early on the morning of the ninth, we crossed the river on a pontoon bridge and were soon winding our way over miniature Alps. Now climbing over huge rocks and now wading through awful mud holes, dead mules and horses completely lined the way, and in one narrow defile[2] through which we passed in the afternoon we counted over sixty dead carcasses in going a quarter of a mile.

That night it rained terribly and in the morning pleasing prospects of mud met us on every side but our march must be concluded that day and so we started about nine o'clock in the morning. We had twelve miles only to go but before we arrived there we found it to be the hardest days march we ever experienced.[3]

We had more then twenty creeks and small rivers to ford and our poor feet were fairly soaking. But there is a sort of stimulant about march that sustained us till we arrived at our camping grounds, and before they could take off their load, I saw dozens of men fall fainting to the ground. We were kept in line with all our things on about half an hour to be reviewed by Maj. Genl. Howard who rode out from his headquarters to see us, and then allowed [us] to stake our tents and rest. I felt some exhausted but still well and thanks to a good constitution I could have endured a great deal more without giving out. I gathered that night a fine lot of pine boughs to sleep on and enjoyed an excellent night's rest in spite of the rain which insisted on dropping down in my face once in awhile.

I feel now just as well as I did when we left Nashville, and have no doubt but that I shall preserve my health.[4] How long we shall stay here is wholly uncertain. Some think we shall soon move to the immediate front soon. Others think we will stay here some months. I do not mention an opinion inasmuch as I have nothing to form one on.

Hooker's and Howard's hdqrtrs. are within three miles of us, and their troops can be seen settling along the valley between the hills looking very much as if their camps were playing hide and seek with each other. Genl. Howard is commanding our corps and Hooker the grand division we are in. Howard is a very pleasant looking man and appears more adapted to the pontoon than the field of battle, though I believe he is a good Genl. He has only one arm.

I wrote to you twice on the march and once to Aunt Sophia. Received one letter from her and one from you containing your photograph which I was very glad of. Think you have not altered much. I believe you will do best to keep the house you are in as long as possible. In a year I may possibly return and then can look up some other home. I do not believe business is going to drop as you fear but I must now close.

With love to all,
Your affectionate son George

Lookout Valley [Tenn.]
March 26, 1864

Dear Mother,

Your letters of the 15th and 19th are both received, and though we are all in confusion here putting a floor inside our tent, yet I will try and answer by spells.

I was sorry to hear you were expecting my arrival in that region of civilization, for owing to certain obligations I am under to Uncle Sam, it is not possible for me to be there; I think for about seventeen months. I *was* however rather expecting to visit Wheaton, before we left Nashville, and sent in an application for a furlough believing it would be granted, as an order had been issued allowing five percent of every regiment furloughs. But we left Nashville before the papers came back and mine overtook me at Tullahoma, *Disapproved*. I did not mention it to you because I wished to surprise you in case I got one, and did not think it necessary to disappoint you as well as myself when they were disapproved.

I have become so used to army life that disappointment does not trouble me, principally for the reason that while here I expect it. My enlistment however is rapidly wearing away and I shall soon be entitled to more than a short—20 day furlough.[5] Still, I do most earnestly hope that before, or at least at that time, the war may be ended and I cannot think otherwise.

You speak of having moved; perhaps your business may be more profitable now as you are on the main street and I am very glad if the situation is pleasant.

With regard to my things which Sgt. Grant took home. I did not expect when I left N——— that he would go home unless I did, for we both sent in applications together, but he obtained his afterwards at the hospital and did not intend to send home my "little tracts" such as I could keep here. The picture you spoke of, in a miniature case, is one of a young lady, of my acquaintance, living in Nashville. She is a very fine young girl and had one brother die in the rebel army. Her mother also recently died, leaving herself and older sister alone with an aged father, who was at one time wealthy and in good circumstance.

I left a small account book with all my photographs in it with Grant; wish you would send them to me also all the other little things which you think I will need. I can't remember them all now. I don't care particularly about the account book, and you can keep it if you wish.

The weather here has been very bad during the last week. Last Wednesday about one foot of snow fell and is now going off with a slow unpleasant rain. The inhabitants never before saw so much snow at one time nor so cold weather and attribute it to the presence of us "Yanks" as they term us. At this time the snow has all disappeared from the valley where we are encamped. But the mountain top is still white and from here looks bleak and cold.

I intended when I wrote my last letter to have visited Lookout Mountain before writing this, but there has been no time when it would be safe to ascend the mountain, since then. I shall go as soon as possible and am intending to have a picture taken on the front of rock where Jeff Davis made his last speech to Braggs' army last winter, and where the brave legions of Hooker made their successful assault. A few days since I saw a Mass. Regiment, two companies of which were from Lowell.[6] Their regiment and an Ohio regt are now camped opposite a hill from which they drove five rebel regiments on the night of "Hookers Midnight Fight." Most of them are pleasant appearing boys and have done nobly for the state they represent.

We are called by the other troops here, "the big brigade." Our brigade being as large as their division. (A division consists of two, three, and four brigades) and we have the credit of being the best and neatest soldiers here. Our camp is really a beautiful spot and the pine trees which we have set out in it would be worth a small fortune in Illinois. The mountains are covered with pines and evergreens, which gives the country [its] fresh aromatic appearance. There is certainly much to be seen as we travel about through this southern country and if we live to get home, I think none of us will regret the hardships we have endured to see it. My proper address is, Company F, 105th Ill. Vol, 1st Brigade, 1st Division, 11th Army Corps, (1st Brig. 1st Div. 11th A.C. *Abbreviated*)

Your affectionate son George

[p.s] This paper you will observe is slightly dirty, but it was not made so by my hands, for they are clean. And we are now in a country where we cannot afford to throw away any paper on account of the looks. I send you a photograph of Arthur P. Rice,[7] one of our boys. George

Give my love to all.

Lookout Valley [Tenn.]
March 31st, 1864

Dear Mother,

Enclosed you will find a letter to Sergt. Grant. I wrote to him to bring my extra blanket which I suppose he brought to Wheaton, as well as my vest. I need them both much and wish you would give him the letter if possible before he returns. There are also several other small things which occur [to me] among my things there which you can pick out. I wrote you a few lines two or three days since to have you send my hat (I believe I have one there). These things with perhaps a few envelopes are about all I am in much need of.

We are now living quite comfortably again. Our bakery is completed and we draw good bread, which we are more than ever convinced is the "staff of life." Indeed I believe a month or two's experience on "hard tack" will convince any one of it. Our . . . [the letter is torn away at the bottom.]

It blew a terrific gale all the afternoon and again before dark a large tree was uprooted and fell striking five tents in the ground. Fortunately the inmates escaped without injury, had it occurred an hour later, many of them would have been killed. But, little notice was taken of the accident and in a few minutes a dozen axes were singing in the sides of the prostrate "monarch," a half hour later the tree had taken into itself legs and walked off to the woodpile. It took the boys all the next day, however, to straighten up their tents and get into a liveable condition.

Our Genl. has established a system of continuous drills, three a day and scarcely any time is allowed us for the ordinary camp duties, but this will probably not last long and we are often obliged in like moments to humor the caprices of a whimsical old General. Strange such men are retained in the service. I shall write again soon.

Your affectionate son George

Goldsboro[8]
April 2nd, 1864

Dear Mother,

I have received three letters from you dated at Aurora. In the last one yesterday you spoke of some business proposition made by Uncle Rufus. When I return home I desire to settle at once in some lucrative and promising business or employment and if what he proposes shall appear to be such, I shall be very glad to accept it.[9] You remember I shall be 24 years old and the last three years have been given away, so it seems essential for me to enter into something productive.

I do not see why you would not find Chicago a place to live in, everything there would be so different from what it was when we lived there last, and prosperity will make anyplace pleasant. The state of affairs may, after the war is over, be very insecure and I think nothing certain should be thrown aside or rejected.

We have now got our camp fixed up so that we begin to enjoy a degree of comfort, long since a stranger to us; a few small pines have been planted in rows about our tents to give a pleasant shade and neat appearance. Our company streets are swept clean every morning and no manner of rubbish is allowed to congregate in quarters.

A liberal supply of clothing is being furnished and instead of wretched rags, new bright colors are seen. I think all that has been said about the desperate clothing of the rebels would hardly describe the situation of Sherman's army when we reached this place. About one fourth were barefoot, scarcely one out of five had a decent pair of pants and such a miscellaneous quantity of rags for coats I never saw before.

We now also draw plenty of rations such as hard bread, pork, sugar and coffee.

Yesterday I picked up an old horse and rode over to the 15th corps; had an excellent visit with Frank Ellis, took dinner with him. He had just arrived at his command a few days before and coming so straight from home it was a most pleasant visit.[10] He promised to return the call this week so we shall have an opportunity to say all the unsaid things.

I was yesterday promoted to Orderly Sergeant in place of Smith who was made 1st Lt. on that day. My pay is $24 per month now, which I am saving for future use. My expenditures are light. There is some talk of our receiving six months pay here but I do not know whether we shall or not.

Much is also said of another sudden move and rumor says pretty strongly that we shall start again by the 10th. I am always cheerful and contented in having no expectation of going home before Sept., though I think the war has been unnecessarily prolonged by a lack of energy on the part of the administration. So, once more, men in the field would sweep the Confederacy from Richmond to the Gulf at one tenth the expense of life. All soldiers *know* this but alas they have no word in the matter.

I rec'd Aunt Sophia's letter and will answer soon.

Your affectionate son George

Lookout Valley [Tenn.]
April 23, 1864

Dear Mother,

I rec'd a letter from you a few days since, by Sergt. Grant and in addition to them, I had quite a good visit with him. It is always a great privilege to see anyone just from our home and feel that a few hours previously, they conversed with our friends. Always when such a one makes his appearance in camp, you will see him immediately, surrounded by an eager, interested group, all intensely anxious to know if anybody said anything about them or if they sent a letter, a line, or a word. And then a little token he brings from home, how they talk about it and show it to all the others and rejoice to see that they are not forgotten.

If there is anything that makes a soldier discouraged and in fact homesick, it is to feel as though he was unthought of. And such is frequently the case too, with our soldiers. The good people at home are too much engrossed in every day matters to care sufficiently for their friends so far away. I write this not for you but for you to read or tell to some of those Mothers and sisters there who have sons and brothers here exposed to dangers and all the hardships of war besides the thousand and one vices of camp life, with far too few cheerful letters from home containing good wholesome advice and words of affection.

We are still in our old camp but great preparations are making for a vast movement and we cannot tell how long we shall remain here. Meanwhile we are not inactive, drills and inspections are the order of the day. A few days since our brigade was reviewed with two others by Maj. Genl. Thomas and day before yesterday he rode through our camp after which he stated that we were the neatest and best drilled brigade he had ever seen, which I have no doubt was the case, since we have done nothing but drill and make handsome camps since we came here. I do not like the appearance of Thomas so well as Hooker or Howard. He is a sort of burly looking man and my convictions are that he passes more of brute courage than military skill, however I may be mistaken.

Our corps has been consolidated with the 12th and we form what is called the 20th army corps commanded by Hooker. We are the 1st brigade, 3rd division, 20th army corps. The brigade is commanded by Brig. Genl. Ward, a regular old Falstaff[11] whose sheer delight is to swill whiskey, etc. No one respects him and all unite in hoping that he will soon be removed.[12]

The division is under the guidance of Maj. Genl Butterfield. He has the appearance of a thorough going man and his previous military career warrants us in respecting him. With regard to Hooker, everybody loves him and to see him as he rides along our lines is only to like him more each time.

The corps is about thirty thousand strong, and will no doubt have an important position in the grand army. We have received orders to have constantly on hand 150 rounds of cartridges to each man. Some of the officers think the rebels are going to make the attack but I do not believe such will be the case, and do not think a battle will be fought yet for some weeks.

Capt. Daniels, while playing ball yesterday, broke his leg so severe that it will be a long time before he will get off the bed, and may cause his resignation.[13] He is in considerable pain and the limb is swelled exceedingly. You won't mention this for he does not wish his wife to hear of it.

Lt. Adams has resigned and gone home. I sent my overcoat with him and he promised to call and see you. He is a good, kind man. This vacancy does not cause any promotion as our company has become so reduced that we are not entitled to our complement of officers.[14]

The health of the regiment at present is better than ever before. I do not think there are five in the regt. too sick to be able to march. The weather is still cold but bids fair to become more pleasant now and the mud is fast drying up. If this continues the roads will be in good condition in a week. Troops are marching by every day in great numbers. I have no doubt there are a hundred thousand men here to take part in the coming battle.

Your affectionate son George

[p.s] direct to me Company F, 105th Regt—Ill Vol., Lookout Valley via Nashville. That will be sufficient direction for the present. I wrote to Uncle Calvin not long since but have not heard from there since leaving Nashville except by way of the numerous papers he sends me. I do not know how to direct to Uncle Rufus. Enclosed you

will find a photograph of Lt. Adams. I receive letters from Ellis often and we have plenty of fun in our correspondence.
—George

Lookout Valley [Tenn.]
April 29th, 1864

Dear Mother,

Everyone in camp seems to be busy today and as I have finished all my morning duties I believe I will fill up the forenoon writing.

We are just now preparing pay rolls, signing clothing accounts and turning over extra clothing and accouterments, preparatory to the coming campaign. Every day we look for the benign countenance of our paymaster, but as yet he doth not appear. It makes little difference to me if we are not paid till next Fall, but many of the boys are desirous of having their pockets refilled.

Yesterday afternoon we had one of the grandest performances that our regiment ever took part in, namely, a division drill and sham fight. The men all went out with thirty rounds of blank cartridges and aiming at the grounds selected for the battle, they were drawn up as follows. The 105th were thrown forward as skirmishers and formed into a double line. At proper intervals behind was the first line of battle consisting of three regiments deployed, extending the line a little over a mile. Behind this line was the second. This was drawn up in column by division, consisting of four regiments. And still behind this line were two regiments at either flank in close column. The artillery were posted on the flanks, taking positions on two small hills, covering our grand advance. First the skirmishing commenced by our regiment and continued till we had advanced about three miles and taken possession of every point. Then the enemy were supposed to be found in force, and our regiment were withdrawn and formed in line with the first line of battle. Now the fight commenced in earnest, and the quick rapid discharge of musketry soon filled the valley with dense smoke. The artillery firing too was executed beautifully and the booming of the cannon echoed from hill to hill and thence to the grim wall of Lookout. Of course, we drove the enemy and took any amount of prisoners, with[out] any loss whatever on our side.

Genls. Thomas, Hooker, Butterfield, Brannan and Whipple were there to witness our movements.[15] Butterfield conducted them.

There seems to be at present no more signs of a forward movement here than there were a week ago, but no doubt preparations are being made as secretly as possible.

The weather still continues beautiful and the trees in this vicinity are leaved out so finely that they continually invite us to recline beneath their sheltering branches, but it is very little time we get to spend in leisure hours for they keep us drilling most immoderately.

The sides of the mountain look especially lovely now. The stately pines present such grand contrast to the other trees that they look like dark spots of beautiful velvet, while the large rocks above form a magnificent background. Almost every morning and evening I walk out away from our smokey, noisy camp and enjoy this scenery. Everything is so still and inviting. I can think of other things than camp discords.

I am sorry I cannot send you the photographs you wish but I have no more on hand, and cannot very well get any more taken at present inasmuch as I should have to go on the mountain, which I could not get a pass again today, and it would be a week before they would be finished at which time we may be far from here, but no doubt I shall be able to get more before I am out of Uncle Sam's employ. That will be just as good as these.

We have not received any mail whatever for two days, though I cannot possibly define the reason. The trains run regularly but bring none of those pleasant little visitors from home. This of course makes the time pass away dull.

The morals of our company I must say are decidedly on the improve. Our good Chaplain holds regular meetings every Sunday and several prayer meetings during the week. Many of our boys are church members and many who are not make it a point and esteem it a privilege to attend these meetings. There seems to be less card playing and swearing than before. Considering the morality of most of the army I am really *proud* to belong to Company F/105th Ill.

And so long as I live I do not think I will ever regret being a soldier. I could cover the rest of this sheet with names of young men in our company who are trying constantly to see how refined, how gentlemanly, courteous and above all how strictly moral they can become. The army *need* not own *any* man if he has brains enough to maintain his self respect.

The general health is better than it has been before in a long while, occasionally we receive a few sanitaries,[16] for which we have reason to love the Northern ladies which certainly we don't hesitate to do (especially the younger ones).

But I have got my sheet about filled up so I will close.

Your affectionate son George
Co "F" 105 Ill Vol
Lookout Valley
via Nashville

CHAPTER 8

"It Was Every Man for Himself"

Gordons Mills, May 3–Battlefield, June 19, 1864

The early Spring of 1864 constituted a period of extraordinary physical labor. Roads were engineered, entrenchments were dug with a fury, rations were reduced and then reduced again. While the 105th Illinois Infantry entered Georgia guarding the rear of the 20th Army Corps, it was within days on the front lines of battle with the 70th Indiana Infantry, 79th Ohio Infantry, 102nd Illinois Infantry, and the 129th Illinois Infantry. This was the first time that the 105th Illinois Infantry had been under direct fire of the enemy.

Running pell-mell into the fury, cutting their eyeteeth on the offensive tactics of military deployment, Sergeant Cram and members of more than two hundred Union regiments were massed in north Georgia, preparing to engage in the minuet of a flanking war. The territory was new and the stakes were high. Claiming Atlanta's Gate City required opening Georgia's front door first. There was no turning back.

Reports of Confederate misconduct seemed to fuel the Union's urgency for trouncing into the Atlanta campaign. Reports circulated that Union pickets and foragers had been murdered by Rebels. Rebel soldiers who had been taken prisoners were heard to say that their plan was to make this Georgia campaign "a Chickamauga" for them. And the horrific atrocities of Confederate General Forrest's massacre of the U.S. Colored Troops at Fort Pillow in April became more widely known. The public and the troops were horrified. Pressure was building on General Sherman to move forward. By May 4, General Grant had crossed the Rapidan and telegraphed to General Sherman that the time was upon them. The next day General Sherman went to Ringgold, Georgia, and declared that the Atlanta campaign had officially begun.

The implementation of the campaign, its marathon days of charging, with hand-to-hand combat at times, through Ringgold, Dalton, Resaca, Calhoun, Cassville, Allatoona, Big Shanty, and New Hope Church cost more than five thousand Union lives before the month was over. Detailed to tend wounded comrades, Sergeant Cram's ghoulish days in the field hospital near Resaca may have settled any earlier notions of becoming a doctor. He wrote in his diary (May 18, 1864), "The camp is a dismal place and presents a terrible sight—legs, arms, hands and feet are lying all around. . . ." The Battle of Resaca was the 105th's baptism by fire. With Resaca the regiment was tested and taught what the sham fights and pleasant Nashville nights could not teach. War was random, unforgiving, deafening, and macabre. Sergeant Cram, Private Arthur Rice, and countless others came to learn this well.

As the summer progressed, General Sherman's army advanced its breastworks, making creeping progress with points and counterpoints, inching toward Atlanta, some thirty miles distant. General Sherman was frustrated by the endless rains during the summer of 1864, and the soldiers already seemed entombed in the triangular mountain fortress between Acworth and Kennesaw Mountain.

Sergeant Cram numbed to the ear-piercing firing, cramped positions, and sleep deprivation. As he wrote of the deaths of comrades with only brief mention, he didn't offer an extra word to ponder either sorrow or implications of their deaths. Doctor Potter, a major influence in all their lives, was killed—a man who had faithfully served the 105th since Wheaton. Doctor Potter became just another volunteer who would never again welcome a June morning on the Illinois prairie. The insensibilities of war were taking their toll.

Camp of the 105th, Gordons Mills [Ga.]
May 3rd, 1864

Dear Mother,

Since I last wrote you, from the pleasant valley at the foot of "Lookout" we have changed our place of residence as you will observe. We started yesterday morning early and after winding around the mountain we turned our backs suddenly on the grim monster and proceeded directly southward on the Lafayette road.

Our entire division was along and the road for miles was perfectly black with troops whose bright bayonets glistened in the bright sunlight, looking very much like a dense thicket of polished steel. The troops all along the road were preparing to move also and I think it is to be a grand advance. We found a brigade here but they left this morning in an eastern direction, probably to strengthen the center at Ringgold. Our division is on the right wing, and we are now only ten miles from the main rebel line and only eight from their outposts.

About one o'clock yesterday we commenced crossing the Chickamauga battle ground and never in my life do I want to see such terrible evidence of human destruction as were there visible. Hundreds of large trees were cut completely into with shot, and hundreds of items of immense size are bored through and through with those iron messengers, while the butts of them were so riddled with bullets that in many of them not a space of a single square inch can be found free from the scar of a bullet.

The battle ground at Stone River I used to think was awful, but compared to this, it seems a mere skirmish. The saddest sight of all, and indeed the most significant, were the little clusters of graves where are buried the fallen heroes.

The distance we marched yesterday is about eighteen miles, very many poor fellows fell out and were left behind. This is our first experience in marching under Butterfield and I must say, we don't love him much. He gave us scarcely a particle of meat and just stopped long enough at noon for us to hastily swallow a bite and then started on again. If we had marched leisurely and had occasional halts we would have arrived here two hours later without being exhausted and without leaving hundreds of our men behind.

The country here is even more beautiful than the valley of Lookout. It is generally level and the grass has grown quite high and looks so fresh, it seems almost a Godsend to our poor horses and mules. We are almost surrounded too by thick woods, now covered with green and beautiful foliage. I think I would much prefer being here than at Nashville even. We were surrounded there by so much of civilized life which we ourselves could not participate in, that it really was not so pleasant as living here in the wild woods with enough excitement to drive off all appearances of ennui.

Some time ago I sent you a confederate twenty dollar note. You did not mention having received it. I wrote a letter to Aunt Sophia just before we left Lookout. I shall write again as soon as opportunity will permit. Respects to all the girls,

Your affectionate son George

Camp of the 105th Ill. Vol., In the field
May 10th, 1864

Dear Mother,

There are some prospects that the mail may go out today so I will try and write a line though we may be called on to move any moment. We are encamped three miles southeast of Gordons Springs and within ten miles of Dalton. I say encamped, that is not exactly the case, for our brigade has stacked arms in line of battle and we are laying beside our guns.

We are about seven miles from Buzzard's Roost where the rebels are in force, our troops have been fighting with them there more or less two days. The 15th Corps has gone around to flank them and we are waiting to go whenever we are most needed.

Yesterday the firing in front was pretty heavy and various reports came back to us. There is however not the slightest possible doubt but what we shall be most eminently successful. We have a super-abundance of troops and very likely our brigade will not be called into the fight at all.

The chaplain says he must go now with the mail, so good by. I am very well. Don't be anxious. Shall write again soon.

Rec'd a line from you this morning. While he has gone I will write more and trust to luck to get it off sometime.

I could hardly tell you in one letter the many scenes through which we have passed since leaving Lookout Valley. The last day we marched we had to reach a gap where we supposed the rebels were. We made a forced march to it but found nothing but a few rebel pickets who made double quick time on our approach. Our brigade was in advance of the column that day. As soon as we began to cross the gap "Old Joe" galloped by to the head of the troops; he looked as calm and leisurely as though he was going to a picnic. Maj. Gen. Sickles was with him, he looked like some insignificant boy beside of Hooker.

We have no firing today and suppose our forces have either whipped the enemy or are waiting to develop some other movement. The corps Ellis is in passed within two miles of us but I could not see him inasmuch as neither of us could have left camp.

There are, I think more than 150,000 troops engaged in this movement and I believe they are trying to trap the rebels. We hear rumors of fighting on the Potomac but can't get any reliable news from their operation. At present we are expecting orders to move from here every moment, they made us get up last night and pack up ready to move, but still we are here. All the boys are in good spirits and perfectly cool; soldiers who have been in the service as long as we have seldom get excited.

As soon as we get through this movement I shall write more and detail our movement from the start. Of course, I can write no more now than a few incomplete sentences just to let you know how I am.

Give my love to Aunt Sophia,
Your affectionate son George
direct as before

Thursday May 12, 1864
[continued from previous letter]

Dear Mother,

I could not send my letter away this morning and the chaplain says he will get it in the bag for headquarters in a few minutes so I pen a line to let you know I am still safe and well.

Our brigade is camped in the southern end of Snake [Creek] Gap. We are southwest of Dalton and form a position of the right wing of the grand army. It is reported that the rebels are greatly reinforced, but I think we have them nearly surrounded and their escape can only be made with heavy loss to themselves of men and munitions of war. We have learned of the great victory on the Potomac and are exceedingly hopeful.

I think there are over 150,000 men in our army. McPherson[1] is a few miles in advance of us entrenching. About 50 rebel prisoners were sent back last night. There has been no general engagement as yet. Our regiment has seen no fighting, we marched 14 miles yesterday. Don't know when we shall advance again. The supply train went back last night for rations. I believe you will soon hear of a great success here.

Goodbye, love to all,
Your affectionate son George

[no location]
Thursday, May 16, 1864

We slept on our arms last night and this morning found the enemy had fled. Our brigade was left to bury the dead and pick up the scattered guns in the afternoon.

I obtained a detail to go to the hospital and take care of Tirtlot, whom I found very low.² The ball or piece of shell had passed through the right leg above the knee breaking the bone. Tuesday morning I got Dr. Potter to come and dress the wound after which he felt much better and happily has been recovering ever since. Dr. P says he will now get along all right. Last Sunday, he was removed to Genl. Field Hospital at Resaca and I left him quite comfortable.

Last Monday morning I started from Resaca and reached the regiment line last evening about four o'clock found all the boys safe with one exception. Hanson Depue had his arm shot off two days ago in a skirmish.³ Quite an amount of bullets whistled over us last night and we lay on our arms all night.

This morning our artillery was pounding away at the rebels who seem to hold a strong position in our front. We are so used to firing and having balls flying over us that not [enough] attention is paid to it at all and the boys eat their hard tack and laugh as unconcerned as though we were safe in camp a hundred miles in the rear.

When I arrived last night I received five letters from you containing two from Aunt Sophia, also one from Uncle Calvin. I do not know when I can get this out or whether it will reach you but write in hopes. I am obliged to drop all other correspondences for the present, but when we get through this campaign, if I am alive, I will write to all.

We expect to take Atlanta within ten days but more time may be required and severe fighting will take place ere that time. I am in the *very best* of spirits and feel it is the greatest honor to have a hand in this great campaign, which I trust will be the last of the war.

Still nothing will discourage me and though it lasts years, I shall remember my time without any feelings of despondency.

We cannot hear much of late from Grant's army in Virginia but hope all is well with him. Just this moment a bullet whistled sufficiently near my head for comfort, but it only quivers us.

The inhabitants of GA are much more hospitable and intelligent than those of Tenn. & KY though they acknowledge themselves our enemy. The women are kind and brought many nice eatables to our wounded at Resaca. The morning I left that place I ate breakfast with a widow who had a son in the rebel army. He came to see her as he passed by in retreat and she implored him to stay with her, but his officers dragged him off though wounded.

The country is much more pleasant than where we have been before. The farmers have planted an abundance of corn and other grain which will be a great blessing to the country now we have possession.

I close not knowing what will be the events of the day. Skirmishing is still going on and considerable artilery shelling.

Your affectionate son George

In our breastworks
May 27th, 1864

Dear Mother,

I hardly know how to write there is so much of intense interest to communicate, but will begin back to May 14th and describe at random what has occurred since. At that date (Saturday) our brigade formed the 1st line of battle on the right center. The rebels in our front held a most formidable position and it was not deemed advisable by Hooker to charge them, though Genl. Ward was crazy all day to do so; so nothing but skirmishing took place during the day by us, though in our left the 14th corps were heavily engaged toward night.

We slept on our arms during the night and the next morning (Sunday) started rapidly to the left where the rebels were ascertained to be massing their might. Our division was all drawn up in line on the extreme left ready for work at 12 midnight and in a few moments we learned from our commander the duty before us which was to charge the enemy's work. We had formed just beneath a hill whose protecting sides covered us from the sight of the enemy and as our regts. were being massed, an almost deathlike silence pervaded the ranks. Every man knew that in a few moments death would be at work among us and all seemed to fully realize the fact, but they all stood up like men and seemed to vie with each other in real courage.

At 12 we fixed bayonets and dashed over the hill. A perfect shower of shot, shell and grape met us thinning our ranks sadly, (Tirtlot fell on the first shot) but without the least check we flew down the hill, crossed the road at the front, climbed over some breastworks the rebels had left and began the run of the hill where they were posted. The 105th was the last regt., but the two in front of us (79 Ohio & 129 Ill.) immediately laid down at the foot of this hill and our regt. ran right over them.

They were behind and in among us which so mixed us up that amidst the tangled underbrush it was impossible to distinguish our lines and keep together, so it was every man for himself. (Grant, Bachelder and I managed to keep together during most of the fight.) After we had arrived nearly on the rebels, we were repulsed and driven back to the foot of the hill, (here one of our boys, John McGilfrey, was wounded by my side) but we rallied here and charging again drove them from their battery and back into their rifle pits beyond.

The scene was grand and awful beyond description; a terrible sheet of lead bridged the air above us and leaden hail flew threw our ranks. Man after man went down, but no fear entered the hearts of the others.

Grant, Bachelder and I laid half an hour within seven rods of the rebel rifle pits from whence a terrific shower of bullets came. A sergt. here was shot on the left and a private on the right of me. Arthur Rice was killed here,[4] a few feet of me, but we managed at length to escape from that position and reached a place which afforded a little cover, but I have not time to write all that occurred on that afternoon. The many escapes, the many acts of bravery I saw, and the thousand little things which might afford conversation a lifetime, but sufficient to say that at five o'clock we were reformed under cover of a hill and the fight ceased, we having captured four beautiful guns which our brigade drew off next morning.

This description is written hurriedly for now the fight here is going on all around us and we expect every moment to be engaged. We are about 35 miles from Atlanta yet.

Camp of the 105th in the field
May 30th 1864

Dear Mother,

Word has just been sent around that the mail will be sent out in an hour, so I write a line again that you may know how I prosper.

Day before yesterday we were relieved from the first line of battle and form the third now, where the enemy's fire troubles us but little though occasionally a stray bullet finds its way through our ranks. A few moments ago, one of Co. D boys was wounded by one and last night while I was making out a clothing list a ball struck the ground within a few inches of where I sat throwing the dirt in my face, but we have become so habituated to hearing bullets fly that no attention is paid to them whatever and even when on the advance line we lay by our guns and slept as unconcerned as though in some quiet spot at home.

Last night at midnight the rebels tried our whole line desperately, but were driven back with great slaughter. The firing was very rapid and heavy, lasting only about half an hour.

We expect to guard on the front line tonight, and in fact I would as soon be there as here, for we have good breastworks and can then fire back at the villains.

Today is the sixth day that we have confronted the enemy here and I don't know what our generals intend to do. Most of the charges so far have been made by the rebels and have resulted greatly to their disadvantage. I feel anxious to wind up the engagement, but am willing to wait here a month if anything can be accomplished by strategy and life saved.

The news we hear from Grant, though not very late, is such as to keep us in the best of spirits. If he can only kill the rebellion there, we can do it here. I do not have the least anxiety about our campaign and I do not believe there is a soldier in this army that has any other thought than that we should be victorious.

We are still situated about thirty-five miles north of Atlanta. Our line of battle extends through a beautiful piece of woods with occasional openings in it. Just such a place as one would desire for a picnic excursion.

There has been none of our boys wounded since I last wrote (last Friday).

I see I must close as the time is about up.

Your affectionate son George
Direct the same

In the field about ten miles from Marietta [Ga.]
Tuesday, June 7, 1864

Dear Mother,

The mail came in today for the first time in a week and I received four letters from you which I immediately set about answering as our chaplain (who is postmaster) says he shall take the mail out tonight at 5.

Since I last wrote we have been beating the bush considerable but have not had any hard fighting, though a few in the regt. have been killed, among whom is Dr. Potter[5] who was instantly killed by a shell while our brigade was changing positions.

When I last wrote our corps and Howard's (the 4th) held the center, but in a few days we were relieved by McPherson and sent to the extreme left, turning the rebel right and compelling them to fall back without much fighting.

We are today in line of battle behind some breastworks which we built last night when we came here. I have no idea how many of the rebels are in our front, but do not think there is a very large force. I believe they are retracting again. Our boys all endure though hardships of campaign very well.

We are now on 3/4 rations but we make them last pretty well and I would be perfectly willing to live on half as much if it would aid in shortening the terrible war. The weather has troubled us more than anything lately. It seems to be a season of showers and rain is the order of the day but grumbling is a very useless thing and especially so when the weather is the object.

The last I heard from our wounded boys they were all doing well. Tirtlot was in good spirits and I have not a doubt of his recovery. Noah Gary received four wounds, all very slight except one in the leg near the knee joint. He is doing well and I believe his mother and sister have no need for anxiety. Noah went into the charge bravely. He was the first sergt. on my left and his position was about two places from mine.

That was indeed a most terrific charge and the more I think of it the more I believe it was a special act of Providence that so many of us are today alive. Genl. Butterfield told our chaplain the next day that few such charges were ever made and I can well believe it. The loss of our brigade during the month of May was 99 killed and 385 wounded, making an aggregate of 484 most of whom received their wounds in that charge. This you will see amount to about the fighting men of one regt.

Tirtlot will not be able to go home for a month yet. Noah Gary will I think as soon as his father can go after him and I do not believe he will have any difficulty in procuring a pass by applying to Gov. Yates.

It is most especially gratifying to me to learn that you are so cheerful, I was so afraid you would be anxious about me. I believe I shall come out of this campaign safe and hope it may last till the peace is secured but whatever the result—I have not a single fear for the final issue. Our army here is confident of victory. We are anxious only for Grant and his Virginia army, if that is victorious. We have faith to hope our soldier life is nearly ended.

Sergt. Grant is well and also Bachelder. Lt. Potter is now commanding our company, 1st Sergeant Smith would have been in command but it required a commissioned officer to account to the government for company property and no promotion can be made in the present state of our company affairs. We are really in a pretty bad situation and I hope something can soon be done to better it. While I am hastily scribbling this, a great shower is slowly coming up from the West and the now distant thunder threatens us grimly.

I shall try and write as often as there is a chance to send mail out for I know how anxious you are, and if we are again called into serious action, I will try and write immediately after.

My address will still be the same and letters will come through, sometimes, although they may be long delayed.

Your affectionate son George

In the field four miles southeast of Ackworth, Ga.
June 15, 1864

Dear Mother,

Letters from you, Ettie & Uncle Rufus came last night. Situated here in this vast wilderness nothing seems so enlivening as letters from home.

Since I last wrote you we have not changed our position. The entire army has been mud bound and save a slight shifting about of some corps and divisions, no movement has been made. And no advance on flank movements can be made for a few days yet.

The weather has been most unpromising. For ten or twelve days it has rained more or less and at one time it rained fifty hours without stopping. This has placed the roads in such a condition that the team cannot get full rations to us and artillery cannot be moved. The weather is still cloudy and threatens more rain, but we hope it will defer it till some more suitable time, for we are very anxious to advance and wind up this, already long campaign by the possession of the prize, Atlanta.

Our corps is situated on the right-center pretty well to the right. The 4th and 23rd are moved here with us. Genl. Howard commands the 4th and Schofield the 23rd. McPherson is on the left ready for a rapid march on the rebel right and when the time comes he is the man to do it. Hooker rides along our lines daily attended by a single orderly and a calm, placid look is inevitable to him. When he passes his troops he always smiles and looks upon them as a father would gaze on his family and it does one's soul good to hear the rousing cheers which greet him. You never saw him but if you get a likeness of George Washington you will have a better picture of Hooker than any I have seen. He is in feature very similar to that patriot of '76.

The country in which we are now placed is a continual forest and the trees seem to have a sad expression as they wave their branches over a desolated country.

The rebels evidently hold a very strong position in front and the river is only about twelve miles distant so they will probably contest every step now to Atlanta unless crushed in the onset by a fierce assault.

Skirmishing is going on all the time about half a mile in front of us and often the cannons growl out their venom at each other and the hissing, screaming shells go tearing through the woods splitting up huge oaks and pines (as if they would vie with the artillery of Heaven) and cutting into the lesser ones.

Ah what a thing is war! And how *little* do the citizens of the North know about it. Last night I could not sleep and so sat by the dying embers of our camp fire and thought of the sad scenes the last month had called us to witness.

I noticed in the *N.Y. Tribune* a letter from one of its correspondents stating that the rebels scalped our dead and wounded on the field at Resaca. I did not know but you might have seen it. The statement is a most maliciously false one, our brigade staid back to bury the dead and care for the wounded and no act of barbarity was seen by any of us. I know the rebels are savage enough, but why seek to stir up more bitter feelings in the North and cause many to find fault with the administration for not retaliating? I don't want my friends to believe I am to be butchered if I should face into the hands of the enemy. Most of this army correspondence is mentioned without a particle of truth in it. Very frequently the rebel skirmishers and ours meet each other half way and spend an hour talking quite amicably, when not ordered to fire and our boys sometimes trade coffee to them for tobacco.

A few days since three of them (the rebels) got hungry and went to kill a pig. They said it was a Yankeefied pig and so ran for the Union lines, but determined to have him, they followed, though without trying to head piggie off and his pigship soon found a number of blue coats to whom he delivered his pursuers. They seemed to enjoy the thing highly and our boys thanked them for the pig, took their guns and brought them in. They were fine looking men and well dressed but had enough of fighting against the old flag.

The news of Abe's renomination was received with intense joy by the army, but the addition of Fremont blasts him[6] forever in the eyes of the soldiers. We who were once his strongest supporters now rank him [Frémont] with the enemies of the country and the special enemy of the soldier. Anything opposing the complete unanimity of the North we regard as prolonging the war and consider all those who favor "side shows" as ambitious politicians and not patriotic men.

I received a letter from Aunt Annie yesterday. And also three papers from Uncle Calvin. So I am pretty well off as regards reading materials at present. I shall answer Ettie's and Uncle Rufus' letters as soon as I can. We have to write here at an hours notice, the chaplain comes around tells us when he can send off a mail and we go at once to writing.

If the weather continues dry another day or two I think we shall move. I shall write as often as possible.

Lt. Potter is in command of our company. He is a still sort of a man and pleasant as a companion. I do not think Capt. D——[7] will resign. He will "lay by" nearly a year drawing pay meanwhile and then if the war lasts, come back to the Co. We are as a company really in bad shape, with no officers of our own and no prospect of any.

I do not hear from any of our wounded boys by any reliable source lately. Sergts. Grant and Bachelder are well. Tommy Holmes is in good health and I believe all the boys generally are in good spirits and hopeful as to the war. None are discouraged but rather as hardships and dangers in the course, they feel more determined to complete the work, now so well begun.

I had heard of the enlistment of the hundred-day men but can't say that I think them very great patriots.

I send you a rebel postage stamp as a relic of Georgia.

Your affectionate son George

Battle Field
June 16th, 1864

Dear Mother,

I have just received a letter from you containing also one from Ettie and Aunt Sophia, and if the rebels will give me a little time I will endeavor to write you a few battle notes, detailing as well as I can our present position and how we came by it; commencing with yesterday at 2 pm at which hour our columns began a general advance upon the enemy. The 20th (ours), 23rd, 4th, and 14th army corps were drawn up in the woods in three heavy lines of battle. The 20th formed the first line; our division at once threw out a line of skirmishes and the 105th was ordered out to support them.

We marched across a large open field and engaged the rebel skirmishers in a belt of timber on the opposite side. They opened so hotly that it became evident they were in heavy force beyond. Our brigade then advanced by us and contrary to Butterfield's orders, Ward ordered us to form on the left and advance. He immediately threw us forward so injudiciously that our regt was on the skirmish line and part of them beyond it with orders not to fire. The enemy saw our position and opened on us heavily but happily there were but few casualties, only one from our company.

We sought shelter in a little ravine a short distance in front, and remained there flat on the ground about two hours and a half while the rebel bullets whistled wildly above us, occasionally coming so close as to fairly glue us to the bosom of Mother Earth. Finally an order came from Genl. Butterfield for us to obtain the cover of the hill in our rear and carry out his first order, try to support the skirmishers. As soon as we arose the rebels poured on a fierce fire but "Johnny" was too excited to aim well and we got over the hill and formed with little loss.

The heavy lines of battle behind now advanced and entered the woods; for a moment a death-like silence prevailed and then an awful roar of musketry broke forth, from right to left a long, heavy and deadly rattle rung through the forest. In a few minutes artillery was in position and the great screaming shells went tearing through the air, now bursting and throwing their fragments among the trees and now burying themselves deep into the ground. At length the sun dropped behind the distant hill, leaving a red, fiery trail behind, which soon merged into the deepening twilight, and the fight ceased.

The "Grey Jackets" had been driven from their outer works. The "Boys in Blue" hold the battle ground and the "red field was won." Our regt. was relieved and going about 1/2 a mile to the rear we laid our weary bodies down to rest. Thus ended the 15th of June, just one month since we made the terrible charge at Resaca.

Early this morning we advanced to the front line and began building breastworks while about two dozen rods ahead our skirmishers were hard at work with the rebel skirmishers. The bullets from them who saw us at work sifted through our ranks and their wild whistle was strangely blended with the cries and groans of the wounded. We worked all the forenoon like beavers carrying logs and throwing up dirt and now little danger is felt save from the sharpshooters who inhabit the trees. A section of battery (2 guns) has just been planted a few rods to our right and is now sending its compliments over to "Johnny." They will probably soon be returned with interest.

It's now 2 pm. If I can get time I will add a few more notes this evening.

Friday Morning, June 17th. I was too busy to write any farther last night. The remainder of the afternoon was occupied by a heavy artillery drill between our batteries and the rebels. We had ten guns planted about 20 rods to our right and I should think nearly as many more 40 rods to the left. There were few casualties on our side.

It is not these huge shells and solid shot that kill men. It is the little leaden messengers sped from rebel muskets that decimate our ranks and find so many southern graves for our boys. Just at dusk I drew rations and had nearly finished issuing them when suddenly a long stream of fire passed over our works a little to the right and buried itself in the forest. This was quickly followed by another and another. It was truly a grand and awful sight. The rebels had commenced shelling us again and in the dark, the shells had the appearance of great balls of fire. We immediately grasped our guns and stood in our works ready for a charge, which this shelling might precede, but they did not come and our deep-mouthed growlers accepting their compliments returned them in double measure. This completely silenced everything but the continuous popping of the skirmishers.

We laid quiet till nine o'clock and were then relieved by our third brigade (Col. Wood's). After marching circuitously nearly a mile we found ourselves half a mile, on a direct line, to the right of our former position, and in the second line of battle with a most wretched apology for breastworks. We would have greatly preferred to have remained behind the secure works our own industry had built, but we are soldiers and know that it is as much a mark of bravery to cheerfully obey orders as to fight unflinchingly in the foremost ranks in battle.

So we laid our tired bodies down and soon slept while happy dreams of home afforded sweet contrast to the stern, sad realities of our waking hours. The total casualties of the 15th and 16th in our regt was 17 wounded and 2 killed. Our company lost 2, wounded Patrick Brennan severely in leg and Patrick McGraw slightly in head. Both excellent boys and brave as lions.

This morning we hear that the rebels have left and the silence broken by only occasional firing from the skirmish line which seems further away, leads us to think that it may be true.

Everything looks propitious and I believe that if the citizens of the North will do their duty in regard to the coming election as faithfully as the soldiers in the field are doing theirs, this may be the last heavy series of battles we shall be called upon to engage in.

We captured two prisoners yesterday who had heard of Lincoln's nomination and seemed to understand the relation of things pretty well. They said that if we took Richmond and Atlanta and re-elected "Abe," their only hope was gone. They were as tickled as little boys on account of their capture, rejoicing exceedingly that they had not any more fighting to do.

We are now momentarily expecting orders to move, and as I have brought my notes up to the present time, I will lay them by taking the earliest opportunity to add what may be developed in the future.

Saturday, June 18th. We remained quietly awaiting orders yesterday till 11 am at which time they came and we quickly filed out to the wood and again marched southward. About forty rods ahead we passed the rebel breastworks, their strongholds, and they were strong indeed. They were built of heavy logs, laid up seven or eight feet thick at the bottom and gradually sloping upwards till they were some fight or six feet high. They were packed solidly together with dirt and would have resisted a heavy artillery fire. In front of them the rebels had placed long poles sharpened at the ends so that they would hare men onto them, in case we had made a charge, and so thick together that it would have been impossible to get through.

To have charged such works would have been madness, and few would have got away alive, but thanks to the strategy of our generals, a flank movement saved us such butchery and the enemy was forced to leave a position he had worked long and hard to render impregnable. And so our troops marched on inwardly thanking God, and giving cheer after cheer as they successively filed by the work.

Going about two miles we had to form line of battle again for the skirmishers were hotly engaged and sweeping through a thick wood soon came out to an open clearing extending for miles on either side, where our batteries were pounding volley after volley at the rebels, who were in the heavy timber beyond. Our corps was massed here, connecting with the 23rd corps on the right and we put up our little tents to shelter ourselves from the rain which now threatened.

Meanwhile the artillery kept up a fierce fire and the advance line was also engaged with musketry. It was a grand scene, the cannon shooting forth their streams of fire and the shells bursting among the treetops while the rush of the iron missiles hurrying through the air sounded like a fierce hurricane, but I must add, that I find "distance lends enchantment to the view" and when one is engaged in making this din and roar of battle, they have very little appreciation of its grandeur.

The fighting continued all night and is still going on this morning notwithstanding the hard and steady rain which has poured down since midnight.

Sunday, June 19. The rain continued all day yesterday and we were not ordered away from our positions in rear of the advance line. In the afternoon we drew two days more rations, and rations of whiskey were issued to the men, singular enough, that when the troops are living on reduced rations, transportation should be used to draw the meanest of whiskey to steal away their brains and injure their systems, but I am happy to add that a large number of Company F refused theirs.

It continued raining by spells all night, as if the elements would equal the storm of man which was being kept up in front, but this morning, there were comparatives and the general calls in advance told us that the rebels had again left. At about 9 am our division took its place in the column and we again moved on. We had marched about a mile when we came to a creek which was greatly swollen by the recent rains, and there being no bridge we waited to lay rails and logs in. It began to rain and in a few minutes poured down a perfect torrent, but we again started on and began the crossing.

As our regiment came to the worst part of the stream, the rails gave way and floated off. We were now thoroughly wet and plunging in soon found the opposite bank drifting with muddy water. The rain now ceased for a time and we again advanced. Our batteries meanwhile were planted on a high eminence a mile or two ahead and were shelling the enemy who had made another stand.

On arriving at this hill we halted and our division was massed. At this point I am now writing these humid notes. The 23rd corps is to our right and the 4th to our left. They are now at work lively and the prospect is that we shall soon move, so for the present I close.

Your affectionate son George

CHAPTER 9

"Perfect Terror"

Marietta, June 25–Near Atlanta, July 31, 1864

Duthere during June 1864, the weather became the armies' enemy. In the thick, wet woods about Kennesaw Mountain the troops had great difficulty executing their commanders' strategies. General Sherman reported to General Halleck that after nineteen days of rain, the roads were impassable and the fields were nothing more than muddy quagmires. Yet with perseverance, creeping progress was made with points and counterpoints. The troops had confidence in General Sherman in spite of the bleak conditions. Another Illinois soldier aptly described the troops' unwavering devotion to the general: "Sherman will never go to hell, for he'll flank the devil and make heaven in spite of all the guards."[1]

During the battle of Peach Tree Creek on July 20 Sergeant George F. Cram and Lieutenant Melvin Smith captured Confederate flags after hand-to-hand combat. Lt. Colonel Dutton claimed that the colors belonged to the 12th Louisiana Infantry. In his diary (July 20, 1864) Cram wrote, ". . . the rebels charged our entire line. We hurled them back and fought til night. The ground was covered with their dead. . . ." When he wrote to his mother, Sergeant Cram down played the significance of his role in the capture of the rebel flag. Yet, army records noted his act of heroism, and it was reported in the *War of the Rebellion: A Compilation of the Official Records of the Union and Confederate Armies*.

Sergeant Cram's tone was hard and cynical when he wrote about the new recruits who were on their way to reinforce the dwindling numbers of foot soldiers. Toughened veteran soldiers that they had become, the men of the 20th Army Corps had earned the right to look down their bloodied noses at young recruits who were both fearful of the action ahead while terrified of missing it altogether.

On the field near Marietta [Ga.]
June 25th, 1864

Dear Mother,

I have a few leisure moments this morning so I thought I would begin another letter to you or rather a continuation of the last and commencing with Monday, June 20th.

We did not remain long on the hill, but moving half a mile to the right formed line of battle and advanced through a dense forest, something over a mile. Here we came upon the enemy and the bullets began to whistle around us. The third brigade held the advance line, 150 paces ahead. The first (ours), the second, and the second [held] the third [line]. One of Genl. Ward's staff officers was drunk and insisted upon moving our regt. where we would probably have been cut to pieces, but fortunately Col. Dustin himself heard Genl. Butterfield's order and refused to move his regiment contrary to them. Meanwhile the rain was again pouring down, completely drenching us, and we had to lay down on the wet ground to protect ourselves from the enemy's bullets.

The afternoon had passed away thus, and we laid silently in battle line without advancing. Why was this? Why did those bullets also come from the right and left, traversing our whole lines? And why did Genl. Butterfield and staff appear so anxious? Night spread her mantle over us and then low humid[ity] came to move to the rear with perfect silence. Our line of skirmishes was kept well out till all the brigades were a quarter of a mile back and sheltering themselves behind some beanstalks which were being rapidly cut up and then it was silently withdrawn.

We now learned our previous position. Our division held the advance of the corps and were to connect with the 23rd Corps on the right but either this corps had failed to push up their advance or some misunderstanding existed between corps commanders and we were pushed on without connecting on either side till we were surrounded on three sides by the enemy and it was ascertained that a heavy force was making a demonstration on our right. Our danger was imminent, but the coolness and skill of Genl. Butterfield saved us and we were removed from immediate danger to where we could defend ourselves from behind good works.

Our regt. was here massed in support of the 129th Ill. which occupied the works. We were ordered to be in readiness to move at a moment's warning. It was about ten pm and breaking off boughs from the trees we threw ourselves upon them and wrapping a rubber blanket around us passed the remainder of the night with occasional snatches of sleep.

This morning the skirmish firing seems to be more distant and more directly in front though there is still considerable to our left, but I think this is accounted for by their changing directions of the entire line to the left.

We made us some coffee and dried our clothes by a good fire, so we feel considerable better. There are yet no orders to move, but we do not know what is before us or how soon we may be called out. The weather is still uncertain and threatens more rain.

Tuesday, June 21st, about an hour after the above was written we moved up to a point of the works which were built the night before. Nothing of interest occurred during the forenoon. Occasional bullets from the enemy's skirmish line passed over us, but we have become so accustomed to the continual whiz of these messengers that no attention is paid to them, except when some poor fellow is struck, which frequently happens whenever many men are together.

In the afternoon yesterday we stood in our works in line of battle from three o'clock till seven while a junction was being formed with the 3rd corps. An eight-gun battery, all brass howitzers was brought up and supported by the 3rd brigade which went out a little in advance of the line of works. Two Parrot guns were brought up to our line also and one was planted directly in view of our company. It appeared that the officers expect an attack while the two corps were being connected, but the rebels have no relish for charging "Yankee" works. And so after remaining in line unmolested save by the rain which pertinaciously attacks us till everything was properly secured we sought the shelter of our tents and prepared our minds for a little sleep. The night was spent comfortably and we were much refreshed this morning. Orders were received at midnight to be in readiness to move at six this morning but, we did not move.

The day has passed away without excitement here. However, who[ever] is on our left has been shelling the rebels very severely all day, but "Old Joe" don't open his guns. Tonight a few brass pieces have been brought up and are now most invitingly contemplating the enemy's position. We are all very anxious to have them charge us, for it is not at all pleasant for one side to do all that kind of work.

The rebels have their own trains; the whistle of their locomotive has been plainly heard by us at intervals, during the day, but whether they bring reinforcements or are taking away the store of a retreating force, we are entirely ignorant.

Wednesday, June 22nd. The enemy did not charge us last night as we some expected and this morning preparations were made for another advance. Everything was in readiness at noon and we rapidly climbed over our works and formed the advancing line. Our corps was drawn up connecting on its right with the 23rd under Schofield. William's division held the right. Geary's the center and Butterfield's (ours) the left. Genl. Howard's corps joined us on the left. Our division was formed in three lines of battle. The third brigade formed the first line. Part of ours the second and the 105 Ill. and 70 Ind. the third line. The second brigade was on our right formed in the same manner.

We skirmished with the enemy about one half a mile when the first line came to an open field which the skirmish line could not cross. Col. Wood immediately fixed bayonets and ordered a charge. His line was about 200 yards in front of us and we could see the men through the timber plainly. With loud cheers they made the charge and the rebels concluding that "discretion was the better part of valor" made fast time for the rear, firing but very little. As soon as the first line was established in the woods opposite, our line, the 3rd was ordered over the 2nd to form on the right of Col. Wood. We emerged from the cover of the thick woods and moved across the open field in glorious style without losing a man. Forming immediately on Wood's right we advanced to within a few rods of our skirmishers and hastily threw up works under the very noses of the rebels and exposed to a severe fire.

I do not yet know how many of our regt. were lost here but it was not a large number. Our company had only one man, James Brady, slightly wounded in left arm by a spent ball.

We had finished our works about 4 pm and were resting behind them when a heavy fire was opened on our right and left and some in our front. We immediately grabbed our guns, stood in the works and awaited the coming "Johnny Reb," but it was only a feint on us and a most desperate conflict was waging on the right. The roar of artillery was the most terrific I have ever heard and between the intervals of the cannon a low deadly rattle told too plainly how heavily the infantry were at work. It is now nearly sundown and the fight still continues on the right but not so severe as it was an hour ago.

Our skirmishers are busily at work in front of us and whistle over our heads on strike solidly against our works doing us no harm if we keep close under our own cover. Our position is most harassing and exhausting, so continually confined, but war is a stern teacher and we have learned patience.

I learn that the hard fighting to our right was caused by the rebels suddenly hurling a charging column on Williams division and post of the 20th Corps. Williams, you will remember held our right and connected the left of the 23rd. On our advance his troops were thrown across a portion of the main Atlanta road, thus flanking the rebel position badly. The enemy of course could not allow this, and while our troops were endeavoring to entrench themselves, thrice heavy lines of battle charged them furiously. Williams advanced line fell back to their support. A terrible and most destructive cross fire was then opened from our batteries which had been quickly brought up into position. Shell, grape and canister were fairly rained upon the downed foe, while a storm of musket balls swept through their ranks. No men could withstand such a withering fire and they stopped. Their lines were shattered from flank to flank and quickly turning they ran for their lives, while our brave boys sent cheers and bullets after them, after they had reached cover a continuous raking fire was kept up till dusk between the two opposing lines. Our brigade was relieved by a brigade of the 4th corps at ten o'clock tonight and we moved to the right about half a mile and passed the remainder of the night in line of battle.

Friday, June 24th. Yesterday morning early we moved a little further to the right and halted. Here we were ordered to make coffee and got ready to move again. We stopped here however till nearly noon and then marching again to the right about two miles we reached the scene of yesterdays fight on the Atlanta road. Heavy works were being completed and artillery so planted as to completely make everything in front. Our entire corps was being massed at this point. Our division was thrown out in advance of this line and facing Marietta (which place the rebels still hold regardless of newspaper correspondents assertion to the contrary). The town is about two miles in front of us, but whether we shall take it by a direct assault or not I cannot tell, probably not as flank movements are the rage now. A light line of works is in front of us and our brigadiers held for support.

This morning everything is still except that inevitable popping of the skirmishers. They keep up one continuous rattle from morning till night and accomplish generally nothing.

I saw four prisoners yesterday who were captured in the fight the previous afternoon. I asked one of them if he did not find a pretty hot place in that charge, and he replied as following, "I reckon we did, you all used us mighty rough there," and concluded by saying that he had much rather be a prisoner in our hands than remain over there (pointing to the rebel position).

Saturday, June 25. Yesterday we quietly rested without changing our position. Our gens. are evidently preparing for the conflict, which may come any day and may not for weeks yet.

A rebel came over in the morning and gave himself up to one of our boys who was out on the skirmish line. He reported the enemy heavily entrenched in our front and considerably reinforced.

One of the deserters from our regiment was brought in this morning having been caught at Bowling Green, Ky. He deserted us at Chicago and I have no doubt but what he will suffer for it now.

Everything is quiet this morning and everybody seems disposed to rest save the skirmishers of the two armies, who watch each other so closely that no one from either side can change position without having a bullet whistle by him and frequently too close for personal comfort. Each skirmisher selects his tree and keeps snugly behind it. The opposing lines are often so close together that they can talk across, but their conversation, not always being the most elegant or polite, a shower of bullets generally ends it.

The reason that so few men are killed in battle is owing to the nature of the ground. This country is a succession of hills, mountain ranges and dense woods, and men in fighting do not stand up only. When advancing or retiring, they either lie flat to load and fire or simply raise up upon their knees. If a battle could be fought upon some of the level prairies of Ill., it would not last an hour, but a great many more would be killed.

Our chaplain is at present back in the hospital assisting with the wounded. The surgeon who takes Potter's place is Dr. Waterman from Naperville. He is a most miserable shiftless man.[2] Sergt. Grant is well. Bachelder is slightly wounded in right shoulder and the last I heard from him he was dong finely. Holmes and Baker are both unharmed and in good health.

I received your letters very regularly and answer as often as I can. I would like to have you send a little black linen thread in your next letter. There is nothing else I need.

Our diet for the last three months has consisted of hard bread, sugar, coffee, salt, pork and beef. We cannot get vegetables here, and if we could we would not be able to cook them.

The sutlers are all very extensively in the rear. When we take Atlanta I think we will have some rest and then a can of rations will be dinner.

Your affectionate son George

P.S. The rebels are now pitching shells at us as if they imagined they were doing us an immense amount of damage.

Sunday, June 26, 1864

Dear Mother,

I received a letter from you and Ettie yesterday dated June 19. You spoke of Tirtlot. I cannot hear a word from him except the rumors that come from Wheaton. When I left him at Resaca he was doing well and was in a fair way to recover and retain his leg. He promised me he would write immediately on reaching some place where he expected to stay and tell me how to direct his letters, (the hospital at Resaca was only a temporary affair) but he has not written a word. If you hear from him I wish you would let me know.

I do not either hear from Ellis though I have no doubt but he is somewhere in our army here, but his corps and ours seldom comes near each other and as yet we have had no chance of meeting.

Everything is now quiet. The weather is hot but we are so well acclimated that it does not trouble us anymore than it did when we lived in the civilized North. I feel rather hopeful that the fighting of this war will close this summer. This is certainly the greatest campaign the world has ever known and I believe Grant means to continue it till one of the armies is destroyed.

I am quite well and shall take good care of my health. I must now close to draw rations.

Your affectionate son George

In the field near Marietta [Ga.]
July 1st, 1864

Dear Mother,

Since I last wrote to you our position has not been materially changed. Occasionally we go out to the front line and relieve a brigade then and are in turn relieved by them. Just at present it comes to our lot to be in the rear and pretty much out of range of the enemy's fire which still continues day and night from his skirmish line.

We have put up our little tents to protect us both from the burning sun and from occasional showers. The boys are lying about in perfect abandon and utterly regardless of looks, protecting themselves from the intense heat by the plentiful use of green leaves.

Sixty days have passed since we left the quiet valley of Wauhatchie over which Lookout Mountain towered so grimly. Sixty long weary days, every one of which has been in itself a lifetime. During that time our regiment has lost in killed and wounded about one hundred and twenty-five men. Our company has had one killed and ten wounded being a very favorable percent of wounded. They are as follows: Lt. Tirtlot (Wheaton), Corp. H. S. Ehle (Bloomingdale); Priv. Wm. Brown (Wayne); Priv. McGifrey (Wayne); Priv. H. J. Depue (Downers Grove); U. B. Keniston (Wayne), Aaron Dissing (Naperville); James Brady (Bloomingdale); Patrick Brennan (Winfield); Patrick McGraw (Bloomingdale); and A. P. Rice, killed at Resaca.

Several of these wounded are still with the company, their wounds not being serious enough to keep them from duty. A large number of the boys in the 105th are becoming sick but most of this class still cling to duty, being too proud to go to the rear at such a time as this.

The last week has been spent in constant fighting at different points along the line, but so far nothing has been gained and no ground lost. Several severe charges have been made by our troops and reported, but I am inclined to think it all been a grand feint, to hide some movement soon to be developed. It certainly does not seem probable or even possible that we are to stay and butt our heads against rebel breastworks for no purpose.

I have been troubled for a few days with my feet which through the poisoning medium of wild ivy swelled badly, but they're now better and in a day or two will be entirely well.

Your letter of June 22nd was received yesterday. I am very glad to see you so confident of the closing of the war. I think it must close either one way or the other in a few months and we can recognize but the *one* way.

Tirtlot is doing exceedingly well. Capt. Daniels wrote to us that he had rec'd a letter from him and said that he expected soon to be at the hospital in Chattanooga. He promised to write to me as soon as possible when I left him, but for some reason he is very reticent.

Our Co. is in a poor condition, and all the work has to be done by those who don't get the pay nor enjoy the position, but for my own part I care very little and am satisfied to return home with life and a whole body.

I would be glad if you would send me some stamps, I have considerable writing to do and am nearly out of stamps. Also send an envelope in each letter. If the campaign lasts many weeks yet, I shall be minus them.

I shall write again soon.
Your affectionate son George

In the field, seven miles north
of the Chattahoochie River [Ga.]
July 4th, 1864

Dear Mother,

I have a few moments this morning to myself and will write what I can before we again take up the line of march after the enemy. Yesterday morning we were ordered here before day break, and making a little coffee, packing up our blankets and filling our canteen, we sat down, awaiting the word, "March." The rebels had been leaving their strong position in our front all night and part of the day before, actually forced out by a brilliant flank movement of Sherman. Our skirmishers had advanced to their works, found everything clear, and we were preparing as I have described, to follow. About sunrise we filed out in the road and our brigade led the advance after the foe.

It was a lovely Sabbath morning and as we marched along the road toward Marietta, our hearts were filled with gladness that the foe had been so compelled to retire, without losing our lives dashing against him in his den (for I can call it no other name). As we marched through the awful slaughter pens he had prepared for us, it was enough to appall the bravest. Had one charged them, such a total destruction of an army would have been chronicled as never before was heard of. Their works consisted of three separate lines. The first was slight and the plan evidently was to immediately retreat from this, at our assault, retire to the second line which was considerable stronger. Here they would have made a greater resistance, but finally, retreat to the last line.

In the meanwhile our boys elated with such victory and confident that their enemy *could not* stand anywhere, would have dashed on headlong after them. Soon they would have been through the thick woods, reach an opening and a quarter of a mile beyond was the "last ditch" of the rebels. With shouts of victory they would have swept on undisturbed by the rebels' fire till within rods of the works, however, an infernal machine similar to a hay rack with stakes sharp pointed, and so arranged that it would have rolled over and over us as we tried to get through just as a porcupine defends itself by rolling into a ball and thrusting its quills out.

At this point a murderous fire would have opened upon us from all three of their lines now concentrated there, a fort also was so constructed as to have raked over the whole line from flank to flank, and in this the enemy had massed his artillery.

You can well imagine what a "graveyard" would have been made there, and you can have some idea with what joy our hearts thrilled as we marched through them without the firing of a gun. I felt as though I could march a thousand miles, jump a hundred feet, or perform any other impossibility, and what furnished us still further cause for exultation was a continual string of prisoners, coming in most of them giving themselves up, declaring that they would follow the running army no farther.

These men seemed just as glad as we were that they were in our hands, and the expressions they used in reply to our interrogations were frequently amazing. One lank fellow in "grey" was asked by "fat boy in blue" if he had "got tired of the show." "You're right, I have!" was the ready and emphatic response. One of them remarked that he had "got tired" following the old Joe (Johnston) and was going to try the new one (Hooker) awhile. Generally they appear at first rather afraid of us, their officers tell them such topics about our treatment of prisoners, but our boys greet them invariably with "How are you boy?" and "why didn't you bring more?" till their faces assume the most intense satisfaction.

A large number of the houses we passed by were deserted. Some families that would remain were informed that the Yankees would "kill them," "skin them," and devise other equally humane and civilized things, but after they had seen us and their fears were quieted, they were exceedingly loquacious, generally informed us that they believed we were human beings. Our soldiers generally treat these inhabitants as well as their own. I always pity them. The rebel army has swept them clean of everything, and they stay, clinging to the old homestead, trembling awaiting the coming of their foe.

Well we passed rapidly on till we came to a slight elevation on open ground, where our boys could see the rebels with a battery nearby a mile distant. Immediately our battery was ordered up to the little hill and our brigade was marched by division behind it: so briskly did our artillery men mark them we had scarcely formed when firing went again, followed quickly by all the others (five) in succession, and six shells went howling over to "Johnny" but "Johnny" was not to be used that way. Away and before the echo of our guns had died away, a report from the distant battery rapidly followed by a shriek high sound above our heads announced that he had accepted our challenge for an artillery duel and, bang, bang, whiz, whiz shells went and came "like lightening from the mountain cloud." Our regiment was in a peach orchard and squarely behind our battery at which the shells were all aimed.

At first I thought I would stand up and witness the fight, not thinking we would be in any serious danger, but the second shell that came convinced me that I was tired and I sat down. The next one caused me to lean down resting on my elbow, and the fourth found me flat on the ground, every shell seemed to come still closer to the ground until they just passed over our backs. By this time, officers and men were panic stricken and running in every direction, exposing themselves to every shot that passed. Others were shouting to them to "lie down for God's Sake, lie down." Thus, everyone who had a particle of coolness did and never, I mention to say, did men ever hug the ground closer.

Meanwhile our poor battery boys were being terribly cut up. In waking up the battery opposite they had indeed "caught a tartar," their horses too were rapidly being killed, many being shot through and through by shell, and now occurred what made many falter even [more] than they had been. The horses had become

perfectly panic stricken and six of them attached to a heavy caisson whirled about starting on a run and threatening to mow a path
through the infantry behind, their course would have been directly
through our regiment, but a stout artillerist seizes them and by
desperate efforts holds them till more help comes to him once the
horses are secured.

Our battery now was nearly silenced but still the boys worked
with steady determination and perfect heroism. One gun was already withdrawn, now a poor boy has his leg shot away, another has
his face blown off by a shell, and one by one they fall.

In the midst of all the dying, the report of their own guns and
bursting of rebel shells, we could distinctly hear the captain giving
commands in a loud clear voice, and the men obeyed them as if they
were unconscious that the next moment might be their last on
earth. Noble fellows! Everyone a hero. But their deeds of glory will
be buried with them and the great mass of humanity in the civilized
North, though, perchance they may read the casual line of some
newspaper correspondent noticing them will scarce give them a
thought beyond tomorrow.

This fight was the most dreadful of anything I have yet seen, although of course it was not so destructive to us as others we have
engaged in, but then we laid, not being able to fight ourselves and
every shell coming near and nearer till they began to burst all
around us. Several burst directly over our company and one so close
to me that the shock fairly raised me from the ground throwing powder and smoke all over me and for a moment I was completed
stunned, but fortunately it injured no one and very soon after this
our regt. was ordered to move to the left, which we were only too
glad to do, and a few rods put us out of range.

We had been about twenty minutes under that terrible fire, but I
have no doubt most of them would strongly affirm it was two hours.
Minutes seem ages when one is in such immense peril of life. The
fighting did not last long after this. The rebel battery was silenced
and after firing the last shot our own boys were glad to quit. It was
the toughest artillery fight I ever heard of.

We then moved on cautiously to take munition but had not advanced far when we suddenly came upon the 4th corps, which had
pushed on like a whirlwind and already held the town. So after an
hours delay the lines were reformed and our corps moved off in a
southwesterly direction. We still held the advance and pushed

rapidly on, now turning one way and now another, continually feeling our way along and winding about very much as a snake travels.

About noon, our company was sent out as flankers. We were deployed about ten paces apart and marched along about forty rods to the left of the column, to protect the flank from a sudden attack or cavalry dash. The day was dreadfully hot and exhausted us considerable, but the excitement of the occasion fully sustained us.

About two p.m. the rebels made a stand again on a long high ridge. The balance of the afternoon was taken upon maneuvering to ascertain the enemy's force and position, and establishing our lines, connecting with the different corps.

Night found our brigade holding the advance to the right, and about a mile from a hill where the rebels had fortified. Skirmishers were sent out to clear our front of any lurking foe and building fires, getting water, etc. we soon had a cup of coffee washed down, a cracker and lying down on the grass gave ourselves up to sleep.

This morning we were awakened early by the music of our regimental and brigade bands playing grand old National airs, and "the fourth of July" was carried from tongue to tongue as the boys successively awoke and listened to the sweet harmony.

We soon discovered that the enemy still occupied the crest in front and the 14th and 4th corps planted batteries and commenced shelling them. This they are still doing and our line has not advanced yet today. We can see the rebel position plainly and above our shells burst in their works. It is now one o'clock and I do not think there will be any advance today.

I rec'd a letter from you last night. Tirtlot is doing well in hospital at Chattanooga. There is nothing I need sent except a few stamps and perhaps some envelopes. I have sufficient underclothing and my knapsack will be the last thing I shall throw away, for it is my house.

July 5th. About two hours after I wrote the above, the bugle sounded and forming in line we again marched southward. The rebels were driven from their position and our army was moving to connect the different corps, and establish new lines. Our division marched about three miles in an irregular course with a general bearing southwest.

Genl. Ward was leading and suddenly he ordered a halt and set us to work building breastworks rapidly. He had seen an immense number of troops about a mile in front and while we were fortifying he ordered up our battery and was about to make the enemy run awfully when he was asked to open his eyes a little wider and observe that the troops he was making such demonstrations against were a swarm of "boys in blue." The entire 23rd corps having swung around in front. We had worked hard but still were not too tired to enjoy a good laugh at Grandfather Ward's expense.

Finding out we were safe, our brigade moved on a short distance and camped in a large orchard, whose trees were heavily loaded with green apples and it would have done you good to see the boys dive for them. In less than half and hour after we stopped, not an apple could be found on the trees. It was the first green thing we have had for a long time and they furnished us a delicious cup of sauce.

The weather is most intensely hot, and a great many of the soldiers were sun struck yesterday. We passed the poor fellows all along the road.

This morning we got rations again and had a good breakfast which we especially relished as we have been out of meat lately.

There are yet no prospects of moving very soon, although we never can tell what moment we may be again on the road.

A few minutes ago the postmaster came around and informed us that the mail would be sent out today so all along our line you see men sitting down with a sheet of paper on their knees, writing to their homes, and visiting in mind the friends around the family fireside. I received a letter from Frank Ellis about a week ago. He wrote from Huntsville and said his division expected soon to reinforce our army here. They were being relieved by the 100 day men.

These prodigies of valor were very much surprised at the reception the three years men gave them, it being quite different from the sweetmeats, flowers, and kisses they received from the camps near home. Those veterans of the 15th Corps who have fought in a dozen battles, failed to see the bravery or patriotism of men enlisting for *100 days,* when there was such a prospect for a draft. When they thought the war was just ending; expecting no fighting, but simply guarding forts that the industry of *others* had built; yes and built at the cost of life; and then when the blood of their brothers in the front had dearly bought a glorious peace, thinking to shout— "See how *we* killed the bear." The sentiment of the entire army here is down on such men and we do not, cannot recognize them as brother soldiers.

Everything here is well, calculated to inspire us with hope. We shall surely enter Atlanta. I have taken add. moments to write these lines and have been physically exhausted all the time, so having no time to copy you must [bear with] a multitude of grammatical, rhetorical, and orthographic mistakes.

From your affectionate son George.

Battlefield, four miles from Atlanta [Ga.]
July 21st, 1864

Dear Mother,

We have had a great battle and routed the rebels most thoroughly. Yesterday morning we left camp and formed on the left of the 4th corps. The day was intensely hot and the forenoon was spent getting up to the line as we were obligated to working slow. About one o'clock we halted a little in the rear of what was to be our position and waited for the skirmishers to clear the way. We remained scouting here in the area about two hours.

At 3 o'clock firing suddenly began heavy on our left and non combattants and stragglers were seen running to the rear. Another minute and the great storm of musketry rolled around to our front and thence far as we could hear to the right. Our brigade was ordered quickly into line. We were lying right under a hill and Loring's[3] rebel divisions charged over the hill upon us, but they caught a "tartar."[4] Our line was ordered forward and forward we went right up the hill at them. They waved their colors and charged madly at us and for a minute it seemed as if they would overpower us, but our line dashed on, met them midway on the hill and hurled back their charging columns.

Now commenced an awful scene, the rebels ran in confused masses from us and the very heavens seemed to tremble at the terrific fire we poured into them. Their dead and wounded covered the ground, and in perfect terror many of them threw down their guns and ran to our lines to escape destruction.

We reached the top of the hill and held our position there, a position of us keeping off the enemy while others carried rails to throw up in front of us. The battle raged meanwhile awfully all around us and at one time we were nearly flanked by the giving way of a brigade somewhere on our right; but we held our ground and fought till night put an end to the conflict. In the dusk the rebels drew off their forces and the "red field was won."

I walked over the ground in front of us when the moon rose and helped take off the rebel wounded. It was nearly morning before they were all brought in. Today we have been carrying the dead, and waiting for another battle but it has not come yet.

Our regt. lost only 14 men killed and wounded. Our boys are very careful, always laying down to load and fire except when advancing and at the command halt and drop flat to the ground. This is the first fair open field fight we have had and it must have been desperation on the part of the rebels. Our boys would not give back an inch and I believe they would have gone in with the bayonets before they would have retreated a step.

The heat was so awful that many of our men went sun struck, but all worked nobly enveloped in a dense cloud of smoke with faces begrimed with powder.

Sergt. Bachelder was wounded by my side in the right shoulder. I think not dangerously.[5] He has gone back to the hospital.

I am very tired and cannot write more at present.

Your affectionate son George

In the field two miles from Atlanta [Ga.]
July 24th, 1864

Dear Mother,

I last wrote on the 21st the day after the battle. The rest of that day we remained on the field strengthening our works and early the next morning our line again advanced. The rebels had left one very strong line of their works and passing them about two miles we again formed line of battle on the crest of a hill. Here the enemy's skirmishers began to fire at us and it was very evident that there was a heavy force on the rising ground about a mile in front. So we proceeded to fortify ourselves, which we have been doing slowly till the present time. The rebels have made two or three advances on us but our skirmish line rallied each time and drove them back. The[y] kept up a more persistant shelling but so far have done no more harm than to kill a horse and knock over an ambulance. We can hear their guns in time to get into our works before the shell comes.

The rebels have removed their best General (Johnston) and Hood now has command. So far his movements bid fair to completely ruin his army. The morning after we had the great fight General Hooker rode around to see us. Oh, it would have done you good to see the boys cheer him. His face looked just like a sunbeam. When he came along to our regt. we brought out a battle flag which we captured, he stopped and coming up to us said, "Boys what regt. is this?" The 105 Ill., we replied. Then said he, "You did splendidly, splendidly but they did just as well on the right, the corps is all right." We gave him cheer after cheer and it was carried from regt. to regt. all along the line as he rode on.

When we went into the fight, wounded, worthless but doting general (Ward) was commanding the division in absence of Butterfield, and when our brigade dashes up the hill and turned the rebel line, he sat on his horse clapping his hands and shouting, See my brigade! See my brigade!

I received two letters from you day before yesterday one of which contained some envelopes and also a week ago received the six stamps. You need not send any more envelopes. I got a lot not long since and have plenty. I must not [now] stop writing as our battery is going to open and we are ordered into the works.

Your affectionate son George.

[p.s.] Monday morning 25

I received last night a letter from you containing a stamped envelope. The balance of the afternoon yesterday was passed dodging the rebel shells and about midnight they made a feint upon us. In less time than I can write a line we were up and ready for them. To witness the shelling at night would be most grand if one did not feel constrained to suddenly prostrate himself. We watch the rebel works and soon a bright flash lights up the sky and a line of fire wings its aerial flight for our line. Now it comes right over us whiz, bang it bursts, and the pieces are whirled on. This continues night and day but in the day time we have to be guided by the sound as we cannot see the flash. Our pickets now are simply a line of skirmishers thrown out about fifty yards. My duties as commissary sergt. excuse me from all guard duty.

In the field, five miles west of Atlanta [Ga.]
July 31, 1864

Dear Mother,

Since I last wrote I have received two letters from you, the latest being dated July 24th. During the last week we have been working pretty hard. On the 23rd we advanced as we supposed for Atlanta. But on arriving at about two miles from that coveted point we found ourselves right in the teeth of their very strongest point and huge 12 lb. shot began to hurl over us. We went to work rapidly, threw up works and waited to develop [our] lines. In the afternoon of that day, they massed on McPherson but after terrible fighting, the noise of which jarred the ground for miles, the rebels were used up and driven back.

On the 28th the army attempted to turn to our right and about 6 pm our division was ordered around to assist them but after marching about two miles we were met by a messenger from Thomas who told us that they had killed and captured so many that they did not need us, so we went back again.

The next morning we started and marched about six miles to the extreme right. Our army is now moving to the right and our division is here to protect the right flank. In the recent battle there has been upwards of twenty thousand rebels either killed, wounded or captured. This may seem a large amount. I am satisfied these figures will come short of their real loss. An official order signed by Genl. Thomas was read to us a few days since. Their own corps alone "put out the fight" of six thousand rebels.

You spoke in one of your letters about the rebel deserters. They are not foreigners but mostly Georgians and are as intelligent as any. The foreigners we captured are the most rabid, particularly Irishmen. Day before yesterday I saw some prisoners from Miss. and they all looked rather corner-ways out their eyes at us, but the most of the deserters and prisoners are only anxious for peace on any terms.

The night after our battle I went over the field and helped with the wounded rebels (Ours were all off before night) and one pleasant looking boy, who was able to walk by leaning on my shoulder expressed great joy at being wounded. He said if we could only kill their generals, that they made them fight against their will, etc.

Our army is now working out some plan, but I have no idea when we shall enter the "Gate City," it may be tomorrow and it may be a month. The works around it are too immense to be taken by arsenal and we can only gain it by strategy. Hood still commands the rebels and if he continues as he has commenced he will have no army in two weeks.

I have received all the letters you wrote lately, and noticed that the last two or three were directed wrong, but the principle direction is the regt. If that is plain they will come right. It is well enough however to put on the rest.

Old Joe has left our Co. and reported to Washington, we are mourning his loss greatly, and expect now to lose some of the fame won under his command.[6] He was in my opinion the best general in this department and jealousy made Sherman and Thomas use him so that he could not stay under them and he asked to be relieved. Well, this we cannot help, but our best wishes will ever attend the dear old man. He obviously had a smile and a kind look for the honest soldier and however he may be used by great men, the soldiers, who fight battles will always love him. I have little faith in Sherman's ability, but a wooden General ought to succeed here against an army one half our strength commanded by a rash man.

You expressed some fears about the regt. reenlisting. If they do, I shall not, so you need not be the least concerned. I am satisfied that when my three years are completed I have done my whole duty and owe the country no further service as a soldier. I have written this hastily as I do all my letters for we expect every moment to move.

Your affectionate son George

CHAPTER 10

"The Very Air Seems
Full of Death and Destruction"

Near Atlanta, August 4–Atlanta, October 23, 1864

Protracted battle fatigue took its toll. The 105th Illinois Infantry remained outside Atlanta skirmishing with rebel pickets sporadically while the Union army's heavy artillery steadily pounded the city. Sergeant Cram, uncharacteristically short-tempered with his mother about postage stamps, plowed through the details of tactical warfare in his letters as though pounding howitzers were echoing between the written words. Deprivation of sleep, sustenance, and normalcy caused officers as well as field soldiers to be anxiously perched on the edge of expectation. Twentieth Army Corps General John W. Geary's letter to his wife (August 15, 1864) expressed his state of mind: "Every thing has been very quiet here for several days, but it is that kind of quietness that the tiger or the cat uses before springing upon its prey. . . . Great God when will all these terrible battles cease. For one hundred days and nights consecutively I have been in the whistle of bullets and blaze of battle; even at this very moment more than 50 cannon are being fired upon the doomed city of Atlanta."

By the end of the summer of 1864, General Sherman began to lob an additional form of hell upon the civilians of Atlanta. General Sherman notified Atlanta's mayor and council on September 12, 1864, that all citizens were required to leave: "Now you must go and take with you the old and feeble; feed and nurse them, and build for them in more quiet places proper habitations to shield them against the weather, until the mad passions of men cool down, and allow the Union and peace once more to settle on your old homes at Atlanta." The war began to leave deep psychological wounds on the lives of non-combatants as well as architectural scars on the landscape of Atlanta. With the momentum of a conquering mob, like gravity itself, marching into Atlanta was only a matter of time.

The presidential elections were deliberated among soldiers and in letters home after the fall of Atlanta. Mrs. Cram's letters likely argued for the position of women's involvement in politics. Her unsympathetic son admonished her, in return, describing his own views on the impropriety of women in political and business affairs. While getting to know Anna Blanchard Cram can only be a deductive process, she seemed to be a progressive suffragette in the making, judging from her son's replies.

The relatively calm fall days of 1864 were in contrast to the action just weeks before. Looking for something to do, George worked on a chimney with the assistance of an old horse he found. But even the beast of burden was unwilling to get lathered up over a chimney on a hot day as Cram's diary noted (October 17, 1864)—"the quadruped had absconded."

Cram speculated about the jealousy of a certain Colonel Harrison of the 70th Indiana over the comfortable quarters of the 105th Illinois. By holding the rear during the Atlanta onslaught, the 105th Illinois Infantry had the time to construct a fine camp along the Chattahoochee River while they awaited further action. He could not know that Colonel Benjamin Harrison would survive this inequity and become the 23rd President of the United States.

Sergeant Cram and the 105th had a chance to observe General Sherman close-up while he visited their camp. The general seemed very agitated as he worked on several telegraph dispatches. Unbeknownst to the men nearby, General Sherman was finalizing the details on October 19 with the chief quartermaster and the chief commissary of the upcoming campaign: "I propose to abandon Atlanta, and the railroad back to Chattanooga, to sally forth to ruin Georgia and bring up on the sea-shore. Make all dispositions accordingly." The March to the Sea had begun.

In the field 2 miles north of Atlanta [Ga.]
August 4th, 1864

Dear Mother,

When I last wrote you I believe our division was on the right flank. Well we marched back night before last and now occupy a position on the right of our corps immediately in front of Atlanta. We are so close to the rebel works that their bullets keep us pretty close and last night men were sent out from each company to build a new line still nearer. That line is now being completed and we are expecting orders momentarily to move up into them. The rebel forces are in plain sight and the worst of all is we are obliged to be quietly here and see their miserable flag float over them.

An important movement is still progressing on our right and the rebels may have to leave Atlanta or do worse most any day. Still, we set no time as to its capture.

I have received several letters from you lately containing stamps and envelopes. The last contained four stamps.

You wish to know something about the Sanitary & Christian Commissions. When I was at Resaca with Tirtlot I had charge of all the sanitary and commissary stores there and we constantly had for the wounded soda crackers, condensed milk, pickled potatoes & cabbage, extract of beef, dried fruit and some other little things furnished by the S.C. while govt. commissary could furnish them nothing but hard crackers, pork, beef (bad), coffee, sugar and beans. Also each badly wounded man was furnished with a clean white shirt. Drawers & socks by the S.C. Also *all* the lint. and bandages and much of the chloroform were furnished by the S.C. Besides these we received many dozen bottles of whiskey, brandy, and different cordials, from the S.C.

On the other hand, I have seen great abuse of these stores by officers high in authority, but if one poor wounded soldier's life has been saved by the Sanitary Commission (and I know there have been thousands) who in the North can say the society is a failure or hesitate to give them mite?[1]

The Christian Commission is also a good thing and we frequently get religious papers through them. They do much good in different ways.[2]

Our regt. is situated on very pleasant rolling ground and while I write our flag is waving proudly over our works. That flag was once beautiful, but now it is rent and torn with rebel bullets and the staff is nearly shot off.

I have seen the call for 500,000 more men, but must say I don't see the policy of calling them out for only one year, at which time the service of all that remains of that 500,000 expires. What will govt. do then for men? Or do the administration think they can end the war then?

I received your letters regularly and letters from home are most pleasant messengers just now, I assure you.

I know nothing more about Bachelder's wound than have told you. He was struck in the right shoulder by a bullet (I think) though a shell passed by at the time. He was sent to the hospital and from there was sent further North. The last I heard of him he was comfortable and doing well. Grant and Holmes are well.

The weather is hot and not very pleasant to men in our circumstances. Give my best respects to Miss Markham and thanks for the very few lines she sent.

Your affectionate son George

[p.s.] I would like to have you send me a skein of black thread.

> In the field two miles from Atlanta [Ga.]
> August 9, 1864

Dear Mother,

Since I last wrote you, we have not moved from our position except to advance our line a few rods which were done without loss. I received yesterday and today five letters from you and an *Illinoian,* also four stamps.

With regard to the rebel flag, there were seven of them taken by our division and this one. Sergt. Smith and myself took it from a rebel sergt. who had been shot dead.

I have seen accounts in the *Tribune* of Grant's repulse at Petersburg. What a pity! When so near the most brilliant victory ever known. Mother, the abolitionists may talk as they please, but I tell you that colored troops cannot be depended on and that evidently caused this great defeat.

Our army is gradually extending its right wing encircling the rebel position here and I hope we shall soon be in a condition to ask the "Johnnies" to "come in." The only way we can take Atlanta will be by flanking it or by seige. Their works are too strong to assault and to make the attempt would be to lose the power of the army. Our works are so close to the enemy that we have to keep pretty well behind them only walking around when obliged to cook, bring water, etc.

Almost every day someone in the regiment is wounded. Yesterday one from our company was shot, bullets are continually whistling and monster shells flying from line to line. In truth, the very air seems full of death and destruction.

Occasionally the rebels make a demonstration on us and we seize our guns, jump down into the ditch (not our last ditch) and eagerly watch for them, but after a great deal of yelling and shooting, they become again silent and we once more throw off the cumbersome cartridge box, lay down our "Springfield" and resume our previous occupation, some writing with a sheet of paper on their knees and others reading, whittling, eating, etc.

It is very dull remaining right here all the time but we can endure anything the rebels can. I get away once in awhile to draw rations and then get out of reach of bullets (for our commissary men keep well in the rear) and speaking of rations, puts me in mind to tell you that we actually drew one days ration of *soft bread* a few days since. Twas a dainty morsel, I assure you after eating nothing but hard crackers for these months.

I received a letter from Frank Ellis yesterday, he was at Kingston, Ga. It is almost night and I must close,

Your affectionate son George

[p.s.] The thread you sent was *very* opportune. Give my love to Aunt Sophia and many thanks.

In the field 2 miles from Atlanta [Ga.]
August 20, 1864

Dear Mother,

The mail came in today for the first time in a week and I received two letters from you dated the 7th and 10th each containing a stamp. Don't *stick* stamps to your letters! I can't get them off without ruining them.

Since I last wrote we have not moved from our old position facing the rebel forts in front of the city. A few days ago we had orders for our entire corps to move back to the river but they were soon countermanded. Hard fighting has been going on at the extreme right—yesterday and day before and it is understood here that our forces have taken the Macon railroads. If so, we shall surely take the city.

The rebels opened furiously on us day before yesterday before daylight with their artillery but after allowing them to have their own way about half an hour, our batteries opened and in twenty minutes completely silenced them. The shells from our battery just pound the rebel fort opposite right through, and they have not dared to fire a gun from it since.

We have noisy times here frequently loud—our ears have become pretty much used to it, so that it disturbs us very little. We are also learning to be early risers as we have to get up every morning at three o'clock and stand in the trenches gun in hand till sunrise. This the boys think is a very useless arrangement, certainly it is anything but pleasant as no sleep can be obtained till near midnight on account of the heat.

I had received a letter from Ellis a short time ago and answered it. He writes excellently and I wish there were more young men in the world and especially in the army like him.

You spoke of a young man there who might be inclined to avoid the draft. You will notice that is the case with all the most rabid abolitionists. And I have noticed here that those who are the bitterest on rebels; the most affectionate to the Negroes; those who continually tell how they want to fight to the bitter end, etc. are always taken suddenly very ill just before a battle and find some reason for being obliged to stay in the rear, very much *of course* against their will. For my own part I am disgusted with Negroes although I think slavery is wrong and hope, as I believe, that the war will end it on this continent or at least in this government.

I expect we shall be paid off when the campaign is over which may be in a week or a month or anytime. What money I get, I shall endeavor to send home as soon a possible, for it is not a very safe place to keep money here.

I suppose of course you have before now heard that Sergt Bachelder is dead. The intelligence caused much sadness with us as he was thought very highly of as a man and soldier by every member of the company. I hear nothing of Tirtlot, he writes of his whereabouts or condition to no one here. Sergt Grant is out on the skirmish line today. His health is good. Tommy Holmes is also well and cheerful.

I have just received a lot of papers from Uncle Calvin. He sends them regularly.

Your affectionate son George

Camp of the 105th near the Chattahoochee River [Ga.]
August 30, 1864
Dear Mother,

You see by my heading that we have slightly changed our position since I last wrote. Last Thursday night our entire regt. vacated the strong position before Atlanta and moved back to the river. The movement was made so quietly that the enemy did not know anything of it till daylight revealed the fact that no Yankees were visible. Of course no commands could be given, so our brigade band went to HdQrts and struck up "Yankee Doodle" at which the brigade filed noiselessly out of their works. We went back about a mile and then formed a new line and waited till the 4th corps had executed their movement to our right and joined the rest of the army. This kept us there till two in the morning and we then started swiftly for the river which we reached at daylight. Our cavalry was still kept out to watch the motions of the rebels when they ascertained our forces were gone and their reports were very laughable.

The rebels hardly knew at first what to think but finally they advanced a strong skirmish line which came on with most profound respect and awe for our truly formidable works. Now creeping up slowly and now lying down and looking first one way and then another till they finally ventured to climb the battlements and gaze over. Then their line of battle came on still cautiously as if they still suspected some Yankee trick. But the Yankees were far way laughing at their fears.

We remained that day on the south side of the river to support the 1st division in case they should be attacked while building works but the next day (Saturday) we came over to the North side and established our camp about two miles from the river in a dense piece of woods which we have now cleared out and transformed into a most helpful camp with charming shade trees. We cut pine poles and made them up into bunks for beds and you can hardly imagine how happy all the boys are at being so comfortably camped after our long weary campaign.

The balance of the army are still working for Atlanta and we were wisely thrown back here to protect the crossing and guard the rear while they finished the campaign. Col. Dustin told yesterday that the reason the 20th Corps was selected for this duty was because they had done more hard work and more fighting and sustained greater loss than any other corps in this department. He said he thought we would stop here some time unless the balance of the army got into trouble and needed us to get them out.

I have not yet received the letter you spoke of sending with Cousin Mary's picture. But it may yet come. I received one from you yesterday of Aug. 20.

You have not mentioned anything lately about the land. Have you received the rent yet for last year or rather for this year and has the taxes been paid? I wish much that I could be there to see to it but that will have to be deferred another year I am afraid.

I am almost disgusted Mother with politics, there is so much rottenness in it. I want Lincoln to be reelected for the benefit of the country, because I think it would be a benefit to the country at the *present time,* but I am far from being satisfied with him or his administration.

The soldiers want a great deal less *talk* and a great deal more *work*. I don't like this call for men for a year and unless the war closes within that time I fear it will be destructive to the country but we can't tell much about the future and it's useless to borrow trouble.

I don't think much of your "League" arrangements for ladies to secure votes. Two years in the army leads one to think still more that ladies should be ladies and not meddle with the contentions of men. Let the women teach their children to be honorable, honest and pure minded, and their boys will develop into honest statesmen, and the girls into social and rational women. There will be fewer demagogues, no traitors and a great many more sensible and refined ladies than the present day affords. Woman should not mingle in the strifes and contentions of the political world. Hers should be a life of gentleness, purity and love.

I meant to finish this sheet but they call of me to come and draw some meat so I must close to get this in today's mail

Your affectionate son George

South bank of the Chattahoochee River [Ga.]
Sept. 9th, 1864
Dear Mother,

Since I last wrote I have received the letter containing Mary's pictures. The mail has failed to come for the last week so I get no late letters from you to answer.

We left our nice little camp last Monday and moved across the river to the old rebel forts which our regiment now occupies. Our position is on a high hill over looking the muddy river and commanding the railroad bridge.

Every day we are expecting orders to go to Atlanta. General Ward says he certainly will have us there today or tomorrow and as he has said the same thing for the last week we begin to believe it. At any rate we hope it may be so for this place is not the most pleasing in this southern clime.

As soon as it begins to get a little dark at night the villainous mosquitoes commence a nervous tenor and as the night advances the bullfrogs chime in an unearthly bass. It was laughable the first night we were here to hear the boys run out every few minutes and throw clubs at these latter pests.

We do not expect a very long rest this Fall, for Sherman has signified his intention of opening another campaign in about a month. He probably means to win the rebel army in his front if possible.

I have just been having a couple of bad teeth extracted and my face is so sore I can hardly write a proper sentence.

There is some little prospect of our being paid off before a great while and I shall endeavor to send most of mine home some way or other.

I sent home last Spring by Lt. Adams of Wayne an overcoat. If you ever get a chance to send anything, send that. I do not need it now, but can any time take care of it till the weather will be cold.

Trains are passing by our camp loaded with supplies for Atlanta nearly all the time, now and then one contains a load of soldiers, mostly those who were sick during the campaign and have now recovered their health, to become again invalids when the army makes another move.

Sherman is clearing out Atlanta sending the disloyal south and the loyal north. I cannot say that I like Sherman much or all his actions but he is our Genl., and we have to submit.

The weather is becoming a little Fall-like and seems much more pleasant than our summer. All our boys are well.

I hope to write my next in the "Gate City." Love to Aunt Sophia.

Your affectionate son George

Chattahoochee River [Ga.]
Sept. 29, 1864

Dear Mother,

I received your last letter for the 18th day before yesterday. In regard to the overcoat, do not worry about it at present. The weather is so warm yet that we do not wear any coat at all during the day time and it will yet be a full month before an overcoat will be at all necessary. If you should get a good chance, send it and if not, why in about a month I think it can safely be sent by express which would be much cheaper than I can get a new one and I would not get one for that time anyhow. We can't draw just what and when we wish down here.

Things now look as though there would be no Fall campaign here. At least one corps of troops have passed this place, bound North within the last few days but whether they are reinforcing Grant or merely going up to protect our rear against the cavalry raids of Wheeler, I have no idea. But whatever may be their object, I don't think Sherman will attempt to move forward after so weakening his post.

We have daily a dozen or two rumors and speculations in the place of news. The papers seldom appear before us till they bear an old date and we never get any of the late news except the most important events which are telegraphed to Sherman and he causes it to be posted in front of his headquarters so that all may see it. We learn in this way that Jeff Davis has sued for peace and many are the speculations concerning it.

Soldiers are generally apt to be over sanguine and hopeful, a very good thing to be sure, for although their expectations are frequently greatly below par, still a hopeful disposition enables one to pass through hardships easily by enjoying all the best and quietly passing over the rough sides.

Yesterday the day was spent in adorning our already excellent camp. Two fine rows of beautiful pine trees were set out in front of every company; one now in front and one in rear of the line officers tents and one now in front of the field officers, so that now the camp has much the appearance of a young forest. Our tent is in the row of line officers inasmuch as we have to act rather officially in the prolonged and continuous absence of our "veteran" captain who "doth not yet appear."

The daily camp routine is as follows: revilee at sunrise. Breakfast to be eaten at seven when the bugle blows. At half past seven the bugle again blows and our sick men report to the surgeon. At 12 N. dinner bugle and roll call. At 5 retreat roll call and supper. At 8 tattoo roll call and at 8 1/2 taps, which means, for every light to be extinguished and the enlisted men to seek their blankets. Officers can do as they choose about retiring, they being considered men of sufficient intelligence to know when it would be conducive to their felicity to seek the covers.

Every Sunday we have a minute and very rigid inspection of arms and occasionally at intervals throughout the week. At the inspections every man is required to have his gun shine like a new dollar.

About every other day it is calculated to have a drill but so much time has been spent in getting camp comfortable and handsome that as yet we have drilled but little. We shall commence that in earnest next week.

There are now a few McClellan men. Alas, copperheads in our regiment, but they are weak-kneed cowards who want him elected merely to stop the fighting so they may not have to endanger their worthless necks anymore. I am most happy to be able to say that Company F has not got a single one of these contemptible sneaks, but on the contrary all are loved for Lincoln and the Union.

I do not believe we shall go home to vote. In the first place, Sherman can't spare so many as it would take from his command at this time without endangering his position and to meet with any disorder now would be worse than a Union victory in those two states (Ill. & Ind.), but I do not think there is any danger of defeat there. Lincoln will certainly carry those states without any outside help.

Last week I had a very pleasant visit with Frank Ellis. He is just the same honest Frank that he was at Wheaton, not a shade the worse for the wear and tear of army life. So much for elocution. I find all the young men here who have had even an insight into book knowledge are not injured in the least by camp vices. Frank looks just as natural as though but a day had passed since we were both at Wheaton. He is now orderly sergeant in his company, having been promoted from private.

I am very glad to hear your business is so good and that land had just yielded so much. It was a good plan not to rent 3 years at that rate however, I think it will bring a larger dividend when I can go there and see to it. I see Uncle Rufus still holds on to his business in Chicago and it seems to me that it would be very profitable after the war, more so than before.

There are a great many citizens living in this region of country yet not withstanding Sherman's order, most of them are women and what we would call up North the lowest specimens of humanity. They sometimes bring in a few articles to trade for our staples, such as bread, coffee, flour and sugar but as they won't sell for money, the trade is confined to officers, we privates not having a surplus of "Uncle Sam's" provender. Rations on hand are hard to get here and Sherman feeds them, but these natives have nothing but a few dried up string beans and a little corn almost wholly unfit for us. We still keep up our stock of pumpkins and find them palatable and healthy vegetables. We draw now once in awhile a little soft bread, 18 oz. per day to a man, the regular portion being 22 oz.

I wrote a letter to Aunt Sophia and directed to Wheaton a few days ago. You can send it to her.

There is no prospect of our leaving this place yet for some time and we are quite contented to stay. The boys are in good health. Grant, Tommy Holmes, Baker and the Wheaton boys generally are well, hopeful and earnest for Lincoln.

Your affectionate son, George.

Chattahoochee River [Ga.]
Oct. 18th, 1864

Dear Mother,

Since I last wrote we have had strange doings in this part of the uncivilized world. About two weeks ago Hood crossed the river a few miles below us with his army and proceeded immediately to try

Sherman's flanking system. So we marched for our suppers, but Sherman, leaving our corps to hold Atlanta and vicinity, started for him with tremendous vigor. Two whole days the road through this place was lined with troops. Great masses of artillery went rattling by, and there came the cumbersome wagon trains. It seemed as if they never would pass.

Sherman spent one whole day here telegraphing back and forward. He honored us by eating dinner with our colonel and then remarked that we had one of the finest camps he had ever seen. He is a very nervous man and can't keep still a moment. He wouldn't sit down in the telegraph office, give the operator a message then jumped up, took off his hat and rubbed his head, then he would pull off his coat and walk the floor, keeping up a continual motion all the time. I begin to think much more of his generalship than I ever have before.

Well of course you know as well as I that communication has been cut off since the beginning of this great raid so we have neither sent out nor received any mail, but I write this expecting to be able to send it tomorrow by an officer, going direct to Chattanooga.

In all, the hurrying to and fro, in this Fall campaign our regiment has so far been more remarkably fortunate, and mostly on account of our former brigade commander Col. Harrison, who having a great dislike to [of] our regt because it is far superior to his own and being jealous of our colonel, when he was ordered to move his brigade to Atlanta leaving one regt here to guard the bridge, he picked upon ours as the one to remain. Of course at that time everyone wanted to go to Atlanta, but we did not grumble, and by hard work soon had a handsome and comfortable camp established. Well as soon as Hood crossed the river the rest of our brigade had to move back here laying out two or three days in a cold storm while we were comfortably housed.

A week ago last Sunday quite a serious accident happened here. It had been raining several days and about midnight—Sat. night—a great quantity of driftwood came down the river carrying away two major bridges which in addition to the driftwood, came against the railroad bridge with such force that more than half of it was carried away. A pontoon was immediately thrown across and before night men arrived to reconstruct the railroad bridge which was finished some days ago and trains are now running over it.

We are daily exulting over a continual string of good news. The capture of Richmond is known to us, or at least we fully believe it this time as it comes through official sources and not from newspapers—said articles not having been seen in camp for a long while—and that Sherman is punishing Hood for his temerity we are daily assured.

The weather is now somewhat cooler though very pleasant. Our boys are kept continually at work perfecting our defenses which are now about impregnable.

All citizens are kept outside our lines, and not allowed to enter camp under any consideration.

We are hoping for a large mail now in a day or two.

Your affectionate son George

Chattahoochee River [Ga.]
Oct. 23rd, 1864

Dear Mother,

Once more we get a mail and in that are two letters from you, one from Uncle Rufus and one from Ettie. I have written nothing for over a week as all communication was cut off and no mail neither could leave the regiment. In your letter you speak of recruits. We are very glad to receive them and shall expect them daily.[3] David Grant was much displeased with his brother for re-enlisting but I think very likely he may stand the service this time as well as the rest of us.

A few days ago we were paid off, in this way. A small amount was paid each man here, what was considered sufficient for his present use, and the balance given in a draft, one to each company, with the entire amount due that company on it. Our company draft will be sent tomorrow by our regt quartermasters to Chicago and given to Thomas B. Bryan. A schedule will also be sent with it containing the amount due each man and the name of the person it shall be paid to. I have sent your name as my assignee and probably soon after this letter reaches you the draft will have arrived in Chicago and you can then get the money. The amount due me is $131.85 (one hundred and thirty-one dollars and eight-five cents.)

I am so glad your business is so prosperous and trust it may continue so. I am afraid before the winter is over there will be a general crash in business of all kinds. With regard to the land, I am inclined to think it would be best to sell immediately if it were possible, but probably the way it is situated, you will not be able to dispose of it, not being there to do the business.

It is difficult to sell land so far away from it. I am afraid myself that land will fall, but real estate is always good property.

I have got along finely without any overcoat yet, and the weather is still so warm that one is not needed. Still I shall be glad to get it the first opportunity. None of the company could have things sent by express yet as communication has so long been destroyed, and when it's again restored so the cars can come through they will be kept leveled with army supplies.

Today an order was received by our surgeon to dispose of his sick and get ready for active field service within fifteen days, so it looks a trifle like work again, and yet I cannot see how Sherman can move forward from Atlanta for we are now on 3/4 rations and not a pound of anything will come down for a week yet. Hood tore up the railroad terribly but is at last driven from it and gone no one knows where.

I received the ginger and pepper you sent but did not particularly need it, though I could of course use it. We draw rations of pepper. I do not need anything that you can send in a letter at present, but whenever you have a chance, send some note paper and envelopes, they are very difficult to get.

We have built a fine fireplace in our tent and are now just as comfortably situated as one could desire in the army. I wish you could just step in a moment and see how truly is "necessity the mother of inventions."

Your affectionate son, Geo. F. Cram

CHAPTER 11

"Terrible Havoc Among the Citizens"

Near Atlanta, October 30, 1864–Raleigh, April 19, 1865

Strategic foraging was sanctioned de facto during the Winter of 1864–1865 when General Sherman ordered that their supplies and communication should be left behind as they began to march again. Survival of the fittest, the fittest of Union soldiers, would depend upon their capabilities to beg, borrow, and steal from civilians along a fifty-mile swath to Georgia's Atlantic coast, the historic March to the Sea. The question of morality might have been a complex one for some soldiers who disapproved of Sherman's strategy in decimating, not just conquering, the Confederate states. General Sherman's objectives were strategic as well as pragmatic; he had to supply an army on active campaign. Destruction of property meant crippling the economic base of the South; railroads were destroyed, cities burned, and civilians were assaulted. Cram wrote in his diary (November 15, 1864), "All houses burned during the march." Both pantries and pride were left empty.

While Cram wrote his mother about the inherent danger to army discipline of mob attacks on Confederate civilians, Chaplain Daniel Chapman's January 1, 1865, resignation letter spoke volumes in its subtlety about his own conflict of being present and bearing witness to a conquering mob's histrionics: ". . . it is my opinion that it will be impossible for a Chaplain to accomplish anything very valuable in the ensuing campaign for the good of the regiment."

With the conquest of Atlanta proudly behind them, the 105th Illinois Infantry, part of the 1st Brigade, 3rd Division of the 20th Army Corps, burned its camp, railroad ties, and bridges behind them and followed General Sherman in marching towards the final stages of war—bringing it to an end. Approaching Savannah, Cram noted in his diary (November 27, 1864) that the course they took was not without its surprises: ". . . marching brought us to the S.C. Railroad. Crossed it and took the wrong road. Had quite an exhibition of General Slocum's temper on the procession."

But as troops wandered from Georgia's peanut fields northward through the Carolinas, from hills to "the famous land of swamps"

(Cram diary, December 1, 1864), then to rice fields, they found themselves on the front lines once again at the Battle of Averysboro in March 1865. En route to Goldsboro three days later they took the extreme left of the 14th Corps that had encountered General Johnston's men in what became the Battle at Bentonville, the last battle between General Sherman and General Johnston. The battles and skirmishes in the Carolinas were more aggressive than Sergeant Cram and his comrades had seen for awhile; it was a fight to the finish and the Confederate soldiers did not lay down their arms quietly. The final embers of fighting were among the most heated of the war.

Chattahoochee River [Ga.]
Oct. 30, 1864

Dear Mother,

Today is Sunday and one week from my last writing day so although I have not heard anything from you, I must proceed to do up the regular writing. This forenoon I wrote to Uncle Calvin, in answer to one received from him a short time since. Our railroad communications are not yet perfect and no army supplies are being got through but the mail continues to get to us every few days in some way probably being conveyed over the break by mule teams.

Last night I received a letter from Frank Ellis, a most intensely interesting one, detailing the terrific battle which occurred at Atlanta where his regiment was stationed. He was indeed fortunate to escape from such a fight with bare life, and he feels it too though he received two severe wounds, one in the right shoulder and one in the left thigh. The rebels drove them from their outer position and were speedily driven back in town, but they captured many of their things for a short time, among which was a letter to me which was enveloped and addressed ready to send. The robbers tore open the letter but finding nothing of money value in it, threw it down and I now have the letter in my hands and shall enclose it with this wishing to keep it for a memento of the war.[1]

Today we have received orders to prepare for a fifty-days campaign. All our company books and papers are to be sent back to the rear together with all surplus baggage. Not a soul knows where we are going or what we are to do, but conjectures are multiplied by mystery. Undoubtedly we shall go somewhere, where it matters little.

Last week I visited Atlanta for the first time. A few other young fellows and myself got an old hand car and arming ourselves with proper passes, we started "our train." About an hours hard labor, for it was all upgrade, brought us to our old line of works where we were nearly a month engaged in dodging rebel bullets while besieging the city.

Here we stopped to take one more look at the familiar old battleground. There was the place where our company was stationed. Oh so natural; the very head log of the breastwork which I had helped to lift there was unmolested and there was the spot where our tent was staked and the remaining of a little side table we made there. A little further to the left was the six silent graves of our dead associates who fell at their posts, pierced by the whistling minnie or mangled by the wildly shrieking shell while all over the ground were fragments of iron which had passed howling over us, fired from that grim monster fort. Sadly we took another lingering look at the scenes around us and then slowly started towards the old rebel line. Long solid lines of breastworks rose up before us, which to have attempted to carry [out] would have insured our regt total annihilation and yet one word from one man would have hurled us upon them.

But now no lines of fire greeted our approach, no Union cheers were mingled with rebel yells and save the rattling of our car, even the dropping of a pin could not be heard. A few more turns brought us to the limits of the city and houses began to multiply. But such houses! Each one riddled and torn by our shells, here a tall chimney knocked down and there a portico carried away. Along each side of the railroad were holes in the bank where families had crawled in to escape our iron showers.

In about the center of town stood the depot and on either side were the ruins of machine shops, commissary stores and many other public buildings, here our siege guns had rained down thirty-two pound shots unmercifully and unceasingly. A once beautiful roundhouse[2] was there, said to contain forty five engines. A little farther up we found what was called a bookstore where a few periodicals of ancient date, some musty old books and a very limited amount of stationery could be obtained at fabulous prices. (It is needless to add that my purchases were confined to one small bottle of ink for twenty-five cents.) On the opposite side of the street was the clothing store where a few hats were to be had at prices from seven to twelve dollars, and near there a few barber shops were established as if to suggest opposition. This comprises the entire list of business houses now in the city.

A few citizens still remain who walk the streets with a mournful absent look or stand like statues gazing at the "Boys in blue" as they pass. The houses are closed; blinds drawn tightly down and everything has a sad deserted appearance. Most of them were carried off south. The handsome streets are dug up in crazy places for fortifications; fine shade trees are hacked to pieces, magnificent stores are smoldering ruins; desolation prevails. Atlanta, the beautiful, the "Gate City" is dead.

We stayed only about two hours and seeing a train about to start out, jumped aboard leaving our old hand car in the city. At about eight in the evening we again reached camp, pretty tired, though well satisfied with our journey.

Those recruits have not yet come,[3] though we are daily expecting them. The weather is still pleasant and free from those northern storms but still I prefer the cold climate, there is much disease here which I attribute to the warm weather.

Your affectionate son George

Chattahoochee River [Ga.]
Nov. 6th, 1864

Dear Mother,

Yesterday I received a letter from you dated Oct. 24. The one you mentioned in that as having sent by Isaac Grant I have not yet had as he has not arrived, and very likely may not for sometime.

For several days back we have been expecting orders to march, and have been packed up all ready nearly a week. Yesterday the army of the Tennessee—15th & 17th corps—arrived within a few miles of us, and we were not surprised to receive word last night to be ready to move at seven this morning. Everything was still as mysterious regarding our intended movement as ever and no one had any idea which direction we were to take.

Well we went at once to work, arranged our knapsacks and also the inevitable "sine qua non," our haversacks. Portfolios too were neatly prepared with writing materials, old letters were re-read and burned; photographs inspected. A few company papers packed a in small box which we are allowed to carry in the regimental wagon; a couple of shovels, pickaxes, and axes, were also packed for the purpose of entrenching against the enemy and we began to think ourselves ready.

A glance around our little tent and oh yes, there is a nice piece of paper we nearly forgot that must go, and there is some soap we shall need washing without doubt, then there is a small package of nice tea which we will put in our knapsack. And certainly there is nothing more, do we take a lingering look at our miniature home, and in that look how much of affection. The little cupboard made by our own hands, the table, stools, bunks, shelves, and fireplaces, evidences of industry which we hoped long to enjoy turning away with much of sadness in our faces we prepared at a late hour for bed, expecting a hard day's work on the morrow.

But soldiers don't always know one day where they will be the next, and so it proved with us, for about midnight, I was woke up by the voice of our sergeant major who came around to inform us that the orders to go in the morning were countermanded, so with a smile of satisfaction I went again to sleep. This morning nobody knew why the order was countermanded and all are as profoundly ignorant as before. The report is that Hood is again getting in our front with his army so our campaign may be different from what was intended.

Trains were running down from Chattanooga all night but they were empty. This is rather significant that Atlanta will be abandoned, but yet, we can't tell. We are still on 3/4 rations, though most of the boys have sufficient. I have not suffered yet for food.

Yesterday afternoon we got some clothing and I drew some nice shirts and stockings for the winter. They will be so comfortable if we march which probably we shall do before long. This month came in with a cold rain storm but it has not passed away and the weather is beautiful and not too cool for comfort.

D [ecember] bids fair to be a pleasant month, which is all we ask for in case we campaign it.

I wrote a letter to Uncle Rufus a few days since. I don't know when I can write again, it will depend on when and where we go and whether our communication is kept up.

Your affectionate son George

Chattahoochee River [Ga.]
Nov. 9th, 1864

Dear Mother,

I have this moment received your letter of Oct. 30th and as we are informed that the mail will go out at eleven o'clock, which is not far distant, I hurry to write a line in answer; we are expecting to march tomorrow though perhaps it may be delayed till day after. This morning Atlanta was attacked and the fight is even now going on. We have just received orders to wear our accouterments and be continually ready for anything. So I write with mine on.

This morning also an order was received relative to our intended campaign. We are to carry 2 days hard bread and pork, 10 days coffee and salt and 5 days sugar in our haversacks, regular forage parties are to scour the country continually on either side of our line of march. And in all probability every enterable house we find will be burned. Atlanta will no doubt be abandoned and mostly destroyed. Where we shall go I know not, perhaps to Savannah, or Mobile, though our destination may depend on circumstances after we start.

I am pained to hear there is so much unhappiness up there where everybody ought to be happy. I think 'twould do everyone good to be a soldier and then home and society would be better appreciated.

The reason I sent to Tirtlot for such an amount of stamps was that he was indebted to me for that sum of money and I preferred the stamps but probably I shall not receive them now, as we shall leave so soon, and I cannot believe that communication will be kept up.[4] Well good bye and be assured I shall write again at the first opportunity, so however long it may be until you hear again from me, don't be alarmed or anxious.

Your affectionate son George

Four miles northeast of Savannah [Ga.]
Dec. 18, 1864

Dear Mother,

Today for the first time in more than a month our little band was made happy with a mail. Sober faces were thus, this afternoon, unearthed in smiles and it was my good fortune to receive two from you, together with several others, among which was one from Uncle Calvin.

We have made a great raid, leaving Atlanta in four columns, marching on four different roads, taking up in a general sweep about an average of forty miles wide through our whole route. At first we struck due East, making a feint on Augusta, tore up miles and miles of the Georgia railroad, then suddenly shooting southward from Madison entered Milledgeville without firing a gun. We stopped there one day and made most terrible havoc among the citizens, then moved again in a southeast direction, making it difficult to tell whether our object was Augusta, Beaufort or Savannah, but it is at last decided.

We arrived here one week ago yesterday. Skirmished with rebel cavalry the last seventy five miles through a country so intersected with mirey swamps and deep morasses that our advance was slow and difficult thus giving the rebels time to assemble a respectable force of mixed soldiery in the city and fortify with great success. Our division led the advance to this point when our progress was stopped by their works in front. We formed line of battle and waited for the other divisions to come up and connect with the other corps, fully expecting to storm the rebel forts in the morning. But morning came and we were still in position, no orders came to advance and we quietly remained by our guns while the 14th corps passed us to the right.

The next day or two was spent in changing our line and tonight we have finished a heavy line of works about one mile from the outer forts of the rebels.

For awhile after we arrived here things looked blue enough. We had taken with us only about eight or ten days rations, and had obtained the rest from the country during our march. This worked very well so long as we were changing camp daily for the country abounded in sweet potatoes, hogs, sheep, meal, flour, and poultry besides producing plenty of sugar, salt, molasses and considerable honey. But when we came to a dead halt in front of an armed city and not a pound of bread or bacon in our entire army, our haversack empty, affairs looked alarming enough.[5]

And yet Providence provided for us, for the next day, a large rice plantation was discovered on an island in the river and men were sent over to thresh out the rice. We had picked up large herds of cattle on the way, so with beef and a small quantity of rice each day, we have lived comfortably one week and are now daily expecting rations from our fleet.

What will eventually be done here is difficult to foresee. We may assault and we may besiege; the latter will be slow and sure with small loss of life, the former uncertain and bloody. Sherman and Foster[6] together have a very large army, I should think from seventy-five to a hundred thousand effective men.

I cannot give you an interesting account of our raid now, but on the march I took a few notes which I shall write out and send you as soon as I can do so. My health was constantly good, I stood the march well, notwithstanding we had some severe times and was often on the road forty-eight hours without rest. I saw and learned much that will always be of interest to me.

I am glad you received the money I sent, and shall send more when we are again paid, though that may not be for some months yet.

Grant and Wilcox have not yet arrived. They will hardly do their country much service during their short year.

I write this in haste in order not to miss the first mail, shall make up for it in my next.

Your affectionate son George.

[p.s.] I omitted, I see, to state just where we are situated. Our regt is camped in line of battle between the C&S Railroad and the Savannah River, being about a quarter of a mile from the former and over a mile from the latter, and between them, four miles from the city. Since I have written this letter we have received orders to fix up our camp most comfortably, so that it seems as if we were going to make a regular siege of it.[7] Direct your letters to me, Co. F. 105th Ill. Vol., near Savannah, Ga.[8]

Camp of the 105th, South Carolina,
Jan. 5th, 1865

Dear Mother,

Well we are in South Carolina and I will try and give you the locality as nearly as possible. First, we are distant from Savannah seven miles, and six miles north of the Savannah River, on the Charleston and Savannah dirt road, near an ancient place bearing the singular name of "Thunderbolt."[9]

On the last day of the last year we were ordered up long before light and hastily throwing our knaps together and eating a hurried breakfast, our division started for the south branch of the river which we crossed on a pontoon without difficulty.

This placed us on an island with one little narrow road to march on and all around us a swamp; marching a mile we came to the other side of the island found the position of the river between us and the South Carolina shore, wide and swelling greatly by the rising tide.

And while the General was directing how to pontoon it, bullets began to whistle from the opposite side, where a number of buildings afforded shelter to some of the rebels. One man in our regt. was killed.[10] A piece of artillery was quickly brought up by hand, and the old houses shelled vigorously which quieted the rebels amazingly. The wind kept rising and a cold rain set in much to our discomfort and the waves were so high that no bridge could be put down, moreover after keeping us out in the storm all day, it was discovered that we had not boats enough in the whole army to bridge it anyhow.

So Genl. Ward sent back for orders and the result was that two brigades of the division went back to the old camp and our brigade staid on the river bank to guard the place. The night was blusterous and ushered in the new year with fury; we did not sleep quite so warm and comfortable.

The morning broke very cold, clear and still windy and the boys sat shivering over little fires till about two o'clock in the afternoon when they had concluded to cross us in boats. Our company and one other got into a large flat boat with only two oars and setting out boldly soon found ourselves going downstream faster than was desirable, and after going down quarter of a mile we succeeded in landing on the same side from which we started. Here a few of us got out and hunted up some oars and long poles while others got little boats and rowed; and in the course of an hour we were all on the main land, on the treasonable soil of South Carolina.[11] I shall always remember my first acquaintance with that state for I got one of my feet gloriously wet in getting out of the boat, which in the overall state of things was not so pleasant.

After our brigade had all landed and got together we started northward and marching about five miles across a large rice swamp went into camp in a pleasant place just in the edge of a hill of pine timber where some fine houses were grouped together. As soon as we stacked arms, the whole brigade rushed hell upon these houses and in half an hour not a vestige of them remained save the chimneys and one house for headquarters. They made us excellent fires and warmed us thoroughly. Such was our entrance in the state.

We stopped there till the fourth, and then moved on this place and camped in an old fort which the rebels built about three years ago when Fort Pulaski was taken by our forces. These works are built around a large plantation which belonged to a Colonel Hardee.[12] This is used by our brigade commander,[13] the outer buildings being knocked to pieces for fire wood.

A large reconnoitering party was sent out yesterday afternoon and found the rebels cavalry occupying a position about six miles from us watching our progress. How long we shall remain here is more than we can tell anything about.[14] Sherman is as secret as a post and no one knows his plans till they are entirely executed. The boys call him "crazy Billy," but there seems to be some "method in his madness."

We get scarcely any mail since we have left northern Ga. I sent you a long letter with something of a description of our march through Georgia, not long since, but don't know whether you will ever get it or not.

I saw a few days ago an alligator which had been killed a short time; the Negroes say they are very plenty in the summer season. This country is all swamp with occasional patches of rising ground covered with pine timber.

If you have not sent my overcoat yet, you need not send it. They only have bitter spells of cold weather here which last but a day or two and in another month the winter will be over. If you ever get a chance to send any little things you may send some mustard. We shall get all salt meat raw and seasoning of that kind will be both wholesome and palatable.

I don't expect we shall be paid off again for some time, and rather hope not for I don't see how we could send it home very well.

We have just received notice that a mail will be sent out in a very little while, which is the reason this is written so hastily.

I shall try to write again soon.

Your affectionate son George.

Camp of the 105th,
seven miles north of Savannah [Ga.]
Jan. 16, 1865

Dear Mother,

I have been daily expecting a letter from you and have consequently delayed writing for several days. But something is amiss with our mail arrangements and although we hear of tremendous mails having arrived at Savannah, yet we never see anything more of them than sometimes two or three letters for a company. So I have concluded to wait no longer.

Since I last wrote we have changed our camp, but only to the opposite side of the river where we are formed into a stronger line of battle. We are now in a large field of waste land as level as the sea and fronting a heavy pine forest. Nothing is yet on this side of the river but our division, though preparations are steadily going on to move the rest of the army over. This is no light job for the long pontoon bridge breaks apart at every high wind and the road this side is so bad that a great amount of labor will be necessary before the heavy trains can be moved on it.

Isaac Grant and Wilcox have arrived and by them I received several nice little remembrances from home, among them the $8.00 in stamps and several letters, which had lost no interest by being long delayed.

Tell Aunt Sophia I will answer her soon. I am anxious to hear from you and know whether you got my last letters before I went to march. Yesterday I received a letter from Uncle Calvin, a very long one too for him to write, and also one from Annie. I think a great deal of their letters, they are so kind, cheering and affectionate.

Uncle has sent me the *NY Tribune* ever since I have been in the army, besides several books and frequently money with which he wanted me to buy some little comfort, so that I am always perplexed to know how to express the thanks I always feel; he is so good and kind.

We are expecting soon to start again on another campaign, perhaps against Charleston; half of the army has already left on transports and we hear they have landed at Beaufort,[15] so that looks as though Charleston was the object. The other half—20th and 14th corps—are ordered to get ready for an "active campaign" at once. This seems to us a trifle ridiculous since our division has been on an active campaign since we left Atlanta.

We have been marched about from place to place, continually clearing up new campgrounds; preparing a way for the army to cross the river, in which operation we had a brisk skirmish and lying about here and there, not daring to fix ourselves comfortable in any one place. The rest of the army, too, have been hard at work, although their camp was stationary. They have put up a line of formidable works around the city, which can never be taken.

This is one of the worst places I was ever in and perhaps it is sufficient description to say it is a grand rice country. In fact it is all swamp with here and there a spot where a man can stand without being in water. Through these places deep canals are cut from the river for the purpose of removing the swamp water from the rice lands and also for irrigating them for rice will not grow on land that is not wholly covered with water a certain portion of the year.

At intervals of two or three miles, we find large plantations where hundreds of Negroes were kept to cultivate and harvest the rice. The Negroes are inhumanely treated, being fed on rice and a little corn, having no meat, save on Christmas and each male and female alike whipped up to a certain amount of work each day. This is the only place I have ever seen slaves really abused, except so far as it is an abuse to make them slaves and I think many novelists, not omitting Mrs. Stevenson, have drawn largely on their own lively imagination for many of the horrors of slavery.

The winter weather here is pretty much like our March weather in Illinois, cold, rainy, windy sometimes pretty warm and at others pretty cold, but none of that severe cold which characterizes our Northern winters and which in my opinion is much healthier and more pleasant and indeed the inhabitants here are living proof of it.

Savannah is considered one of the finest cities in the South, but I was greatly disappointed in it. There are a great many beautiful buildings in it certainly and some large stores but both stores and residences have an old dilapidated appearance that makes one long to see again some of the lively cities of the North. The streets instead of being nicely paved are two or three inches deep with heavy sand so that it is difficult to cross them.

The stores are now open and trade is beginning to stand up quite brisk, but all for "Greenbacks" in fact you couldn't buy a shoestring with a bucket of confederate notes. Everything is exorbitantly high but this will soon be regulated.

For the present—good bye,

Your affectionate son George

Robertsville, S.C.
Jan. 30, 1865

Dear Mother,

I am sitting in front of my tent writing by firelight as I understand the mail will be sent out tomorrow. We left Hardeeville yesterday morning, marched seventeen miles and camped in a pine forest, for such is the whole country. In the entire day's march we only passed one plantation but what was burned, either by troops preceding us or our division. This morning we started early and arrived here about noon, distance eight miles. This town consists of eighteen houses, one store and one church. The buildings are yet standing though I wonder at it.

We are now over forty miles from Savannah and about ten miles from a landing on the river to which place our boats now run up. We shall stay here tomorrow and probably next day to draw rations and prepare for a rapid move which I believe will take us to Augusta.

The rebels are encamped about three miles in front of us watching our movements. One of their darkies came in to us tonight and he says the private soldiers all want to come back into the Union and stop the war but the Generals won't hear a word of it. His master was a private and at home owned a hundred Negroes.

A detail of men has just come, to go off foraging in the morning and I must go and find the men.

Back again—I put another stick of dry pine on the fire and write again. The weather is what we call cold, though doubtless you would not. Each night the ground freezes about an inch and the swamps are continually sealed over with ice, as the sun never reaches them.

We put up tents at night and sleep generally three together, by that means having an extra blanket.

Our recruits stand it well. Isaac has been out foraging all the afternoon. Wilcox has got a lame foot, but a few more days march will toughen it. We are camped in the midst of a gloomy forest north of the village. The timber is all pine and the ground is nearly all swamp. We have to break off pine boughs to sleep on, to keep off the dampness. Everyone in camp is cheerful and all are joyfully counting the months yet to serve, slowly they pass away and the end draws near.

My health is excellent and I never was in better spirits. Tell Aunt Sophia I received her last letter, will write to her as soon as possible. I may not be able to write again for some time.

Your affectionate son George

Fayettesville, N.C.
March 12, 1865

Dear Mother,

It is now noon and we have just had notice that a mail will go out at one o'clock so I'll sit down instantly to write a line, knowing how anxious you will be to hear. To give any particulars of our long tedious march will be impossible this time.[16]

We started from Hardeeville on the 29th Jan. On the 2nd of Feb. Our regiment was the advance guard and we had a pretty severe fight with Wheeler's Cavalry.[17] Only one man however in our company was wounded; this was the only engagement we have been in, for a few days passed but with the relevance that we had a brush with them.

The roads have as a general thing been very bad and great delays were often as necessary in building bridges, etc. We have lived entirely from the country with the exception of a little coffee occasionally.

All the boys in our company are well and cheerfully awaiting the mail, which we expect will come in few days. Tommy Holmes, Baker, Sayer, the three Grants, Wilcox and all the Wheaton boys stood the march finely. You would hardly know Wilcox; he has grown so much stouter than when he came to us.

We reached this place yesterday. It was taken with but very little fighting and the best possible feeling seems to exist between the citizens and our army. The houses were not plundered and a guard was sent to each. It is a very fine place of probably ten or fifteen thousand inhabitants.

. What we are to do next is just as much a mystery as ever, many think we shall go to Goldsboro, others, that we shall stay here. A few days, perhaps will make it more definite. We know but very little of what has been done since we swung clear of our communications.

Citizens tell us of a great battle in Virginia and that Charleston and Wilmington is ours, the latter of course must be.

When we were near Augusta, I received two letters from you, which came in a mail brought through by one of our divisions which left the river some two weeks after we did. You spoke in one of them of buying a house there, perhaps it would be a very good plan; you can judge better than I can. Real estate is generally good property and perhaps Wheaton will be as pleasant a place to live in as any we can find, at least for some years to come. I am thinking much of the time, now fast approaching, when I shall again enjoy the comforts of a home.

You can scarcely imagine how anxious all the boys are to receive the mail and their eagerness creates a thousand rumors regarding it.

The weather for the last two weeks has been constantly rainy but I will tell you more in my next which I hope to write very soon.

Your affectionate son George

Goldsboro, N.C.
March 28, 1865[18]

Dear Mother,

At last we have found a limit to our campaign and are now busily engaged fitting up a camp for a short rest. Day before yesterday we received our first mail and you may well imagine that there were more happy, cheerful faces here that day. Men were seen everywhere reading and smiling.

I received a number of letters from you, telling of your intended removal to Aurora. I would rather you could have remained at Wheaton till I returned; changes are so uncertain, but business may be so brisk now during the war that you will prosper. I think houses will be plenty enough in Wheaton when peace comes again.

Of your letters I got none later than Feb. 26: probably shall, however, by tomorrow.

I wrote you a short note from Fayetteville some two or three weeks since and as our progress from there to here was the most exciting of any I will endeavor to describe it. After resting a couple of days at Fayetteville our column again pushed forward on the 15th— Wednesday—the rebels had been concentrating on our march which was the extreme left of our army, so our train was sent with the corps on the right and two divisions of ours and two of the 14th corps moved forward unencumbered by any, save a necessary number of ammunition wagons.

My feet had become very sore and so I mounted one of the forage mules and went out in advance with the foraging party. There were some fifty of us, pretty well mounted, and as we were confident there were rebels near, we joined forces with another squad of about the same number. We rode rapidly about ten miles without turning off the road, when we came to a sudden halt at seeing the road ahead filled with a confused mass of horsemen running back at full speed. A minute more and they flew by us shouting that the rebels were right after them.

We immediately dismounted, left every fifth man with the animals and deploying on each side of the road advanced to reconnoiter, as we moved slowly up our number was augmented by other squads that came up, so when after advancing a full mile, we came in sight of the rebels, entrenched, we had quite a respectable little force. After exchanging bullets about half an hour with them we got around their right-flank and drove them out, killing one and wounding some others, without having a man hurt on our side. This was but the commencement of a series of fights we had with them that day and at night. We had taken a mill from them twice, and been intense[ly] driven away so we went to camp with but little forage.

In the affair at the mill, I got my right hand grazed by a bullet which just knocked off the skin from the knuckles making them a little sore for a few days.[19] The next day—16th—we spent about the same way, but the column had a severe battle with the rebels who disputed their crossing Black River. Wilcox was wounded slightly in left side, the only casualty in our company.[20] Our brigade took three guns from the rebels.

The 17th and 18th passed by tedious marching through the

"Great Dismal Swamp." On the 19th, my feet were pretty well and I marched with the column. Our division was in the rear of everything. About noon, heavy artillery firing was heard about eight miles ahead and we were started off in a very rapid walk which was not slackened till we marched the advances, then a fierce fight was going on. The 14th corps had been attacked and driven back a long distance with the loss of three guns. Our 1st division arrived just before we did, were thrown forward and had then checked the rebels and established the line besides taking back the captured guns but the roar of musketry accompanied by the sharp terrible discharges of artillery was almost deafening. Our brigade was double quickened to the flank where we quickly threw up some light works to guard it. Half the men working and the other half standing at arms. Every moment we expected to be engaged in the bloody work but darkness came and the rebels withdrew from the attack leaving us in quiet.[21]

The 20th passed off with scarcely a shot fired. Our division extended the flank half a mile. The morning of the 21st our regiment was sent out to reconnoiter and feel the enemy. We found them about a mile in advance, received a few bullets and returned. That day all the wagons were ordered to Goldsboro and we prepared for a retreat the next day. Morning of the 22nd came and the rebels had gone, so we went also on our road to Goldsboro which place we reached after three days marching through the mud without any more opposition. We formed on the 23rd, part of the 24th, and part of the 25th, all in this vicinity.

When we reached this place I suppose we were about the dirtiest, raggediest lot of men that ever made up an army, but now the clothing begins to come in and soap is daily expected.

This great campaign has kept us so constantly busy that I was not able to write anything from which I can give you my journal of events. There were many times that we were not allowed time to get our meals and had to swallow pancakes, half dough, with but twenty percent chewing, but time is fast passing away and I shall take much more pleasure in relating than writing. We have subsisted entirely on the products of the country having, generally, flour, or potatoes, meat, hams, and often, sugar and honey in abundance.

The roads we have passed over have been mostly a succession of swamps. In South Carolina we ruined the principle railroads and I am sorry to say, destroyed a great percent of dwelling houses; this kind of campaigning is just as vicious to our army in its discipline as it is to the enemy.

I do not need any shirts as we draw mostly cotton shirts now. The mustard came all right and I am going to have some for dinner.

The boys in the company are all well and in good spirits. Wilcox is at division hospital doing finely. He is an excellent soldier.

I received a letter from Uncle Edwin which I shall answer tomorrow. I expect Ellis is now with his corps and shall endeavor to see him in a few days. Will write again soon.

Your affectionate son George

Raleigh [N.C.]
Apr. 19, 1865

Dear Mother,

Your letter of Apr. 2 containing Ellis' was received yesterday. That was the first mail we have received since leaving Goldsboro. There have been no very exciting times with us during our campaign here; we were but four days on the march and entered this place the 18th without any show of resistance. The rebels had a line of pretty fair works around the city, but we should have gone over them easily enough.

We received the happy news of Lee's surrender when we were at Smithfield[22] and I never saw such wild enthusiasm, the columns were just starting out of town when the dispatch came. Everything was stopped; officers rode back and forth proclaiming the glad news and the air was rent with cheers.

We laid here just one day and then started out again after Johnston but we had not advanced over a mile when a flag of truce came in and we were ordered back to camp, where we have been ever since, waiting in the profoundest suspense, the result of negotiations, which we are pretty confident, are going on between Sherman and Johnston.[23]

Yesterday our camps were filled with intense sorrow over the death of Mr. Lincoln.[24] A shadow was thrown suddenly over our rejoicing and the feeling in the entire army is deep mourning. The citizens of this place held a meeting yesterday and made some resolutions expressing their sorrow at the occurrence and even the old rebels seem to feel a kind of horror at such a dastardly deed.

Frank Ellis was over to see me yesterday, he still stands the fatigue and looks well; we are now quite close together and shall be as long as this army is kept together.

I wish I could say something definite of what the rebel army in our front is going to do, but of that, we are still in the dark, though it is the general opinion that it will surrender if it has not already; if they do, the war is over and we shall have no more fighting, but if they do not, they can prolong the war some months and cause us much loss of life.

Of course we hope for and expect the best, everything is going on finely here, the same civil officers are conducting the city affairs; and the same editors are conducting the same papers under auspices of the old government; and they do it in the most loyal manner too. This is really cheering. I do not know however the case may turn out, as it will shorten our time of service any, for many soldiers will be needed yet some time, but the surrender will soon pass.

I am glad you like Aurora.

In my last I wrote you concerning the proposition Uncle Rufus made you. You have not told me what it is and I am much interested. I can see no reason to reject any fair business arrangement.

Your affectionate son George

CHAPTER 12

"Extremely Well Paid for the Trip"

Raleigh, April 28–Washington, D.C., June 1, 1865

General Sherman's attempt at negotiating peace with General Johnston in April 1865 did not set well in Washington. Thanks to Secretary Stanton and General Halleck, then Chief of Staff, not only was the signed proposal of peace rejected, but the public heard of General Sherman's embarrassing chastisement before he was even notified.

George wrote about his surprise at seeing Lieutenant General Grant, who was in camp. Secretary Stanton, on behalf of President Johnson, had ordered Grant to resume military hostilities against the Confederates. Arriving in Raleigh, Lieutenant General Grant was directed to assume the reins of Sherman's command. Adding insult to injury, General Halleck telegraphed General Sherman's generals and ordered them to disregard any of Sherman's orders.

In spite of these last minute disputes, within a few days the war was over. Soldiers turned themselves to marching rapidly to Washington to participate in victory parade appearances for the Grand Review in the capital. George and thousands of western troops worked hard to demonstrate their skills one last time.

The country had endured a great deal of grief, stress, and hardship in just a month: a presidential assassination and investigation, a new administration, the end of an unthinkable war, and the resumption of business and trade within the country. Perhaps the capital city needed a parade as much as the heroes who marched in it.

The process of separating from the army seemed to have a life of its own. Sergeant Cram was responsible for much of the paperwork. The 105th's last days among the Union Army were filled with bureaucracy, storytelling, and, no doubt, fond farewells. Washington, D.C. from May 15–June 15 was a melting pot of men from all companies, regiments, brigades, cultures, and walks of life. And Washington, D.C. launched the return of these seasoned war veterans to their farms, shops, colleges, churches, homes, friends, and families awaiting them.

Sergeant Cram probably didn't know if he would ever visit Washington again, so his sightseeing venture was predictable. Buildings, doors, and artifacts were of keen interest to him. As he stood in the U.S. Patent Office admiring the relics of invention, he may not have known that this building served dual duty to the country; its upper floors had also served as a hospital for Civil War soldiers.

Sergeant George F. Cram, just one of the Wheaton men of the 105th Illinois Infantry Regiment Volunteers, was about to become a veteran while opening up new chapters of his life back home in Illinois. General Sherman's Special Field Order Address No. 76, on May 30, left the veterans with words of encouragement for building productive lives after the war: "Your general need only remind you that success in the past was due to hard work and discipline, and that the same work and discipline are equally important in the future. To such as go home, he will only say that our favored country is so grand, so extensive, so diversified in climate, soil, and productions, that every man may find a home and occupation suited to his taste; none should yield to the natural impatience sure to result from our past life of excitement and adventure. You will be invited to seek new adventures abroad; do not yield to the temptation, for it will lead only to death and disappointment."

George F. Cram, veterans of the 105th Illinois Infantry, and thousands of other veterans from Chicago, Indianapolis, and towns all across the country took General Sherman's message to heart, got on board their freedom trains, and headed for home.

Raleigh [N.C.]
April 28th, 1865

Dear Mother,

I received your letter of April 8 some four or five days ago but amid the turmoil here have had no opportunity of answering and even now am obliged to trust to good fortune for an opportunity to send this off.

I think I wrote you that we were expecting peace about ten days ago. Genl. Sherman made an agreement with Johnston which would bring peace when finally ratified. He told us in an order that he hoped and expected to conduct us to our homes in a very few days.

So we waited and were filled with joyful anticipation but one day Genl. Grant suddenly made his appearance and we received orders to prepare immediately to march on half rations the following morning.[1]

Here was trouble for us and it was quickly known that we were to march in the direction of the rebel army. I have never in my life seen such intense disappointment nor experienced it—joy was quickly changed to gloom and sorrow and a great black cloud served to hang over us all.

While in the morning (25th) we started there were sober faces there too—our division marched in the rear and we reached camp at night some twelve miles from Raleigh. We remained there the 26th in suspense and the 27th (yesterday) till four o'clock, when our entire train was ordered to town and our regiment was sent as guards.

We started and reached our old camp here at eight o'clock, having made a very rapid march; and reaching camp the glad news was spread that hostilities had ceased, Johnston had surrendered; news that nobody could so well appreciate as tired, weary soldiers.

I was very tired but could not sleep for hours after wrapping my army blanket around me, and this morning the birds awoke me with the dawn. I never heard them sing so sweetly, and never saw them flit about so merrily. The green ground in which we are camped had a peculiar beauty and freshness and as the sun rose above the city steeple it seemed as if we could float right up with it.

The general expectation is that a few days will start us for the north of course we shall march through and I assure you we shall not grumble at the transportation.

I have only written this to let you know how we are situated and shall write again when anything new transpires and occasion offers.

Dear Mother, don't think anymore of my wasting any precious time at school; I never intend to stop studying, but life with me will now be real, earnest, practical. Give my love to Aunt Sophia.

Your affectionate son George

Near Richmond [Va.]

May 9, 1865

Dear Mother,

I have a few minutes this afternoon and our regt. postmaster informed us that he will endeavor to take a mail out tomorrow so I thought you would be interested in knowing where we are by this time. Our entire corps is camped within five miles of Richmond, we arrived here yesterday about one o'clock after nine days march from Raleigh; distance about 175 miles, so you may judge going towards home did not in any degree lessen our speed.

The country we passed through was very beautiful and rich until we entered Virginia and we then found bounty enough both in soil and people, though in some sections were a few of them rich nabobs so eminent for chivalry. Our army moved without any damage to the country and was as orderly as if we had been marching through Illinois.

The people flocked through to the roadside to see us pass and much happiness was manifested by them at the end for the war. We start tomorrow morning early for Alexandria. At eight o'clock we pass through the city of Richmond. As we pass the army will be reviewed by Genl. Halleck. We shall probably be at Alexandria by one week from today perhaps before this letter reaches you. But of course you will hear of our arrival through the papers.

What will be done with us when we get there I do not know but think we shall be sent home as fast as the necessary papers can be made out; this however, may take some time for all military matters are conducted as slowly as possible and great delays are always considered necessary.

When we get through I shall write again and then perhaps we shall know something more about it; so goodby for the next week. I only write this line that you may hear from me.

Your affectionate son George

U.S. Christian Commission

"This is a faithful saying, and worthy of all acceptation,
that Christ Jesus came into the world to save sinners; of whom I am chief."

[stationery letterhead]

Near Washington [D.C.]
May 26, 1865

Dear Mother,

For several days past have wanted to write and let you know our progress homeward, but our time has been so completely used up by the great service of which you have heard through the papers that I could not do so till the present moment. We arrived in this vicinity a week ago, camping between Alexandria and Washington on the west side of the river. Immediately on our arrival, we received orders to prepare for the great review of the two armies.

It was very necessary that we should prepare for the immense amount of hard work our army has done was not particularly conducive to a neat and plentiful supply of clothing. A liberal issue was made and we went to work polishing guns and brightening up accouterments. The general impression was somehow that Sherman's army was a pretty good army to march and perhaps could fight tolerably but that they were entirely unmilitary and undisciplined as you will see by one of the pieces I send you from the *Washington Chronicle* and we had some pride in surprising the people somewhat. We were well prepared and the service came off day before yesterday.

Thousands of people lined the sidewalks and the city seemed entirely covered with banners. So large an army necessitated frequent stopping and during these we came to an "order arms." At one of these our regiment which has often been called the best drilled regiment in the service brought down their guns with such precision that the audience immediately manifested their delight by cheers and clapping of hands. You will notice this circumstance in the little slip I send although it does not state the regiment. Well the review passed and all have been surprised and we are justly proud of our army.

We are now camped northeast of town in a beautiful pine grove awaiting the necessary forms for muster out. Muster rolls are sent for already. The order is that after the muster out rolls have been made out and properly authenticated by the proper officers here, each regiment will be sent to its state, there to be paid and discharged. This will probably occupy about two weeks and by that time we hope to be on our way home.

Enclosed you will find an article vindicating Genl. Sherman. I have never in my letters to anyone said anything suspecting his agreement with Johnston because I saw by all the papers that a majority at least of the northern people were ready to condemn him without hearing but one side of the story. But my respect for that great and . . . [missing page]

United States Sanitary Commission

[stationery letterhead]

Washington, D.C.
June 1, 1865

Dear Mother,

I received your letter of May 27 last night. For the last week we have been very busily engaged making out muster out rolls and doing other company writing necessary to dissolving the company. You can hardly imagine how busy we have been and are yet. I have just completed the last muster roll and take a moments interim to answer your letter.

I am sorry Uncle Calvin is expecting me to visit them for it will not be possible. We shall not go within some hundreds of miles for New York. Our course home will probably be by the Baltimore and Ohio railroad passing through Indianapolis.

A few days more will doubtless see us on the road. It is not known yet whether our place of rendezvous will be at Chicago or Springfield. Of course, we all desire the former. To one or the other we shall go I think, these to turn back to the state authorities our arms, equipment, etc. and receive regular discharge. This will occupy us some ten or twelve days so I think you may look for me home somewhere near the middle of the month.

All here are impatient in the highest degree to get off. And everybody is expecting the most perfect happiness, the day home again meets their eye. I suggested last night to a friend here that if ever a man might be excused for making a fool of himself it would be on that day.[2]

Notwithstanding our haste, I took one whole day and made an exploration of Washington. I passed through the capitol building into the senate chamber and house of representatives and cabinet; saw the beautiful clock of the senate, the superb oil paintings that decorate the rotunda and the world renowned brass door, designed in Rome and executed at Munich.

After going through the capitol I went to the patent office. Here I saw among the wonders Genl. Washingtons personal effects.

To describe the marvels would be impossible and so I will just say that I felt extremely well paid for the trip.

But I have not time to write more. So good by,

Your affectionate son, George

Two weeks after his last letter to his mother, Sergeant Cram drew
this "Fruit of War," a memento of the battles in which he fought.

(Courtesy of John Hoskins)

Afterword

The 105th Illinois Infantry was mustered out of the U.S. Army in early June 1865 and began their long journey home by means of the Pittsburgh, Fort Wayne and Chicago Railroad. In Pittsburgh they were greeted with a brass band and generous refreshments at 2:00 A.M. Their homecoming to Chicago, however, grievously disappointed them. When they arrived in the rain on June 10, no attempt had been made to provide a welcoming ceremony. General Dustin had telegraphed Chicago officials of the 105th's upcoming arrival, but folks there had been attending to the affairs of the arriving generals instead. No provisions had been made for the rank and file.

Without a place to rest or a morsel to eat, the men spent a dispirited and uncomfortable night on the floor of Union Depot. With hunger now their primary enemy, the troops began to march the next morning to Camp Fry at Wrightwood and North Clark Street. Some returning veterans claimed that a Chicago policeman ordered them off the sidewalk and into the street.[1] Insulted, some allegedly considered firing on the "foe," but reason prevailed and they continued to the camp. Yet, Camp Fry had not been used in quite some time and the rations there were spoiled. The men grew unruly and the *Chicago Tribune* reported that some troops, indignant over their homecoming, caused $5,000 damage to a saloon. A bill for $78 had also accumulated to cover the damages (broken windows, sashes, doors) at Camp Fry.[2]

Apologetic about the lack of welcome and philosophical about these urban skirmishes, the *Chicago Tribune* (June 13, 1865) reported: "Many of the boys feel very sore at the fact that they are neglected on their arrival in this city; they do not meet with that warm reception which they have a right to expect; they have been allowed to drop off the trains here tired and hungry, and with no one to welcome them, and marched off to camp without anything to eat or drink. These things ought not so to be. . . ."

Approximately 460 of the 105th Illinois Infantry came home with George F. Cram. Four hundred ninety-four others had fallen in battle or were already mustered out on disability, among them some of George's friends of the "gentlemen's tent."[3] Kingsley had died more than two years before in the merciless winter of 1862–63 at South Tunnel. Bachelder, who stood next to George in battle, died from the effects of wounds received in the summer of 1864. However, Martin Griswold not only survived and married his schoolmate sweetheart, Elizabeth, he joined George in business for a couple of years. Martin died in 1903.

Ogden Whitlock moved to Colorado late in the century. His letter to a pension commissioner indicated that he still upheld principles of the gentlemen's tent: ". . . I have been free of tobacco and liquors all my life. I do not even eat meat, and my habits are strictly temperate. When whisky rations were issued to us in the army, I gave mine away and was always on duty, never having had a furlough during near three years of service to the end of the war."[4]

William M. Tirtlot, perhaps the most enigmatic of George's former comrades and friends, later married a former Wheaton College student, Lydia A. Fleming. Tirtlot's war-injured leg was so bad that "it used to drive him insane at times," according to his wife.[5] For many years doctors treating his leg insisted that an amputation was necessary, but Tirtlot refused. He died in 1889 in Oregon among fellow veterans of the Grand Army of the Republic (G.A.R.) from the effects of the long-postponed amputation.[6]

Frank J. C. Ellis was perhaps George's best friend. Although he was not a member of the 105th Illinois Infantry, nearly every letter home mentioned Frank. Their mutual moral support and heroic efforts to find each other across miles of hostile territory and to enjoy each other's wit and wisdom was near boundless. However, Frank's postwar life was tragic. The lingering effects of wounds and rheumatism limited his mobility and capacity to earn a living. When he died in 1894, Frank was receiving a federal pension of only $4 per month. His daughter was permanently disabled from birth and his widow subsequently died in an insane asylum.[7] War years, difficult as they were, might well have been the best of times for Frank.

George F. Cram had a much happier future ahead of him. On October 4, 1865, four months after returning home, he married Martha "Mattie" Hiatt. Judging from a common wedding date with the Griswolds, the friends may have shared a double ceremony. George and Mattie had three daughters over the next seven years—Juliette, Anna, and Helen. Juliette Cram Iliff, her daughter Dorothy Iliff

Hoskins, and her granddaughter Deborah Hoskins Edwards preserved the collection of George F. Cram's letters; George's mother, Anna Blanchard Cram, the recipient of the letters, had died in 1888.

George joined his uncle, Rufus Blanchard, in map publishing in Chicago and became the commercial success that his uncle wasn't. Uncle Rufus Blanchard returned to historical writing with a passion for the next forty years until his death in 1903. By 1867 George was a partner in Blanchard & Cram and two years later he formed his own map publishing business, The George F. Cram Company. Manufacturing maps, atlases, globes, and educational charts, George successfully ventured into several other publishing arenas as well. In 1886 George and R. A. Tenney of Chicago published a handbook for veterans and their dependents, *Pensions: Who Are Entitled to Them, and How They May Be Obtained*. Perhaps motivated by the considerable difficulties facing veterans and their survivors in realizing their federal pension claims, George wrote that "all laws promising pensions for wounds, injuries, disease or death incurred in the military or naval service of the United States, which were in full force and effect when a soldier entered the service were contracts, implied contracts; that Congress has no right to pass other laws impairing the validity of or the obligations arising under those contracts." He added that "the pension system, viewed as a whole, presents a beautiful picture. It is founded upon right, upon the brotherhood of man, the fatherhood of God. Its background is justice . . . every honest soldier who has a just claim upon the bounty promised by the government should not feel that he is asking alms when he makes his application for pension. It is not charity that he will receive, but 'blood money'—earned by many a pain, many a hard march, many a privation and hardship."[8]

From 1899–1901 George published the monthly magazine, *Cram's Magazine,* which featured educational and popular topics of the time. A contributor to the magazine as well, George wrote on diverse subjects, such as his Civil War days ("Reminiscences: The Battle of Resaca," reprinted in the appendix), cross-country train trips ("Reminiscences—Episodes of '96"), and futurism ("Will Science Furnish the Evidence of Eternal Life"). In 1901 George even published a novel, *Minette: a Story of the First Crusade.* Set in 1096, the romantic tale reverberates with parallels to George's Civil War days.[9]

George and Mattie were living with Juliette and her family when Mattie died in 1907. Two years later, George, then 67 years old, married 39-year-old Leonia Wilson. In 1928 George died of a heart attack while visiting a relative in Spokane, Washington. Newspapers throughout the country—Davenport, Seattle, and Chicago—marked George F. Cram's passing: "He was a man of business ability and sterling integrity with a genius for making warm and intimate friendships. . . . Mr. Cram maintained a keen interest not only in business but in all public affairs right up to the close of his 87 years. . . ."[10]

The freshness with which George F. Cram's Civil War experiences stayed alive in his heart and mind for decades was testimony to the searing nature of the Civil War's life-defining moments. In 1902, thirty-six years after the Battle of Resaca, George reminisced in a magazine article about the survivors' fraternity: "Very quietly we ate our supper of hard tack, bacon and coffee, and looking into each other's faces felt that a new band of brotherhood had been drawn around our hearts. We had passed through our baptism of fire. . . ."[11] The evolution of students into soldiers and of boys into men was borne through communal moments as this.

George also recalled his exhilaration at the start of his journey into battle, and one voice in particular that bade him farewell: "As I turned to step on board an old man grasped my hand, put his arm around my neck and kissed me, saying, 'Good-bye, my boy; God bless you and bring you safely home.' I feel that bearded face against my cheek to this day. It was the one kiss I never forgot. It burned into my memory and was with me on the march and on the field of battle."[12]

Patience, pragmatism, prayer, and principled conduct guided George's return as Uncle Rufus Blanchard had hoped. "Gentleman of the old school,"[13] and pioneer of American map publishing, Rufus Blanchard awaited the return of his soldier, his nephew, his imminent protégé and their bright future together charting the world.

Remininscences

The Battle of Resaca

Geo. F. Cram.

Why did I enlist? Well, I have often been asked the question, have often asked it of myself. Was it patriotism? Was it pride? Or was it the contagion of excitement that had swept over the land ever since the memorable battle of "Bull Run"? I do not know; perhaps it was partly all, and as I looked at the regiments of young men marching to the depots to be borne to the front in our late war with Spain I asked myself again the question.

Be the reason what it may, I was one of those who in the fall of '62 found ourselves singing "We are coming, Father Abraham, six hundred thousand more."

It was on the second day of September I stood at the depot in the little town of W—— waiting for the train which was to carry us away to face unknown dangers for "three years or during the war." There were a thousand splendid fellows, and we held aloft a silken banner that had been made and presented to us by the ladies of the village. We looked proudly upon it as it floated unsoiled in the gentle autumn breeze—but not so proudly as the three hundred and fifty of us who three years later brought it back and gazed at what was left of it, draggled, soiled and torn with shot and shell. We went away, many of us, boys. We came back—such as were left—men.

There were fathers there who gravely held the hands of their sons while giving them the parting advice, and sisters full of sympathy, and sweethearts whose pretty eyes were filled with tears and love, and there were mothers, gentle, loving mothers, who struggled to keep back the flood that would have eased their aching hearts as they kissed their boys good-bye, some of them for the last time.

A whistle, a column of smoke, a rumbling which deepens into a roar of wheels and in another moment the train rounds the curve and stops. As I turned to step on board an old man grasped my hand, put his arm around my neck and kissed me, saying, "Good-bye, my boy; God bless you and bring you safely home." I feel that bearded face against my cheek to this day. It was the one kiss I never forgot. It burned into my memory and was with me on the march and on the field of battle.

Thirty-eight years! What scenes they have shifted! What landmarks they have left here and there! What cares! What love! What winters with their hoary frosts! What summers with their gentle dews! But looking back tonight, 'twas only yesterday.

During that long night ride what thoughts were busy in those crowded cars among those who in one brief moment had passed from the citizen to the soldier, were never told. They were hours of realization that not all of that company would return, and with it the query, who?

Morning found us at Louisville, and we had no more than left our cars when we were ordered to prepare for immediate advance. Then came the drawing of guns, knapsacks, and all the accoutrements of the soldier, packing and finding our position in line, and at four o'clock that same afternoon we took our place in the column and marched out of the city, out along the broad turnpike leading south; out toward the foe.

Sundown, and dark, and still the steady, monotonous tramp. Nine o'clock, ten; one by one these untrained boys dropped out and fell exhausted beneath the sixty or more pounds they were carrying. Midnight, and still no signs of rest. One, two, and three o'clock. I could endure no more and caring nothing for discipline or orders, dropped by the roadside and was soon asleep.

The following morning we tramped on, that army of stragglers, footsore, weary still, unwashed and uncombed, and about noon found the camp and rested the balance of the day. Why that night march, I think not even the general who ordered it ever knew.

To come to the story of Resaca we must pass over the first eighteen months that followed; the advance through Kentucky, the scenes at Scottsville, at Tunnel Hill, at Gallatin, Lavergne, and Murfreesboro, at Nashville, and Chattanooga, at Chicamauga and Lookout Mountain. All the memorable incidents of those days and months, interesting enough, would fill a book and a large one and still "the half would never be told."

It was on the 6th of May, in '64, that we marched out of our camp in the Wauhatchie Valley, passed around the eastern end of Lookout Mountain, and turned southward. Across the broad valley Missionary Ridge stretched along for miles, and back of us the broad Tennessee wound around the little city of Chattanooga. At "Buzzard's Roost" and "Snake Creek Gap" we had a smart brush with Johnston's army, which determinedly opposed our movement toward Atlanta, but it was not until within a few miles of Resaca that stubborn battle was offered. On the 8th, McPherson's command attacked on the right but was repulsed and driven back. Thomas then advanced, with Schofield on the left, and our twentieth corps, commanded by "Fighting Joe Hooker," in the center. Nearly a week was passed moving for position, and all this time the artillery was constantly at work, the great guns incessantly booming, and shifting position until on the 15th all was in readiness, and the solid lines of infantry began in the early morning to prepare for the assault. At about eleven o'clock our brigade was marched a short distance to the left and just under the brow of the long range of hills, exactly opposite a masked battery of four large guns, a few yards in front of the Confederate line of battle, which was well entrenched on the opposite hills. We formed in five solid lines of battle, and all the time we were getting in position cannon were thundering their appalling music to prepare the way.

And now with the order to "fix bayonets," there comes a moment of perfect silence; the very leaves of the trees seem to droop and all nature waits in expectation. It was exactly 12 o'clock when four short bugle notes sounded. Those four notes were the command, "Column forward," and like the movement of a gigantic machine we passed over the brow of the hitherto protecting hill, onward to the charge. One quick glance revealed the entrenched enemy on the ridge in front, a quarter of a mile away, and then we were rapidly descending the hill toward them. What a scene now bursts forth; Indescribably grand! Unspeakably appalling! From every sheltered spot all along the hills we are swiftly leaving behind us, and from those in front comes the thunder of the big guns that are hurling streaks of fire across the sky. The screaming shells now begin to burst among us; home and friends are forgotten; pain and death are unnoticed; the soul of the man is lost in the glory of the soldier. Some one says our lieutenant is killed; I look back; he is lying upon the ground, and in that quick glance I see others falling. We seem to be descending into an abyss of shrieking demons, but we heed them not. Onward, still onward; we have reached the little valley and begin to ascend. And now from all along the crest of the ridge in front there is a sheet of flame. The roar of ten thousand rifles accompanies the boom, boom of cannon, and the four-gun battery toward which we are surging is hurling shell and grape. Rifle balls and shot are raining about us. The five splendid battle lines are no longer in order, but one crowded column struggles forward. We begin firing. The whole valley is a cloud of sulphurous smoke. It is not a scene of the inferno, or hades, or sheol, or gehenna; it is hell. Half way up the hill we stagger beneath the terrible storm of iron hail. For a moment even in the mad excitement the heart sickens and falters. A moment only, for here is brave old General Ward waving his sword and shouting words of encouragement. He is holding up one arm, for a bullet has passed through it, and the grand old man is more proud of that wound than is the mother of her first born. A few paces more we fire and fall, only to load again. Firing and crawling a few yards at a time, we are almost at the summit. We can see the heads of the enemy as they fire from their entrenchment. A comrade is by my side sheltered by a stump. He has just loaded his rifle and is taking aim, the gun resting on the top of the stump. The shot was never fired, for a bullet passes through his head and he falls against me, dead. A minute more we have sprung over the embankment, and have captured the four guns that have been hurling ponderous missiles of death upon us. Every one of those brave gunners lie dead beneath the brass monster he will never fire again. Splendid fellows! Foes! Brothers! What homes are broken! What hearts shall mourn! What mothers, what wives, what sweethearts shall listen for the footsteps of him who never comes! What pen shall write the story of their death! What poet sing the song of their glory.

The battle was by no means ended. The position we had carried was neither a bastion or lunette in its exact character. It was a natural hollow, nearly circular, fifty or more yards in front of the enemy's entrenched line, partly concealed by trees and low brushes. Within this hollow a few of us were lying, partly protected from the bullets that were cutting through the air with that wicked zip, zip, that no soldier will ever forget, watching a chance to crawl forward and rush in when the moment came for the final act. There were no more bursting shells, no more booming cannon, for we were at too close quarters for the great guns to be used by either side. Suddenly the rattling roar of rifles in front increases; the line of flame bursts forth afresh; dense clouds of smoke again curl upward and redden the face of the descending sun, and a storm of lead sweeps over us. The foe has been re-enforced and with renewed courage and determination is making a desperate stand for victory. Little Arthur Rice, on my left, raises his head to try for a shot; 'twas only a moment, but a bullet passes through the center of his forehead; his head droops, his fingers relax their hold upon his rifle, and he sleeps without a quiver. Human nerve and heart can endure no longer, and springing to our feet we leap back down the hill. Half way down our uneven line stops and turns again. What is it that has turned aside that momentary panic? Ah! Here is General Hooker, "Fighting Joe." Never was more splendid figure on the red field of battle. He is not shouting, nor is his sword even unsheathed. It hangs by his side, but he is walking erect while he moves forward now in the very front, and he points toward the foe as, without a word, he looks along the line to the right and to the left.

Like magic the scene changes, and we turn back. We must reach the summit, pass over into the enemy's lines and silence that murderous fire. Our own rifles begin again to roar and the death skeleton rides upon the leaden messengers that cross each other in the mad search for victims. We would rush to the supreme conclusion, but cannot. Americans are opposed to Americans, and both sides with natural pride and courage are determined to snatch victory from defeat. Our reserves come up and fill the gaps that are being made in our lines, and all that fated afternoon we fight back and forth over the hillside, slowly, steadily, approaching nearer and nearer, and as the sun is sinking behind the ridge from whence we began the battle at noon we stand in the entrenchments of the foe, covered with dust, begrimed with smoke—exhausted, but victors.

Were we exultant? Did we shout forth ringing cheers of victory? No! Were we grateful? Yes! And as the twilight shadows gathered, what a scene we gazed upon. All about us were the Confederate dead and wounded, and back over the hills were the countless spots of blue dead and wounded comrades, now being gathered up on hundreds of stretchers. Four thousand killed tells the dreadful story. Sitting here tonight at this distance of years from that silent May evening, that awful scene is as vividly pictured out before me as it was when I stood among the dead and wondered that I was living.

In the gathering darkness our little company assembled at roll call, seventeen only answering to their names. Of the rest, some were killed, some wounded, and others had been swept away with the surging human tide and were mixed up with other commands. Very quietly we ate our supper of hard tack, bacon and coffee, and looking into each other's faces felt that a new band of brotherhood had been drawn around our hearts. We had passed through our baptism of fire; entering with the eager flush of soldierly pride, but never again did we hear the ominous sounds of approaching battle without that feeling of unspeakable dread born on the field of Resaca.

Notes

ABBREVIATIONS USED

NA—Orders   Records of the Adjutant General's Office, Record Group 94; Orders, Muster Rolls, and Returns; National Archives.

NA—Pensions   Records of the Adjutant General's Office, Record Group 94; Records of the Record and Pension Office of the War Department, 1784–1919; National Archives.

NA—Service   Records of the Adjutant General's Office, Record Group 94; Compiled Military Service Records; National Archives.

CHAPTER 1: "CITIZENS NO LONGER"

1. A village in a township of the same name in Bureau County (north-central Illinois). Wyanet was located on the Chicago and Rhode Island Railroad line and its local farmers shipped thousands of bushels of grain and livestock annually. Wyanet, adjacent to Princeton township, is a short distance due south of the site of Camp Dixon where the 105th Illinois Infantry first organized. N. Matson, *Map of Bureau County, Illinois with Sketches of its Early Settlement* (Chicago: George H. Fergus, Book and Job Printer, 1867), 44–45; 84–85.

2. Twenty-eight-year-old Frank Ellis was perhaps George's closest friend. By serving in a different regiment, Company G of the 106th Illinois Infantry, most of their contact during the war was through letters. E. E. Blake, a Wheaton College student from Winfield, was two years behind George in school. *Catalogue of Wheaton College, 1861–1862* (Wheaton: Wheaton College, 1862), 5–6. David K. Bean joined Company C, 105th Illinois Infantry. This was the only mention of Bean who, two years later, was mistakenly considered a deserter when he was captured by the Confederates. After he escaped, Bean died of disease at a Chattanooga hospital. NA—Pensions.

3. Rather than an idle report of conditions of the area, this land is likely the Cram family's farm land. The property was mentioned throughout his letters. While it is uncertain, the possibility that this land may have been granted as bounty for military service performed by Blanchard or Cram ancestors during the Revolutionary War and the War of 1812 cannot be ruled out. James W. Oberly, *Sixty Million Acres* (Kent: Kent State University Press, 1990), 130–45.

4. There were other George Crams enlisted in other Illinois regiments during the Civil War, and George F. Crams were also listed in New Hampshire (where he was born) regiments. Perhaps one of their misfortunes was the source of the grapevine's misreporting.

5. A chemical used in making black dye and some medicines.

6. Private Henry Kingsley was a twenty-three-year-old Wheaton College student when he enlisted with George F. Cram in Company F. Leonard Dewolf was a twenty-three-year-old Wheaton College student in the fall of 1862. He had previously been a high school teacher in Mt. Carroll, Illinois, and hoped to enter Yale or Harvard when the war broke out. *Catalogue of Wheaton College, 1861–1862,* 5; NA—Pensions; NA—Service.

7. Soldiers were entitled to an enlistment bounty of $100 and a county-raised bounty of $28. David E. Maas and Charles W. Weber, eds. *DuPage Discovery 1776–1976* (DuPage County Bicentennial Commission, 1976), 115.

8. A small Chicago Army camp named for Congressman H. C. Childs. Camp Childs had short-term use since Camp Douglas, nearby, grew to accommodate the processing of a large number of soldiers. Rufus Blanchard, *History of DuPage County, Illinois* (Chicago: O. L. Baskin & Co., 1882), 104.

9. Camp Douglas, on the south side of Chicago, was established to train Illinois volunteers but also served as a Confederate prison camp later in the war. *Historical Encyclopedia of Illinois* (Chicago: Munsell Publishing Co., 1912), 74. Sergeant Thomas Jefferson Pierce, Company E, 105th Illinois Infantry wrote about Camp Douglas in his letters home (September 20, 1862): "The rats and lice are plenty, and I was homesick while I stayed at that place that day! The rats came out on dress parade in full force about sundown. Camp Douglas is the filthiest place that I ever saw—the maggots fairly climb over the ground." Ellen K. Korbitz, comp., *Letters Home and a Roster of Descendants of Charles and Catharine Pierce* (Burlington: Illinois State Historical Library, 1957), 2.

10. Princeton was largely settled in the late 1830s by members of the Congregational Church community originally from Northampton, Massachusetts. Percival Graham Rennick, "The Peoria and Galena Trail and Coach Road and the Peoria Neighborhood," *Journal of the Illinois State Historical Society* 27 (January 1935): 407–9.

11. Thirty-eight-year-old Captain Seth Daniels was recruited to command Company F by commission from the governor. Back home in Wheaton, he had been involved in a variety of civic roles, including serving as a county judge before the war, as he would again after the war. Blanchard, *History of DuPage County,* 643. However, it remains a mystery what it was that Daniels did or didn't do that so angered his troops from the beginning.

12. President Jonathan Blanchard of Wheaton College was an active leader in the anti-slavery movement. While President Blanchard's papers do

not record an overnight visit to camp, George's letter reflected the buoyant spirits left by a personal visit from the head of their beloved campus. Wheaton College Archives, Buswell Memorial Library, Wheaton, Illinois.

13. The Garys were members of one of the founding families of DuPage County. George was probably referring to Mrs. Gary's son, Erastus Noah, who subsequently changed his name to Noah Erastus. Gary was enrolled in Company D. Blanchard, *History of DuPage County,* 312; NA—Pensions.

14. Slang term for secessionists, those who had seceded from the union or were sympathetic to Confederate causes.

15. Brigadier General William T. Ward, a veteran of the Mexican War, had been a Kentucky attorney before the war. NA—Pensions.

CHAPTER 2: "IF YOU EXAMINE THE MAP"

1. This is the only letter from George to Uncle Rufus Blanchard that was preserved among the collection of letters to George's mother.

2. Haversacks were the all-important bag used to carry food rations; usually made from a sturdy cloth or leather and worn over the shoulder.

3. East Wilton, New Hampshire (Hillsborough County).

4. Union General Don Carlos Buell, also an Ohioan, was forty-four years old at the start of the war. Mark M. Boatner III, *The Civil War Dictionary* (New York: David McKay Company, 1959), 96–97.

5. Likely describing a fever with frequent peaks and related discomfort such as nausea, leaving a bilelike aftertaste. J. M. Da Costa, M.D., *Medical Diagnosis,* 7th ed. (Philadelphia: J. B. Lippincott Co, 1898), 884–86.

6. George's diary entry for October 29, 1862, described the soldiers' misery more clearly: "Many of the boys are nearly used up, their feet are sore and their backs are almost broke carrying those heavy knapsacks. I have seen them walking along encumbered by nearly 60 lbs. weight, the tears rolling down their cheeks poor fellows. I know there is no one here to care for them, all is selfishness here, everyone for himself."

7. The outskirts of Bowling Green fall within the range of the Mammoth Cave region. Other accounts indicated that it was the area of Horse Cave, Lost River Cave in particular, although George did not specifically refer to the proper name. Henry L. Boies, *History of DeKalb County, Illinois* (Chicago: O. P. Bassett, Printer, 1868), 118.

8. Lieutenant Samuel Adams, forty-four years old, was detailed back to Chicago to bring forward the convalescent sick and deserters who were left behind when the regiment left Illinois. In addition, he had the task of accompanying home the body of Company F's Sterling D. Aiken (thirty-three years old) who died of typhoid fever just before the regiment left Frankfort. NA—Pensions.

9. Three brothers of the Canadian-born Grant family were members of Company F: David J. Grant, Sr., was the oldest at twenty-eight when he enlisted; Isaac J. Grant was twenty-one; and Orris W. Grant was just nineteen. NA—Pensions.

10. Twenty-year-old Martin Griswold was a Wheaton College student with George before the war. Student Rosters, Buswell Memorial Library, Wheaton College. Twenty-three-year-old Ogden Whitlock was a printer in Wheaton at the time of enlistment. Those skills were put to the Army's good use.

11. Settled in the late 1700s and incorporated in 1815, Scottsville is the county seat of Allen County. The octagon-shaped courthouse, located in the center of the public square, was constructed in 1819 and survived until its demolition in 1903 when a new courthouse was built. Records of the Allen County Historical Society, Scottsville, Kentucky.

12. Whether a common event or simply a frequently mentioned vignette of camp folklore, variants on the postage stamp incident were commonly reported in many Civil War letters, diaries, and reminiscences.

13. According to George's diary entry for November 18, 1862, it was Lieutenant [Captain] Lucius B. Church, Company B, who sang, "The Sword of Bunker Hill." Captain Church's talents were frequently noted: "Church has charmed the sense of thousands in and out of the army by his magic voice. Stand him on a barrel in the streets of Gallatin or in any of the Corps and he would bring every regiment and every detachment within the radius of a mile inside the circle of his song vibrations." Boies, *History of DeKalb County*, 124.

14. Twenty-five-year-old William Tirtlot joined Company F as Sergeant. Thirty-seven-year-old John Batchelder [also Bachelder] was married and a farmer before the war. NA—Pensions. Batchelder was also an ancestral surname in George F. Cram's family, raising the possibility of their kinship. Dennis Donovan and Jacob A. Woodward, *The History of the Town of Lyndeborough, New Hampshire, 1735–1905* (Tufts College, Mass.: Tufts College Press, H. W. Whittemore & Co, 1906), 710–14.

15. Private Nicholas R. Kenyon of York was twenty-three-years old and a farmer when he enlisted in Company B. NA—Pensions.

CHAPTER 3: "THE GENTLEMEN'S TENT"

1. James A. Ramage, *Rebel Raider: The Life of General John Hunt Morgan* (Lexington: University Press of Kentucky, 1986), 134.

2. The *Independent* was Henry Ward Beecher's weekly religious newspaper. William Harlan Hale, *Horace Greeley: Voice of the People* (New York: Harper & Brothers, 1950), 242.

3. Marshall Meacham, 27, died of typhoid pneumonia. His family was one of the early families to settle in Bloomingdale Township, DuPage County. Newton Bateman, *History of DuPage County* (Chicago: Munell Publishing, 1913), 2:625. Meacham was survived by his wife and minor child in Vermont. NA—Pensions.

4. Henry F. Vallette was the county treasurer back home. NA—Pensions. George's diary entry for December 4, 1862, noted more explicit disfavor: "Vallette is a feverish sneak and a political opponent to [Captain] Daniels."

5. Union General Ambrose E. Burnside was just days away from a repulse at Fredericksburg as George wrote this letter. Burnside lost more than 10 percent of his troops and his rank as commander of the Army of the Potomac. General Grant had less faith in Burnside: "He was not, however, fitted to command an army. No one knew this better than himself." W. E. Woodward, *Meet General Grant* (New York: Garden City Publishing, 1928), 312.

6. The brigade of Colonel Moore of Illinois at Hartsville, Tennessee, were surprised and captured by a small cavalry company led by John Hunt Morgan. Robert N. Scott, *War of the Rebellion: A Compilation of the Official Records of the Union and Confederate Armies,* series 1, vol. 20, pt. 1—Reports (Government Printing Office, 1890), 50; and *New York Times,* December 9, 1862.

7. George had serious (and valid) concerns for his friend Frank Ellis. Within a short time, Frank was taken prisoner of war. NA—Pensions.

8. Grant's secondary supply base, a few miles south of the Tennessee-Mississippi border, was said to have suffered the loss of $4,000,000 worth of supplies when it was destroyed by rebel forces just ten days from this writing. Alfred H. Guernsey and Henry M. Alden, *Harper's Pictorial History of the Great Rebellion* (New York: Harper & Bro., 1866–1868), 318.

9. George's first revelation to his mother that he was thinking of not returning to college after the war.

10. Lieutenant Porter Warner, twenty-seven years old and from York Township, was permitted to go home a few days later. NA—Orders; NA—Pensions; and NA—Service. Discussion of the men's attitude about Lt. Warner are extensively covered in Sergeant Lysander Wheeler's manuscript covering December 1862 to March 1863 (Lysander Wheeler Collection, SC 2003, Manuscripts Department, Illinois State Historical Library, Springfield, Illinois). Circumstances of the incident of the shooting are more candidly discussed in George's diary entry for December 18, 1862, in which he insinuated that the shooting incident may not have been accidental as it seemed: "It is good for him [Warner] that he is an officer."

11. By this time, Ogdon Whitlock was in charge of the army's printing office at Gallatin that published a 6-column newspaper, the *Courier,* with a circulation of 1,200. Boies, *History of DeKalb County,* 123.

12. Captain Enos Jones (Company I, 105th Illinois Infantry) of Milton

resigned December 17, 1862, and accompanied wounded Lieutenant Porter Warner home to Illinois. NA—Orders; NA—Pensions; and George's diary entry for December 31.

CHAPTER 4: "ASLEEP IN JESUS"

1. James A. Congleton, "Reminiscences of the Civil War," 16, [n.d.] Manuscript Division, Library of Congress.

2. Private George W. Kinyon of York, Illinois. NA—Pensions.

3. Scott, *War of the Rebellion,* series 1, vol. 23, pt. 2—Correspondence, chap. 35:58.

4. Confederate General John Cabell Breckinridge, a Kentuckian, had also served in the state legislature and the U.S. Congress. Boatner, *Civil War Dictionary,* 82–83.

5. Mr. Brennan was the father of Patrick Brennan of Company F, 105th Illinois Infantry. NA—Pensions.

6. Private Daniel V. Geer, Company F, left a widow, Cassandra Proctor Geer, and one son, Daniel Beron Geer, who was born just a month after Daniel's death. NA—Pensions.

7. Doctor Potter received a medical leave of absence which said, "He is slowly convalescing from a severe attack of pleuro pneumonia in connection with great nervous prostration brought on by overworking during the whole time of his service." Doctor Potter was permitted twenty days' leave and was "to be removed from the vicinity of the army and the sick and [to] go North beyond the limits of this Department." NA—Pensions.

8. Lieutenant Samuel Adams struggled with bronchitis, eventually the source of his veteran pension claim. NA—Pensions.

9. Saleratus was a compound similar to modern-day baking soda.

10. While the name Copperheads' invoked the image of a well-known venomous snake, during the Civil War the label was used as a disparaging nickname for northern Democrats who wanted Lincoln to negotiate peace.

11. Annie Hall Blanchard was the second wife of Uncle Rufus Blanchard. (His first wife was killed during a train accident on their honeymoon.) Frederick Latimer Wells, "Rufus Blanchard: In Memoriam," *Transactions of the Illinois State Historical Society for the Year 1904,* Publication Number 9 (Springfield: Phillip Bros., State Printers, 1904), 392.

12. While George actively provided medical care to many of his comrades, this was the only known occasion in which he speculated about becoming a physician after the war.

13. Henry Kingsley's father, Reverend Kingsley, had arrived the evening of January 30, 1863, to visit the men for a few days and to see his ill son. Instead, he accompanied Henry's body back to Illinois for final inter-

ment. George's diary entry of January 30, 1863; and Boies, *History of DeKalb County,* 122.

14. George's first diary, covering the period September 12, 1862, through February 28, 1863, probably traveled home to Illinois through his comrade, Nick Kenyon.

CHAPTER 5: "I WOULD PREFER A COPY OF SHAKESPEARE"

1. Luther L. Hiatt to Statira Elizabeth Jewett, June 28, 1863, Luther L. Hiatt Collection, DuPage County Historical Museum, Wheaton, Illinois.

2. William H. Bradbury to Mrs. Bradbury, January 23, 1863, William H. Bradbury Collection, Manuscript Division, Library of Congress.

3. Scott, *War of the Rebellion,* series 1, vol. 20, pt. 2—Correspondence, chap. 32:118.

4. The Union League was one of several patriotic publication societies that emerged during the war and printed more than four million copies of its tracts for mass public consumption. J. Matthew Gallman, *The North Fights the Civil War: The Home Front* (Chicago: Ivan R. Dee, 1994), 118–21.

5. The battle of Stone's River, also called the battle of Murfreesboro, extended over the New Year's holiday of 1862–1863. Henry M. Cist, *The Army of the Cumberland: Campaigns of the Civil War* (New York: Charles Scribner's Sons, 1903) 7:102–35.

6. Edwin Blanchard was another brother to Rufus Blanchard and Anna Blanchard Cram. Edwin worked in the office of Rufus's map publishing business. *Chicago City Directory, 1861–1862* (Chicago: Office of the City Directory, John Gager & Company), 25.

7. Company F comrade Patrick Brennan painted a more colorful description of the troops' easy access to fruit and the like in his letter home (September 2, 1863): "I like to stand picket around Nashville; we make the old citizens give us all the watermellons that we wont and we serch the wagons and if they have whiskey we make them fork it over till we have all we wont and it takes a prity good lot to do us." NA—Pensions.

8. Military equipment carried in addition to arms and ammunition.

9. Even though performing out of rank as an enlisted man, George won't earn additional pay or recognition for such service. Throughout most of his army career, in order to keep his promise to his mother to not become an officer, however, George's personal capabilities frequently positioned him in roles beyond his official rank.

10. Kentucky-born Cassius Clay was a staunch abolitionist, editor, and a Union general early in the war. He was appointed minister to Russia from 1861–69. Boatner, *Civil War Dictionary,* 157.

11. The mythological god of dreams or sleep.

12. Confederate General Joseph ("Fightin' Joe") Wheeler's cavalry units of 5,000 effective troops were hearty opponents to Union cavalry and were imagined as an even larger command. Boatner, *Civil War Dictionary*, 910–12.

13. Another "Fightin' Joe," Joseph Hooker, on the heels of a mix of successes and failures in the east, was sent west and given the command of the 20th Corps, September 24, 1863. Boatner, *Civil War Dictionary*, 409–10.

CHAPTER 6: "WHAT CAN'T BE CURED MUST BE ENDURED"

1. Sergeant Thomas Jefferson Pierce, *Letters Home*, comp. Ellen K. Korbitz (Springfield: Illinois Historical Library, 1957), 23; and NA—Pensions.

2. The reference was to Rosecrans's removal from the head of the Army of the Cumberland.

3. A twenty-one-year-old farmer at the time of enlistment, Private Lewis G. Stover had both legs amputated after his fall. While guarding the Nashville & Chattanooga Railroad near Murfreesboro, Tennessee, riding atop the cars, Stover fell between two cars while the train was in motion. NA—Pensions.

4. George's sister Juliette "Ettie" Theresa had married a Mr. Poole of Chicago sometime before or during the war. No additional information was found on Mr. Poole. This reference is to their twin daughters. Blanchard and Cram genealogy worksheets: courtesy, Deborah Hoskins Edwards.

5. George's sharing of his own picture with his men probably explains the absence of one among the letters preserved. While he frequently wrote to his mother that he would send her a photograph, none of the letters indicated that it was sent during the war.

6. Benjamin Harrison would become the 23rd President of the United States. Boatner, *Civil War Dictionary*, 378.

7. Major General Carl Schurz was in command until February 25, 1864, followed by Major General O. O. Howard who was in command until April 18, 1864, when Major General Joseph Hooker assumed command. Frederick H. Dyer, *A Compendium of the War of the Rebellion* (New York: Thomas Yoseloff, 1959), 1:455, 458.

8. Incidence of smallpox death among the 105th Illinois Infantry, as reported to headquarters, was five. NA—Orders.

9. Uncle Calvin Blanchard, author of *The Religion of Science: or The Art of Actualizing Liberty, and of Perfecting and Satisfactorily Prolonging Happiness* . . . (1860) published another book in 1864, *The Art of Real Pleasure: That New Pleasure for which an Imperial Reward Was Offered* (Jefferson Library, Library of Congress). Mr. Pool was likely a reference to sister Juliette's husband or her father-in-law; elsewhere spelled "Poole."

10. While George left us to our imaginations with his droll remarks

about Captain Daniels and Lieutenant Tirtlot's dancing, perhaps it was because the former was married and the latter had a girlfriend (Lydia) back home at Wheaton College. NA—Pensions.

11. Whatever Anna Blanchard Cram's interests were in the possibility of moving to Virginia remains a secret of history; but none of the family did so.

12. Probable reference to land the Cram family owned, which was tenant-farmed by someone named Hamrick or Ha[e]rrick (a familiar name in northern Illinois) in or near Wyanet (Bureau County). Several Hamricks were farmers in that area according to *The Voters & Taxpayers of Bureau County, Illinois* (Chicago: H. F. Kett & Co., 1877), 278.

13. Unable to locate Hardeville.

14. The diaries from August 1862 to April 1863 and 1864 were kept by the family and have been used to clarify details in the letter collection.

15. While this seems like an improbably large number of stamps, George was writing to many people including his aunts and uncles, college professors, Lieutenant Adams, Frank Ellis, and probably unnamed girlfriends back home.

16. Major General Howard did not officially take command until February 25, after the date of this letter. Dyer, *A Compendium of the War of the Rebellion,* 1:455.

CHAPTER 7: "THE BIG BRIGADE"

1. Dexter Parker, thirty years old, was one of the company musicians. Due to illness, he had been sent to duty at the Soldiers Rest in Nashville. Upon returning to the regiment he probably carried many items normally mailed directly to the field but that might have been delayed due to the restrictive use of the trains to build supply stores between Chattanooga and Atlanta. NA—Pensions.

2. A narrow passage.

3. The recollection of a solider of the 104th Illinois Infantry also confirmed, "The creeks were much swollen, but managed to get our stock across. We moved on and in some places had to swim the animals." William Wirt Calkins, *The History of the One Hundred Fourth Illinois Volunteer Infantry* (Chicago: Donohue & Henneberry, 1895), 195.

4. George's diary entry for that date indicated instead that he did not feel well. Not surprisingly, his cheery tones often belied the accuracy of his circumstances when it came to communicating about his welfare to his mother.

5. George may have been entitled to a furlough, but there is no evidence that he ever took one.

6. The significance of Lowell was that it was where George was born and raised before moving to Illinois. *Vital Records of Lowell, Massachusetts,*

to the End of the Year 1849 (Salem, Massachusetts: Essex Institute, 1930), 39.

7. Likely Arthur Rice's last photograph. NA—Pensions.

8. Unable to locate Goldsboro in the region where George was located at that time.

9. Reference to an apprenticeship with Uncle Rufus Blanchard in his map publishing business.

10. Frank Ellis was taken prisoner of war in the winter of 1863 in Carroll Station, Tennessee, by Confederate General Forrest's men. When George wrote of meeting Frank in early April, it was apparently after Frank and others of the 106th Illinois Infantry had just returned to rejoin the 15th Army Corps, after being home briefly after parole. NA—Pensions.

11. Reference to the Shakespearean character here meaning a drunken, swaggering, brazen soldier without scruples.

12. General William T. Ward had staying power in spite of his shortcomings. NA—Pensions.

13. Captain Daniels did not resign, but he was transferred to the Invalid Corps in Ohio for the balance of the war. NA—Pensions.

14. The implication of this remark is that George and others will assume the duties of officers, without the commission or pay.

15. General John Milton Brannan was Chief of Artillery for the Army of the Cumberland. Boatner, *Civil War Dictionary,* 81–82. General William Denison Whipple was General George Thomas's Chief of Staff at this time. *Ibid.,* 912–13.

16. "Sanitaries" were commissary items provided for by private donations to the U.S. Sanitary Commission. This usually would include food that was not made available through government issue. The "Northern ladies" were those women devoted to providing improved support of the troops for their physical welfare and morale. The ladies were leaders in conducting large fund-raising events in the form of fairs that were held in major Northern cities in order to supply these items. J. S. Newberry, *Report on the Operations of the U.S. Sanitary Commission in the Valley of the Mississippi, for the Quarter Ending Oct. 1st, 1864* (Washington, D.C.: s.n., 1864), 219–30.

CHAPTER 8: "IT WAS EVERY MAN FOR HIMSELF"

1. Union General James Birdseye McPherson, thirty-five years old and a fellow Ohioan, was General Sherman's favored commander as head of the Army of the Tennessee. Boatner, *Civil War Dictionary,* 538.

2. Lieutenant Tirtlot suffered a gunshot wound to the leg on May 15, with serious consequences. NA—Pensions.

3. Hanson Depue, a farmer upon enlistment, was just twenty-one years old when his arm was amputated in Georgia. According to records,

Depue was shot on May 20. NA—Pensions.

4. For George's more extensive description of Arthur Rice's death, see the Appendix, "Reminiscences: The Battle of Resaca."

5. Other comrades left a more vivid description of Doctor Potter's death: "We were advancing on the enemy. The doctor came up riding his horse. A shell fired from a rebel cannon hit the ground a short distance in front of him, bounced striking him on the head...I was just a short distance from the doctor when he was killed. He was good-hearted man." Congleton, "Reminiscences of the Civil War," 43.

6. On May 31, some 350 self-described "radical men" of the Republican party who were dissatisfied with Lincoln met in Cleveland in the style of a national convention. While those attending did not actually represent anyone other than themselves, they nominated General John C. Frémont for President and General John Cochrane for Vice President. Guernsey and Alden, *Harper's Pictorial History of the Great Rebellion,* 664.

7. An apparent reference to the shortage of on-site officers due to Captain Seth Daniels's baseball injury and subsequent transfer to the Invalid Corps.

CHAPTER 9: "PERFECT TERROR"

1. Charles W. Wills, *Army Life of an Illinois Soldier* (Washington, D.C.: Globe Printing Company, 1905), 256.

2. It is unclear why George disliked Doctor Waterman so intensely.

3. Confederate General William W. Loring was Corps Commander in Atlanta. Boatner, *Civil War Dictionary,* 492.

4. George was wrong in his estimate of John Bachelder's wounds. NA—Pensions.

5. With McPherson's death, Sherman needed a general who would "obey orders and execute them promptly and on time." Major-General O. O. Howard, not General Joe Hooker, was the unanimous choice among Sherman, Halleck, and Lincoln. Hooker, greatly offended, resigned his command in the heat of July's battles, giving credence to Lincoln's earlier worries and admonishments to the general. William Tecumseh Sherman, *Memoirs* (New York: The Great Commanders, 1994), 396–97.

CHAPTER 10: "THE VERY AIR SEEMS FULL OF DEATH AND DESTRUCTION"

1. The U.S. Sanitary Commission was a privately funded effort to improve upon the hygiene conditions of the camps and soldiers' diet. *The Soldier's Friend* (Philadelphia: Perkinpine and Higgins, 1865) was a pocket-size

tract that provided a wide array of information and counsel to soldiers.

2. The Christian Commission, another privately funded effort that started during the war, donated Bibles, stationery, and other comforts designed to promote improved moral conduct of soldiers. Lemuel Moss, *Annals of the United States Christian Commission* (Philadelphia: J. B. Lippincott & Co., 1868), 716–23.

3. George's pragmatic acceptance of new recruits was in contrast to the diatribe that he wrote earlier. No doubt his personal acquaintances with these recruits made the concept more acceptable.

Chapter 11: "Terrible Havoc Among the Citizens"

1. Unfortunately, Frank Ellis's letter to George was not found among the collection.

2. A storage facility for train cars.

3. The recruits, also termed "one hundred day men" included friends and comrades Herbert Wilcox and Isaac Grant.

4. Indebtedness may explain the estrangement between Tirtlot and George.

5. Having served as Commissary Sergeant, George was likely more aware of the resources necessary and available to maintain an army on the offensive.

6. Union General Jonathan Gray Foster was in command of the Department of the South, headquartered at Hilton head. Foster was pivotal in helping open up supply lines to the rear of the army up the Ogeechee River. Sherman, *Memoirs,* 512–14.

7. Just nine days later, General Grant's dispatch to General Sherman clarified the duration of the encampment in Savannah: "Without waiting further directions, then, you may make your preparations to start on your northern expedition without delay. Break up the railroads in South and North Carolina, and join the armies operating against Richmond as soon as you can." Scott, *War of the Rebellion,* series 1, vol. 44—Operations, chap. 56:820–21.

8. George's diary noted the tremendous quantities of guns, cotton, and commissaries left by the rebels when they fled Savannah. Enough so that Sherman sent his famous Christmas message to Lincoln: "I beg to present you, as a Christmas-gift, the city of Savannah, with 150 heavy guns and plenty of ammunition, and also about 25,000 bales of cotton." Sherman, *Memoirs,* 507.

9. Thunderbolt, one of the forts that protected Savannah from naval assault, was more correctly described as part of the state of Georgia.

10. Spafford Deford, Company A, 105th Illinois Infantry of Palmas, Illinois was "mortally wounded by a rebel ball fired from the South Carolina

shore, supposed to be the work of a reb sharpshooter." Congleton, "Reminiscences of the Civil War," 77.

11. James Congleton ("Reminiscences of the Civil War," 79) elaborated on the feeling of entering the state, "South Carolina, why did you do it? You have sown to the wind, you will reap the whirlwind."

12. Confederate General William Joseph Hardee had the command of South Carolina, Georgia, and Florida and was the general who was in Sherman's way. With Fort McAllister nearly surrounded, Hardee managed to slip away to join General Johnston in the Carolinas. Sherman, *Memoirs,* 493–95.

13. The First Brigade commander was Colonel H. Case. Sherman, *Memoirs,* 591.

14. George's diary entry for December 29, 1864, noted, "No reliable news. No mail. Passed a pleasant evening discussing war prospects. Concluded the war was about over."

15. The 17th Army Corps had a memorable sea journey from Thunderbolt to Beaufort, South Carolina, remembered by Sherman, "I was really amused at the effect this short sea-voyage had on our men, most of whom had never before looked upon the ocean. Of course, they were fit subjects for sea-sickness, and afterward they begged me never again to send them to sea, saying they would rather march a thousand miles on the worst roads of the south than to spend a single night on the ocean." Sherman, *Memoirs,* 513.

16. Thanks to a Union gunboat that came up the river, soldiers had a quick chance to send a letter home—the first opportunity in weeks. Yet, it was not a time for relaxed writing because, as Congleton noted, "the whole army is in this vicinity. The roads are almost impassable." Congleton, "Reminiscences of the Civil War," 88.

17. During this encounter at Lawtonsville, South Carolina, eight members of their regiment were wounded. Congleton, "Reminiscences of the Civil War," 80.

18. This same day, General Sherman was visiting with General and Mrs. Grant and President and Mrs. Lincoln at sea off the coast of Newbern. This was Sherman's last talk with Lincoln. Sherman, *Memoirs,* 576–83.

19. The extent of George's war injury.

20. The regiment, however, suffered three deaths and twelve wounded during the Battle of Averysboro. Congleton, "Reminiscences of the Civil War," 90–91.

21. The Battle of Bentonville claimed 191 Union men and officers, the majority of them from the Left Wing, composed of the 14th Army Corps and the 20th Army Corps. Sherman, *Memoirs,* 562.

22. They were sent to guard the railroad bridge at Smithfield where Confederate General Johnston was known to be with some thirty-five thousand men. Ibid., 596.

23. Sherman's attempt to execute a document of peace with Johnston

backfired. Not only was Sherman directed to commence hostilities once again against Johnston, but within days Sherman would suffer considerable public embarrassment and accusation while Stanton would direct Lieutenant General Grant to take over Sherman's command in the field. Ibid., 600–620.

24. Sherman had delayed announcing news of the assassination as he had a great concern that soldiers would retaliate against the South. He worried that soldiers might believe that there were Southerners involved in the murder of the president. Ibid., 599–601.

CHAPTER 12: "EXTREMELY WELL PAID FOR THE TRIP"

1. Lieutenant General Grant arrived per Secretary Stanton's request. Sherman, *Memoirs,* 607.

2. A somewhat prophetic note; the homecoming was not the way George imagined.

AFTERWORD

1. Congleton, "Reminiscences of the Civil War," 106–9; and Boies, *History of DeKalb County,* 186.

2. An invoice found in NA—Orders.

3. One hundred eighty-eight men died due to mortal combat, wounds, or disease. William F. Fox, *Regimental Losses in the American Civil War 1861–1865* (1889; reprint, Dayton: Morningside Books, 1985), 508.

4. NA—Pensions.

5. *Ibid.*

6. *Ibid.*

7. *Ibid.*

8. George F. Cram and R. A. Tenney, *Pensions: Who Are Entitled to Them and How They May Be Obtained* (Chicago: George F. Cram and R. A. Tenney, 1886), 8–9.

9. George F. Cram, *Cram's Magazine* 2, no. 1 (May 1900): 637–40; 1, no. 5 (March 1900): 435–43; and 1, no. 3 (January 1900).

10. Davenport *Democrat and Leader,* May 30, 1928, "George F. Cram, Map and Atlas Publisher, Dies. Expires at Spokane, Buried at Chicago, Scene of Business Career."

11. George F. Cram, "Reminiscences: The Battle of Resaca," *Cram's Magazine* 2, no. 1 (May 1900): 640.

12. *Ibid.*

13. *Journal of the Illinois Historical Society* 27 (January 1935): 425–27.

Bibliography

UNPUBLISHED SOURCES

Bender, George A., 1st Lieutenant, Company I, 105th Illinois Volunteer Infantry. "Diary." Chicago Historical Society.

Blakeslee, G. H. "Sumner County, Tennessee" [ms. map]. 1862, Record Locator 446.2. Geography & Map Division, Library of Congress.

Blakeslee, G. H. "Middle Tennessee" [ms. map]. 1863, Record Locator 389.7. Geography & Map Division, Library of Congress.

Bradbury, William H. Letter Collection, Manuscript Division, Library of Congress.

Chapman, Daniel. "Daniel Chapman's Autobiography written at the request of my only daughter, Mrs. William Chapman Kincaid . . ." January 23, 1883. Illinois State Historical Library, Springfield.

Congleton, James A., "Reminiscences of the Civil War" [ms. Diary of James A. Congleton], 1862–65. Manuscript Division, Library of Congress Control Number: mm 79005909.

Cram, George F. Diaries. Personal collection of descendants.

——. Civil War Letters. The George F. Cram Company archives, Indianapolis, Indiana.

——. Family Letters. Personal collection of descendants.

Harper, Denise. "Rural Hamlets of Upper Sumner County." November 14, 1983. Sumner County Library and Archives, Gallatin, Tennessee.

Hiatt, Luther. Letters. DuPage County Historical Museum.

ARCHIVES

Records of the Adjutant General's Office. Record Group 94—Records of Volunteer Soldiers [105th Illinois Infantry] who served during the Civil War: Records of the Record and Pension Office of the War Department, 1784–1919; Orders, Muster Rolls and Returns; Compiled Military Service Records; Regimental Orders and Descriptive Books; Court Martial Records; and Letter Books. National Archives, Washington, D.C.

Record Collection of Henry Suzzallo; E. S. Meany Papers, "Mount Tacoma Club, March 6, 1924." Box 42, folder 24, 106-70-12; Copy of letter from George F. Cram to Mrs. M. G. Mitchell of Tacoma, Washington, August 1, 1927, regarding the movement to restore the name of Mount Tacoma (receipt stamped by Seattle Chamber of Commerce). Manuscripts & University Archives Division, University of Washington

Libraries, Seattle, Washington.
Student Rosters. Buswell Memorial Library, Wheaton College, Wheaton, Illinois.

PUBLISHED SOURCES

Periodicals

Chicago Tribune, 1861–1865.
Cram's Magazine, 1899–1901.
Davenport (Iowa) Democrat & Leader, May 30, 1928.
Grand Army Journal 1, no. 21 (September 17, 1870).
Harper's Weekly 3, no. 401 (September 3, 1864); 7, no. 320 (February 14, 1863); 7, no. 354 (October 10, 1863); and 8, no. 392 (July 2, 1864).
Journal of the Illinois State Historical Society 27, no. 3 (October 1924): 407, 425–27; 35, no. 3 (September 1942): 288–94; 47, no. 1 (January 1954): 64–65; 56, no. 2 (June 1963): 150–63.
New York Herald, January 15, 1864; April 7, 1864.
New York Times, 1861–1865.
New York Tribune, April 15, 1863; May 9, 1863; May 21, 1863; June 20, 1864.
Wheaton Illinoian, October 11, 1895.
Wilmette Life, June 1, 1928.

Articles and Books

Adjutant General's Office. *Report of the Adjutant General of the State of Illinois,* Vol. 5. Springfield: Phillips Bros. State Printers, 1901.
———. *Volunteer Force of the United States Army for the years 1861, '62, '63, '64, '65.* Washington, D.C., 1865.
Alotta, Robert I. *Stop the Evil: A Civil War History of Desertion and Murder.* San Rafael: Presidio Press, 1978.
Angle, Paul M., ed. *The Lincoln Reader.* New Brunswick: Rutgers University Press, 1947.
———. *Prairie State: Impressions of Illinois, 1673–1967, by Travelers and Other Observers.* Chicago: University of Chicago Press, 1968.
Athearn, Robert G., ed. *Soldier in the West: The Civil War Letters of Alfred Lacey Hough.* Philadelphia: University of Pennsylvania, 1957.
Bateman, Newton. *History of DuPage County.* Vol. 2. Chicago: Munell Publishing, 1913.
Bechtel, Paul M. *Wheaton College: A Heritage Remembered, 1860–1984.* Wheaton: Harold Shaw Publishers, 1984.
Blair, William Alan, ed. *A Politician Goes to War: The Civil War Letters of*

John White Geary. University Park: Pennsylvania State University Press, 1995.

Blanchard, Calvin. *The Art of Real Pleasure*. 1864. Reprint, New York: Arno Press, 1971.

———. *The Religion of Science*. New York: C. Blanchard, 1860.

Blanchard, Rufus. *Discovery and Conquests of the Northwest*. Wheaton: R. Blanchard & Co., 1879.

Blanchard, Rufus. *History of DuPage County, Illinois*. Chicago: O. L. Baskin & Co., 1882.

Boatner, Mark M., III. *The Civil War Dictionary*. New York: David McKay Company, 1959.

Boies, Henry Lamson. *History of DeKalb County, Illinois*. Chicago: O. P. Bassett, 1868.

Bowers, John. *Chickamauga and Chattanooga*. New York: Avon Books, 1994.

Brooksher, William R. *Glory at a Gallop*. Washington: Brassey's, 1993.

Bruce, Robert V. *Lincoln and the Tools of War*. Indianapolis: The Bobbs-Merrill Company, Inc., 1956.

Buck, Stephen J. "A Contest in Which Blood Must Flow Like Water: DuPage County and the Civil War." *Journal of the Illinois Historical Society*. 87, no. 1 (Spring 1994): 2–20.

Calkins, William Wirt. *The History of the One Hundred and Fourth Regiment of Illinois Volunteer Infantry*. Chicago: Donohue & Henneberry, Printers, 1895.

Chicago City Directory, 1859–1860, 1867–1868, 1870–1871.

Cist, Henry M. *The Army of the Cumberland*. Vol. 7 of *Campaigns of the Civil War.* New York: Charles Scribner's Sons, 1903.

Civil War Times: The Campaign for Atlanta. Special Edition. Eastern Acorn Press, 1986.

Cogswell, Elliott C. *The History of Nottingham, Deerfield, and Northwood*. Manchester: John B. Clarke, Printer, 1878.

Conzen, Michael P., ed. *Chicago Mapmakers*. Chicago: Chicago Historical Society, 1984.

Cowley, Charles. *Illustrated History of Lowell*. Boston: Lee & Shepherd, 1868.

Cram, George F. *Minette: A Story of the First Crusade*. Chicago: J. W. Iliff & Company, 1901.

Cram, George F., and R. A. Tenney, *Pensions: Who Are Entitled to Them, and How They May Be Obtained*. Chicago: 1886.

Da Costa, J. M. *Medical Diagnosis*. 7th ed. Philadelphia: J. B. Lippincott Co., 1898.

Dannett, Sylvia G. L. *Noble Women of the North*. New York: Yoseloff Publishing, 1959.

Davis, Burke. *Sherman's March*. New York: Vintage Books, 1988.

DeRosier, Arthur H., Jr., ed. *Through the South with a Union Soldier*. Johnson City: East Tennessee State University Publications, 1969.

Donovan, Dennis, and Jacob A. Woodward. *The History of the Town of Lyndeborough, New Hampshire, 1735–1905*. Tufts College, Mass.: The Tufts College Press, H. W. Whitemore & Company, 1906.

Dornbusch, C. E. *Regimental Publications and Personal Narratives of the Civil War*. New York: New York Public Library, 1971.

Durham, Walter T. *Rebellion Revisited: A History of Sumner County, Tennessee from 1861 to 1870*. Nashville: Parthenon Press, 1982.

Durham, Walter T., and James W. Thomas. *A Pictorial History of Sumner County, Tennessee, 1786–1986*. 3rd ed. Nashville: Sumner County Historical Society, 1991.

Dyer, Frederick H. *A Compendium of the War of the Rebellion*. 3 vols. New York: Thomas Yoseloff, 1959.

Edwards' New Chicago and County Records [Chicago City Directory]. 1869–73, Chicago Public Library.

Eklund, Karl. "In Forty or Eight to Rosecrans: The First Wartime Use of Railroads for Strategic Purposes." *Military Review* 30 (February 1951): 12–21.

Fish, Carol. "The Northern Railroads." *American Historical Review* 76, no. 3 (June 1971): 738–43.

Fleharty, S. F. *Our Regiment: A History of the 102nd Illinois Infantry Volunteers*. Chicago: Brewster & Hanscom Printers, 1865.

Fox, William F. *Regimental Losses in the American Civil War, 1861–1865*. 1889. Reprint, Dayton: Morningside Books, 1985.

Franklin, John Hope, ed. *Civil War Diary of James T. Ayers*. Springfield: Illinois State Historical Society Occasional Publications, 1947.

French, Ella M. *History of the Department of California and Nevada Women's Relief Corps: 1883–1934*. Modesto, California: Cavell, 1934.

Gallman, J. Matthew. *The North Fights the Civil War: The Home Front*. Chicago: Ivan R. Dee, 1994.

Ganoe, William Addleman. *The History of the United States Army*. Ashton: D. Palleton Century Co., 1942.

Gardner, Charles K. *Dictionary of the Army of the United States*. 2nd ed. New York: D. Van Nostrand, 1860.

Gary, Olin J. "Wheaton Seventy Years Ago." *Journal of the Illinois Historical Society* 20, no. 1 (April 1927): 129–37.

Guernsey, Alfred H., and Henry M. Alden, *Harper's Pictorial History of the Great Rebellion*. New York: Harper & Bro., 1866–1868.

Hall & Co. City Directory. 1849–50; 1854–55; 1855–56.

Halsey, Ashley, ed. *A Yankee Private's Civil War*. Chicago: Henry Regnery Company, 1961.

Harrison, Lowell H. *The Civil War in Kentucky*. Lexington: University Press of Kentucky, 1975.

Hatheway, O. P., and J. H. Taylor. *City Directory and Annual Advertiser.* Chicago, 1849–1850.

Heath, John Timothy. *Morgan's Daring Raid: The Battle of Hartsville, Tennessee.* 1997.

Herr, Kincaid A. *The Louisville & Nashvill Railroad, 1850–1940, 1941–1959.* 3rd ed. Louisville: *L & N Magazine,* 1959.

Hicken, Victor. *Illinois in the Civil War.* 2nd ed. Urbana: University of Illinois Press, 1991.

Historical Encyclopedia of Illinois and History of DuPage County. Vol. 1. Chicago: Munsell Publishing, 1913.

Hoehling, Adolph A. *Last Train from Atlanta.* New York: Thomas Yoseloff, 1958.

Holzer, Harold. *Dear Mr. Lincoln.* Reading, Mass.: Addison Wesley Publishing, 1993.

Hoobler, James A. *Cities Under the Gun: Images of Nashville and Chattanooga.* Nashville: Rutledge Hill Press, 1986.

Horn, Stanley F., ed. *Tennessee's War 1861–1865: Described by Participants.* Nashville: Tennessee Civil War Centennial Commission, 1965.

Howard, Oliver O. *Autobiography of Oliver Otis Howard.* Vol. 1. New York: Baker & Taylor Company, 1908.

Instruction for Field Artillery. Washington: Government Printing Board, 1864.

Illinois Military Units in the Civil War. The Civil War Centennial Commission of Illinois, Springfield, 1962.

Kaiser, Leo M. "Letters from the Front." *Journal of the Illinois State Historical Society* 56, no. 2 (June 1963): 150–63.

Kennegott, George F. *The Record of a City: A Social Survey of Lowell, Massachusetts.* New York: Macmillan Co., 1912.

Kilby, Clyde S. *Minority of One: The Biography of Jonathan Blanchard.* Grand Rapids: Wm. B. Erdmans, 1959.

Klein, Maury. *History of the Louisville & Nashville Railroad.* New York: Macmillan Co., 1972.

LeBaron, William, Jr. *The Past and Present of Kane County, Illinois.* Chicago, 1878.

Lonn, Ella. *Desertion During the Civil War.* Gloucester: American Historical Association, Peter Smith, 1966.

Lowry, Thomas P. *The Story the Soldiers Wouldn't Tell: Sex in the Civil War.* Mechanicsburg, Penn.: Stackpole Books, 1994.

Moss, Lemuel. *Annals of the United States Christian Commission.* Philadelphia: J. B. Lippincott & Co., 1868.

Newberry, J. S. *Report on the Operations of the U.S. Sanitary Commission in the Valley of the Mississippi, for the Quarter Ending Oct. 1st, 1864.* Washington: s.n., 1864.

Oberly, James W. *Sixty Million Acres: American Veterans and the Public Lands before the Civil War*. Kent, Ohio: Kent State University Press, 1990.

Parrish, Randall. *Historic Illinois: The Romance of the Earlier Days*. Chicago: A. C. McClurg & Co., 1905.

Pierce, Thomas Jefferson. *Letters Home*. Comp. Ellen K. Korbitz. Springfield: Illinois Historical Library, 1957.

Portrait and Biographical Records of Cook and DuPage Counties, Illinois. Chicago: Lake City Publishing Co., 1894.

Portraits and Biographies of the Governors of Illinois and of Residents of the U.S. Chapman Brothers, 1885.

Quimby, Rollin W. "The Chaplains' Predicament." *Civil War History* 8, no. 1 (March 1962): 25–37.

Ramage, James A. *Rebel Raider: The Life of General John Hunt Morgan*. Lexington: University Press of Kentucky, 1986.

Register of Marriages of DuPage County, Illinois. Vol. II, 1839–1889. Hollywood, Calif.: Hollywood Chapter of the Daughters of the American Revolution, 1947.

Richmond, C. W. *History of DuPage County*. Aurora, Ill.: Knickerbocker & Hodder, 1877.

Rowell, John W. *Yankee Artillery Men: Through the Civil War with Eli Lilly's Indiana Battery*. Knoxville: University of Tennessee Press, 1975.

St. Clair, Helen, ed. *Greater Chicagoland Cemeteries*, Guide #3. Worcester, Mass.: Association for Gravestone Studies, 1994.

Scott, Robert N. *War of the Rebellion: A Compilation of the Official Records of the Union and Confederate Armies*. Washington, D.C.: Government Printing Office, 1890.

Shannon, Fred Albert. *The Organization and Administration of the Union Army 1861–1865*. Vols. 1–2. Cleveland: Arthur H. Clark Company, 1928.

Sherman, William Tecumseh. *Memoirs*. New York: The Great Commanders, 1994.

Smart, Charles. *Medical and Surgical History of the War of the Rebellion*. Part 3, Vol. 1. Washington, D.C.: Government Printing Office, 1888.

Strong, Robert Hale. *A Yankee Private's Civil War*. Edited by Ashley Halsey. Chicago: H. Regnery Company, 1961.

Taylor, Richard S. "Beyond Immediate Emancipation: Jonathan Blanchard, Abolotionism, and the Emergence of American Fundamentalism." *Civil War History* 27, no. 3 (September 1981): 260–74.

Vital Records of Lowell, Massachusetts, to the End of the Year 1849. Salem, Mass.: The Essex Institute, 1930.

The Voters and Taxpayers of Bureau County, Illinois. Chicago: H. F. Kett & Co., 1877.

The Voters and Taxpayers of DeKalb County, Illinois. Chicago: H. F. Kett & Co., 1876.

Warner, Ezra J. *Generals in Blue: Lives of the Union Commanders*. 3rd ed. Baton Rouge: Louisiana State University Press, 1995.

———. *Generals in Gray: Lives of the Confederate Commanders*. Baton Rouge: Louisiana State University Press, 1959.

Weber, Thomas. *The Northern Railroads in the Civil War, 1861–65*. Westport, Conn.: Greenwood Press, 1952.

Williams, T. Harry. *Lincoln and His Generals*. New York: Vintage Books, 1952.

Wills, Charles W. *Army Life of an Illinois Soldier*. Washington, D.C.: Globe Printing Company, 1905.

Index

acetate of copperas, 5, 182
Adams, Lt. Samuel, 15–17, 22, 54,
    89–90, 138, 183, 186
adjutant, 28
Alabama
    Bridgeport, 66, 70, 81–82
    Huntsville, 63
    Mobile, 150
    Stevenson, 52, 57, 60, 80
Alice, 8
alligators, 154
Alps, miniature, 82
ambulances, 22
Arkansas, 65
    Holly Springs, 25
Army Corps:
    4th, 104, 106, 110, 115, 122, 125,
      136
    11th, 63, 74, 81, 85
    12th, 88
    14th, 106, 151, 156, 160, 193
    15th, 124, 148
    17th, 18, 193
    20th, 75, 88, 106, 109–15, 130,
      136, 145, 156, 188, 193
    23rd, 104, 106, 109–12, 115, 124
    Invalid, 191
    Veteran, 62, 78
Army of the Cumberland, 64
assassination, of Abraham Lincoln,
    162, 194
Atlanta Campaign, 76
Atlanta Road, 115
Austrian-rifled muskets, 4

babies, 61
Bachelder, John, 18, 31, 100, 103, 106,
    116, 126, 133, 135, 172, 184, 191

Baker, Silas, 116, 141
ball (gala), 64
baseball, 89, 191
Bass, Mrs., 5
bathing, 27, 47–48, 76
batteries, artillery, 55, 98, 121–23,
    127, 130, 135, 153, 177
Bean, David K., 4, 181
Beardsley, Professor, 38
bears, 30
Beecher, Henry Ward, 28, 184
beef, 15, 35, 63, 68, 77, 152
berry picking, 48
"Big Brigade," 75, 85
blacks, 15, 34, 45, 54, 66, 135, 154–57
Blake, E. E., 4, 181
Blanchard, Aunt Annie Hall, 40, 72,
    105, 155, 186
Blanchard, Uncle Calvin, 46, 62, 64,
    69, 72, 78, 89, 98, 105, 125,
    135, 146, 151, 155, 169, 188
Blanchard, Uncle Edwin, 49, 69,
    162, 187
Blanchard, Pres. Jonathan, 8, 54, 182
Blanchard, Uncle Rufus, 8, 36, 46,
    48, 56, 62, 74, 76, 78, 89, 103,
    105, 141, 143, 149, 173–74,
    183, 186–87, 190
    business proposal of, 86, 163
Boone, Daniel, 9
Booth, John Wilkes, 58
boots, 39
bounties, 5, 36, 66, 181
Boutwell, Sgt. George, 60
Bradbury, William, 187
Brady, James, 114, 118
Bragg, Gen. Braxton, 12, 32, 52
Brannan, Gen. John Milton, 90, 190

Breckinridge, Gen. John C., 34, 186
Brennan, Mr., 36
Brennan, Patrick, 108, 186–87
Brown, William, 118
Bryan, Thomas B., 143
Buell, Gen. Don Carlos, 14, 183
bullfrogs, 138
Burnside, Gen. Ambrose E., 23, 27, 185
Butterfield, Gen. Daniel, 89–91, 95, 102, 106–7, 112, 127
butternut, 17

caisson, 122
calomel, 40
Camp Childs, 7
Camp Dixon, 7, 181
Camp Douglas, 7, 182
Camp Fry, 171
Canada, 13
Capitol, U.S., 170
Case, Col. H., 193
cavalry, 25
caves, 15
    Mammoth, 183
chaplains, 5, 43, 64, 78, 91, 96, 102, 116
Chapman, Daniel, 39, 49, 145
Chicago Tribune, 3, 21, 42, 133, 171
Chickamauga, 57, 75, 93, 95, 176
Christmas, 28–29, 33, 156
    Sherman's message to Lincoln, 192
churches, 6, 22, 54
Church, Lucius B., 184
Clay, Cassius, 51
Clay, Henry, 51
Cochrane, Gen. John, 191
coffee, 27–28, 79, 105, 113, 119, 123, 158, 179
college, returning to, 26, 166, 185.
    See also Wheaton College
"Colored troops." See U.S. Colored Troops

Commission, Christian, 43, 132, 168, 192
Commission, Sanitary, 43, 132, 169, 190–91
communications, difficulties of, 146, 159
Congleton, James, 32, 75, 186, 192
Congregationalists, 182
Congress, U.S., 173
copperheads, 40, 45, 140, 186
cotton, 79
Courier, 185
court martial, 13
courtship, 58
Cram, Anna Damon Blanchard, 131, 173, 189
Cram, Juliette "Ettie," 8, 28, 31, 36, 38, 42, 46, 51, 53, 59–61, 103, 106, 117, 143, 172, 188
Cram, Leonia Wilson, 174
Cram's Magazine, 173
Cram, Martha "Mattie" Hiatt, 172–73
Cumberland Gap, 16
Cumberland Mountains, 52

dancing, 189
Daniels, Capt. Seth, 7, 15, 32, 38, 41, 54, 73, 77, 89, 105, 119, 182, 185, 189–91
Davenport Democrat, 194
Davis, Jefferson, 85, 139
debt, 150, 192
Deford, Spaford, 192
Depue, Hanson, 98, 118, 190
deserters
    Confederate, 128
    Union, 12, 40, 116, 183
Dewolf, Leonard, 6–7, 16, 18, 22, 31, 182
diary, 15, 23, 41, 70, 187, 189
diphtheria, 64
Dissing, Aaron, 118

"Dixie," 3
doctors, 35, 40–41, 186
dogs, 31
draft, 135
drunkenness, 6, 112
Duke, Basil, 12
Dustin, Col. Daniel, 3, 64, 66, 112,
    136, 171
Dutton, Lt. Col. Everell, 111

Edwards, Deborah Hoskins, 173
Ehle, Cpl. H. S., 118
elections, presidential, 105, 108,
    130–31, 140
Ellis, Frank J. C., 4, 7, 25, 63, 66, 70,
    73, 76, 82, 87, 96, 117, 134–35,
    140, 146, 162–63, 172, 181,
    185, 190, 192
Emancipation Proclamation, 4
Enfield rifles, 4
England, 51
Ettie. *See* Cram, Juliette

feet, sore, 15, 160, 183
fever, 1, 14, 41
fire, 45, 58
flags
    rebel, 133
    regimental, 132
foraging, 145, 151, 157–58, 160
Forrest, Gen. Nathan Bedford, 93, 190
Fort McAllister, 193
Fort Negley, 44, 53
Fort Pillow, 93
Fort Pulaski, 154
Foster, Gen. John Gray, 152, 192
France, 51
freedmen, 19
Fremont, Gen. John Charles, 105, 191
furlough, 5, 7, 61, 66, 83–84

Gary, Mrs., 8
Gary, Noah Erastus, 102–3, 183

"Gate City," 93, 128, 139, 148
Geary, Gen. John W., 114, 130
Geer, Cassandra Proctor, 186
Geer, Daniel, 37, 186
Geer, Daniel Beron, 186
"gentlemen's tent," 19, 21, 172
Georgia
    Acworth, 94, 103
    Allatoona, 93
    Atlanta, 75, 98, 100–101, 104,
        108, 124–56
    Augusta, 151, 159
    Big Shanty, 93
    Buzzard's Roost, 96, 177
    Calhoun, 93
    Dalton, 93, 97
    Gordon Mills, 93
    Gordon Springs, 96
    inhabitants of, 98, 106
    Kennesaw Mountain, 94, 111
    Kingston, 134
    Madison, 151
    Marietta, 102, 112, 115, 118–19
    Milledgeville, 151
    New Hope Church, 93
    Peach Tree Creek, 111
    Resaca, 93–98, 104, 107, 117–18,
        132, 173–80
    Ringgold, 93, 95
    Savannah, 145, 150–57
    Snake Creek Gap, 97, 177
    Thunderbolt, 153, 192
Gilbert Judd, 58
Giles, Henry, 4
Giles, Mr., 5
ginger, 28, 51, 144
gloves, white, 75
Grand Army of the Republic (GAR),
    172
Grand Review, 164
Granger, Gen. Gordon, 44, 53, 63
Granger, Gen. Robert Seamen, 63,
    72, 57

Grant, David, 15, 63, 84–85, 88, 100,
    106, 116, 133, 135, 141, 143,
    158, 184
Grant, Isaac, 15, 70, 148, 152,
    154–55, 158, 184, 192
Grant, Orris, 15, 158, 184
Grant, Ulysses S., 57, 66, 78, 93, 98,
    101, 103, 117, 133, 139, 164,
    166, 185, 192–94
Griswold, Elizabeth, 172
Griswold, Martin, 6, 16, 18, 22, 31,
    37, 172, 184
guerillas, 40, 60

Halleck, Gen. Henry W., 13, 20, 33,
    44, 111, 164, 167
Hamrick, 56, 59, 69, 189
hand car, 147
Hardee, Gen. William Joseph, 154,
    193
hard tack, 35, 86, 98, 134, 179
Harrison, Col. Benjamin, 58, 63, 81,
    131, 142, 188
Henry, William, 61
heroism, 111
Hiatt, Luther, 43, 187
Hiatt, Martha "Mattie," 43, 172
Hiatt, Statira Elizabeth Jewett, 187
hollow square, 17
Holmes, Tommy, 106, 116, 133, 135,
    141, 158
homecoming, 167–71
homesickness, 15, 23, 35, 37, 171
Hood, Gen. John Bell, 127, 129,
    141–42, 144, 149
Hooker, Gen. Joseph "Fighting Joe,"
    63, 75–79, 83, 88, 96, 120, 129,
    177, 188–91
Hooker's Corps, 55
Hoskins, Dorothy Iliff, 172
houses, private, 44
Howard, Gen. Oliver O., 74, 82–83,
    88–99, 104, 114, 188–91

hundred-day men, 106, 124, 192

Iliff, Juliette Cram, 172
Illinoian, 23, 29, 48, 133
Illinois
    Aurora, 86, 159, 163
    Bloomingdale, 39, 118, 185
    Cairo, 53
    Chicago, 2, 5, 8, 11, 24, 62, 76, 86,
        116, 141–43, 169–73
    Downer's Grove, 118
    Milton, 185
    Mt. Carroll, 182
    Naperville, 116
    Palmas, 192
    Princeton, 7, 181–82
    Springfield, 4, 169
    Wayne, 118, 138
    Wheaton, 1, 3, 5–6, 8, 16–17, 54,
        68, 71, 83, 85, 158–59
    Winfield, 37, 118
    Wyanet, 4, 181
    York, 184–85
Illinois Infantry Regiments
    102nd, 25, 93, 191
    104th, 76, 189
    106th, 7, 190. See also Ellis, Frank,
        J. C.
    129th, 22–23, 29, 48, 93, 100, 112,
        133
Independent, 21–22, 28, 42, 48, 184
Indiana, Indianapolis, 165, 169
Indiana Infantry Regiment, 70th,
    45, 93, 114, 131

Johnson, Gov. Andrew, 62, 64
Johnston, Gen. Joe, 127, 162,
    165–66, 169, 193
Jones, Capt. Enos, 31, 185
Julius Caesar, 68

Keniston, U. B., 118
Kentucky, 10, 14–15

Allen County, 184
Bowling Green, 13–14, 31, 17,
116, 183
Frankfort, 1–2, 9–10, 15, 183
inhabitants of, 9
Louisville, 176
Munfordville, 48
Scottsville, 12, 16, 21, 176, 184
Shelbyville, 3, 8
Kenyon, Mrs., 22
Kenyon, Nicholas, 18, 31, 41, 184, 187
Kingsley, Henry, 6–7, 16, 36–37, 41,
172, 184, 186
Kingsley, Mr., 41, 186
Kinyon, George W., 186

Lafayette Road, 94
libraries, 43
Lincoln, Abraham, 20, 33, 57, 78,
108, 137, 140–41, 162, 191, 193
living, manner of, 10, 18, 21, 23, 47,
68, 117, 140
Lookout Mountain, 75, 82, 84, 118,
176
Lookout Valley, 76, 81–82, 85, 88–90,
94–96
Loring, Gen. William W., 125, 191
Louisiana Infantry Regiment, 12th,
111

McClellan men, 140
McGilfrey, Pvt. John, 118
McGraw, Patrick, 108, 118
McLellan, Lieutenant, 55
McPherson, Gen. James Birdseye,
97, 101–2, 128, 190
mail, 33–34, 69, 76, 103, 124, 132,
138, 143, 150, 154–55, 159,
167, 193
mansion, destruction of, 34
map publishing, 173–74, 187, 190
March to the Sea, 131–45
Markham, Miss, 133

Mary, Cousin, 137–38
Massachusetts, Lowell, 85, 189
Meacham, Marshall, 22, 185
Minette: *A Story of the First Crusade,*
173
Mississippi
Corinth, 61
Vicksburg, 56
Moore, Col. Absalom, 20, 185
Morgan, Gen. John Hunt, 12, 19, 22,
24, 26–27, 29–30, 33, 39
Morpheus, 11, 53, 187
mosquitoes, 138
mustard, 154

Napoleon, 46
"Negroe Regiments." *See* U.S. Colored
Troops
"Negroes." *See* blacks
New Hampshire, East Wilton, 13
newspapers, 14, 16, 20–21, 27, 31,
46, 49, 77, 139
New Year's Day, 33, 61–62, 65, 153
New York Times, 12, 19–20, 104
New York Tribune, 104, 155
North Carolina
Averysboro, 146, 193
Bentonville, 146, 193
Fayetteville, 158–60
Goldsboro, 146, 159–62
Raleigh, 162–67

officers
bad, 12, 23, 26, 41
cowardly, 12
quarreling, 41
refusing to become, 43, 71, 187
shortage of, 103, 105
Ohio Regiments
stacked arms, 24
79th Infantry, 93
Olsen, Aunt Sophia Blanchard, 49,
55, 59–60, 65, 69, 72–74, 83,

87, 95, 97–98, 106, 134, 139, 141, 155, 158, 166

opium, 23

Oregon, 172

Paine, Gen. Halbert Eleazer, 12

pancakes, 28, 38, 161

paper, writing, 28, 66, 73, 144

Parker, Dexter, 80, 189

Parker, Miss, 4

parrot guns, 112

Patent Office, U.S., 165. 170

Patton, Judge, 45

pensions, 32, 172–73

pepper, 23, 28, 144

photographs, 55, 56, 62–63, 71, 84–85, 89, 91, 188

Pierce, Thomas Jefferson, 182

pig, "Yankeefied," 105

pine(s)
  boughs, 82, 158
  bunks, 136
  camps, 140
  trees, 85, 87, 91, 139, 154, 157–58, 168

poison ivy, 118

politics, 131, 137

pontoons, 71, 83, 142, 153, 155

Pool(e), Mr., 64, 188

pork, 5, 11, 13, 18, 28

Porter, Adm. D. D., 33

postage stamps
  "don't lick," 134
  legendary incident, 16, 184
  "send," 72, 119, 150, 189

Potter, Lt. Harvey, 105

Potter, Dr. Horace, 1, 8, 10, 32, 37, 40, 51, 64, 94, 186, 191

Powell, Mr., 8

printing establishment, 65

prisoners, 18, 97, 108, 116, 120, 125

Providence, Act (or Ways) of, 61, 102, 151

Railroad
  Baltimore & Ohio, 169
  Chicago & Rock Island, 181
  Chattanooga & Savannah, 152
  Georgia, 151
  Louisville & Nashville, 12–40
  Macon, 134
  Nashville & Chattanooga, 188
  Pittsburgh, Fort Wayne & Chicago, 171

railroads
  destruction of, 145, 161, 192
  guarding, 30, 50

Ready, Mattie, 20

real estate, 144, 159

recruits, 132, 148, 152, 158, 192

reenlistment, 66, 129

Republican Sentinel, 45

reviews, military, 53
  Rice, Arthur P., 85, 94, 118, 179, 190–91

rice fields, 146, 152, 156

Richard III, 58

River
  Big Black, 48
  Black, 160
  Chattahoochee, 136–49
  Cumberland, 20, 33
  Kentucky, 9
  Mississippi, 16
  Ogeechee, 192
  Ohio, 59
  Potomac, 56, 96
  Rapidan, 93
  Savannah, 152
  Tennessee, 33, 176

Romeo & Juliet, 68

Rood, Lieutenant, 76

Rosecrans, Gen. William Starke, 12, 14, 26, 32, 44, 52, 55–57, 59

roundhouse, 147

Rousseau, Gen. Lovell Harrison, 57, 72

Rufus, Uncle. *See* Blanchard, Uncle
    Rufus
rumors, 8, 11, 18, 139, 159
Russia, 51

Sabbath, 7, 119
saleratus, 38, 186
Samples, Nelson, 13
Sayer, Warren M., 158
scalping, 104
Schofield, Gen. John M., 104, 114, 177
Schurz, Gen. Carl, 58, 188
scurvy, 48
"secesh," 9, 16, 49, 183
sergeant, commissary, 41, 50, 66,
    107, 117, 124, 127, 134, 192
Seymour, Gov. Horatio, 45
Shakespeare, William, 20, 24, 43–44,
    46, 58, 68
sham battles, 75, 90–91, 94
Sherman, Gen. William Tecumseh,
    75, 81–82, 87, 93, 111, 119,
    129–31, 138–45, 152–54,
    162–69, 190, 193–94
    "Crazy Billy," 154
Shurtleffe, Mr., 5
Sickles, Gen. Daniel, 96
singing, 184
slavery, 2, 42
slaves, 10
    inhumane treatment of, 156
sleighing, 65
Slocum, Gen. Henry W., 145
smallpox, 57, 64, 188
Smith, Lt. Melvin, 63, 73, 87, 103,
    111, 133
snuff, 54
soft bread, 24, 33, 63, 134, 141
Sophia, Aunt. *See* Olsen, Aunt
    Sophia Blanchard
South Carolina, 161, 192–93
    Beaufort, 151, 156
    Charleston, 156

Hardeeville, 157
Lawtonsville, 193
Robertsville, 157
specimens, 31
Stanton, Secretary of War Edwin,
    164, 194
Stevenson, Mrs., 156
Stone River, Battle of, 32, 47, 95,
    187
Stover, Lewis, 57,
Strong, Robert Hale, 13
Stubb, Mrs., 4
sutlers, 117
swamps, 151, 156–57, 161
swearing, 24, 91
sword presentation, 17

tea, 28
temperance societies, 5
Tennessee
    Buck Lodge, 32
    Chattanooga, 75, 78, 119, 131,
        142, 149, 176
    fortifications of, 25, 29
    Franklin, 62
    Gallatin, 12, 19, 21–22, 38, 44, 46,
        48, 176
    Hartsville, 20, 27, 185
    Highland Rim, 19
    Knoxville, 71
    Lavergne, 46–49, 176
    Murfreesboro, 20, 32, 35, 176, 187
    Nashville, 14–15, 34, 43, 51, 57,
        61, 65, 67, 70, 72, 76, 83–84,
        176, 187
    Shelbyville, 78
    South Tunnel, 19, 26–33, 36–38,
        176
    strategic aspects of, 26
    Sumner County, 12
    terrain of, 19
    Tullahoma, 39, 52, 79–80, 84
    Wauhatchie, 82, 118, 176

Tenney, R. A., 173

tents, 7, 10–11, 23, 37, 67, 72, 118, 144

theater, 58

Thomas, Brig. Gen. George, 57–58, 72, 88, 90, 128–29

thread, 29, 117, 133–34

Tirtlot, Lydia A., 172, 189

Tirtlot, William, 7, 28, 31, 41, 43, 46, 49, 54, 63, 68, 73, 77, 80–81, 98–99, 102, 117–19, 123, 132, 135, 150, 172, 184, 189–92

tobacco, 54, 105

tooth extraction, 138

Tucker, Colonel, 6

Two Gentlemen of Verona, 24

typhoid fever, 12, 32, 183, 185

Uncle Sam, 7

Union Depot, 171

Union League, 45, 187

U.S. Colored Troops, 60, 93, 133

Vallette, Lt. Col. Henry, 22, 185

Vallette, Mrs., 28

Vermont, 185

vices, 49, 73

Virginia, 67, 98, 103, 159, 189
   Alexandria, 167
   Fredericksburg, 27, 185
   Petersburg, 133
   Richmond, 35, 87, 108, 143, 167, 192

Ward, Brig. Gen. William T., 17–18, 57, 63, 72–73, 76, 80–81, 86, 89, 99, 106, 112, 123–24, 127, 138, 153, 178, 183, 190

Ward's Brigade, 12, 57

Warner, Lt. Porter, 27, 185–86

Washington Chronicle, 168

Washington, D.C., 77, 129, 164–65, 168–69

Washington, George, 104, 170

Washington, Spokane, 174, 194

water filter, 17

Waterman, Dr., 39, 69, 116, 165, 168–69, 191

water tank, 16

Westerville, 54

Wheaton College, 55, 76, 140–42, 181, 182, 184
   "boys" of, 68, 76, 141, 158

Wheeler, Sgt. Lysander, 60, 185

Wheeler's Cavalry, 55, 139, 158, 188

Whipple, Gen. William Denison, 90

whiskey, 109, 132, 172, 187

Whitlock, Ogden, 6, 16, 27, 37, 63, 70, 76, 172, 184–85

widow, 99

Wilcox, Herbert W., 70, 152, 155, 158, 160, 162, 192

William's division, 114–15

Willow Copse, 58

women
   Northern, 92, 190
   roles of, 131
   Southern, 54, 141
   voting rights of, 137

Wood, Colonel, 108, 114

"Yankee Doodle," 136

"Yanks," 84

Yates, Gov. Richard, 103

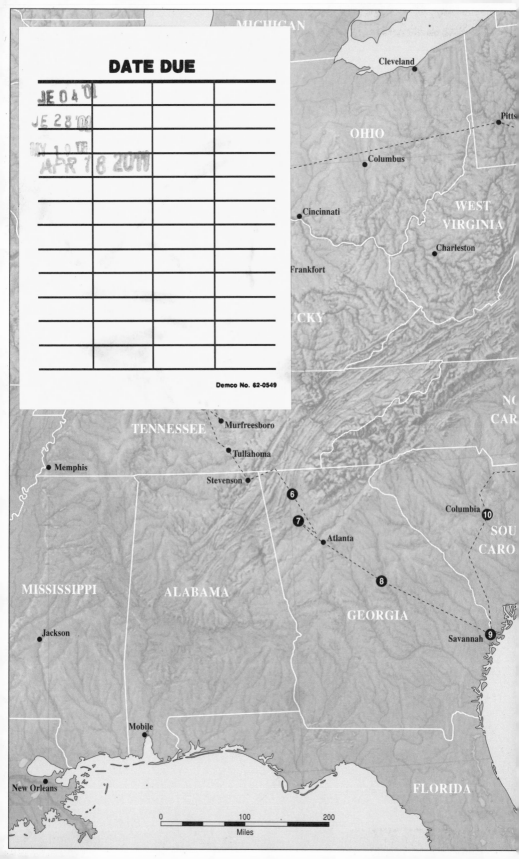

DATE DUE

JE 04 0		
JE 28 00		
MY 1 9 VH		
APR 1 8 2011		

Demco No. 62-0549

MICHIGAN

Cleveland

OHIO

Pitts

Columbus

WEST
VIRGINIA

Cincinnati

Charleston

Frankfort

UCKY

NO
CAR

TENNESSEE
Murfreesboro

Memphis

Tullahoma

Stevenson

Columbia

10

6

SOU
CARO

7

Atlanta

MISSISSIPPI

ALABAMA

8

Jackson

GEORGIA

Savannah

9

Mobile

New Orleans

FLORIDA

0   100   200
Miles